Praise for
Learning Transformed

"Given how quickly and profoundly the world is changing, there are few more urgent challenges than the transformation of our schools and education systems. Some people are still unconvinced of the need for this transformation: others are unsure how to make it happen. *Learning Transformed* is addressed to all of them and to every other educator, administrator and policy maker with a serious concern for the future of our children and our communities. It draws on the best research about the need for change and on the strategies that work and those that don't. More than that, it's seasoned throughout with deep, real world experience of teaching and learning, policy and practice in innovative schools and pioneering districts across the nation. *Learning Transformed* is both a compelling manifesto for the schools our children need now and an inspirational blueprint for how to bring them about."

Sir Ken Robinson
Author of *The Element;* TED speaker; education and creativity expert

"In *Learning Transformed*, Sheninger and Murray provide an ambitious, yet achievable, research-based blueprint for school leaders to lead the needed change in today's schools. Rarely has a book provided so many compelling evidence-rich strategies, as shared through the lenses of leading practitioners, to empower educators to redesign the learning experience so that every child, regardless of their socioeconomic status or zip code, is provided a world-class education."

Arne Duncan
Former U.S. Secretary of Education

"Sheninger and Murray combine some of today's most compelling research, evidence-based practices, and innovative ideas to provide a dynamic blueprint for redefining student learning experiences. They demonstrate how students' participation in authentic, real-world experiences can disrupt inequality and increase access to critical learning opportunities. *Learning Transformed* serves as a handbook to implement actionable, sustainable change in schools so today's students can thrive in tomorrow's world."

Linda Darling-Hammond
President, Learning Policy Institute
Professor Emeritus, Stanford University

"In *Learning Transformed*, Sheninger and Murray deftly combine the past and the future by offering eight keys to the schools of tomorrow, while lodging their insights into the history of the school reform movement. Read this book to be enlightened—and to put fun, excitement, and real learning back into your school or classroom."

Daniel H. Pink
Author of *Drive* and *To Sell is Human*

"Theory and research provide the foundation for change, but it is the actions undertaken by school leaders that drive transformation. Sheninger and Murray move well beyond the buzzwords and latest hype by providing a well-grounded, scholarly book that links theory, research, practical strategies, and evidence to move schools forward. The credible argument articulated is made even more impressive with the practical solutions found throughout *Learning Transformed*."

Robert J. Marzano
Cofounder and CAO, Marzano Research

~

"Our team has been immersed in deep learning for five years, and I can say without a doubt that Sheninger and Murray don't miss a trick. *Learning Transformed* has it all: eight keys that are concise, clear, and comprehensive. Great insights across the whole book. The chapter on learning spaces and design is a gem—an innovative treasure trove of new ideas. The use of successful practitioners at the end of each chapter to bring home the points is especially powerful in consolidating the lessons learned. Put *Learning Transformed* on your short list to read and use!"

Michael Fullan
Author and Professor Emeritus, University of Toronto

~

"What are the needs of the whole child in a digital world? How do you get jobs and joy? Will disruptive educational practices create more opportunity and equity or less? Eric Sheninger and Thomas C. Murray don't shy away from the big questions or shield their readers from the most promising and productive educational strategies either. This book is hopeful but not far-fetched; practical without being pedantic. If you want to approach the future with just the right amount of fear (the kind that prompts you to act with purpose rather than panic)—this is the book for you."

Andy Hargreaves
Brennan Chair in Education, Boston College

~

"If you are an education leader K–12 seeking detailed guidance on how to modernize your school for today's learner, take a deep dive into Sheninger and Murray's *Learning Transformed: 8 Keys to Designing Tomorrow's Schools, Today*. Grounded in dynamic examples coupled with engaging design thinking approaches, the authors provide a blueprint for shifting our old schools into new schools."

Heidi Hayes Jacobs
President, Curriculum Designers, Inc.

~

"Eric Sheninger and Tom Murray get to the heart of what matters most when leading change in today's schools. We all know that leadership and school culture, grounded in long-lasting, dynamic relationships are the clearest path to school improvement. In order to systemically shift K–12 systems, school leaders must model the way and provide the guidance to do this effectively and efficiently. *Learning Transformed* gives us the research-based evidence and tools to do just that. Eric and Tom are two of the leading innovators in education today and they share their expertise in this excellent book. It is a must read for leaders who are guiding change in their schools."

Todd Whitaker
New York Times Best-Selling Author

"In working with thousands of schools and districts, Murray and Sheninger have honed a great sense of where education needs to go and how to get there. In response to the challenges of the automation economy—and with equity firmly in view—the authors offer a sensible path forward beginning with a redesigned learning experience so that student agency is the norm, not the exception. *Learning Transformed* is a must read for education leaders considering what it means to be future ready."

Tom Vander Ark
CEO, Getting Smart

"Who do you trust? When it comes to school leadership, look no further than Eric Sheninger and Tom Murray—both professional educators who have devoted their lives to making learning better for students and educators. In *Learning Transformed*, Sheninger and Murray turn tightly honed concepts into practice. They have a compelling message for us all: 'You are part of the solution.' And with this book, they set out lanterns to light the paths for school leaders who are building vibrant and relevant school experiences for all learners."

Betsy Corcoran
Cofounder and CEO, EdSurge

"At the heart of *Learning Transformed* is a vision of authentic, high-level learning experiences for all students, particularly for those that are traditionally under-served. Sheninger and Murray provide a dynamic roadmap for school leaders to fundamentally shift teaching and learning in schools, while keeping all decision making laser focused on the needs of today's modern learners. The decisions of school leaders in the coming years will have an economic impact for generations to come, and this book will help guide them in that process."

Gov. Bob Wise
President, Alliance for Excellent Education
Former Governor of West Virginia

"Remodeling schools for a new day requires much more than a single intervention. While many communities seek the silver bullet, Tom Murray and Eric Sheninger make the essential case that transformation is a pervasive and ongoing activity. It requires leadership for a new culture that prompts us to reconsider instruction, time, learning spaces, technology tools, and the various other dimensions that contribute to student learning. Tom and Eric don't mince words on the hard work of school transformation, but the expression of that work is the most cogent, future-focused, and inspiration you will find. These are two great leaders discussing great leadership, and I encourage all principals to join their conversation."

JoAnn Bartoletti
Executive Director, National Association of Secondary School Principals

"This is the book that educators who want to transform learning with technology need to read. It starts, as do many books about education technology, about the vision and promise of technology—what might be called the 'why.' But Sheninger and Murray go well beyond that and dive deeply to the 'how.' As CEO of CoSN, the professional association of school district technology leaders, this is exactly the sort of practical how-to handbook that educators, especially those who want to be technology innovators, have been looking for. It sparks imagination while giving concrete, next steps. There is an old saying that if you want to solve big problems, you have to first stop proving that you can't. This book provides a roadmap for transforming learning that is ambitious yet also realistic and doable."

Keith R. Krueger
CEO, CoSN – the Consortium for School Networking

"While it's trendy for teachers to talk about 'tomorrow's schools,' renowned educators and thought leaders Tom Murray and Eric Sheninger separate the wheat from the chaff in *Learning Transformed*. Small wins, cultures of innovation, and student agency are just three important points of emphasis the authors underscore in this carefully researched and pragmatically designed blueprint for turning tomorrow's schools into today's learning environments. If you want student-centered learning, modern classroom design, 21st century professional growth, and impactful change at your school, *Learning Transformed* is the path you must take, and Murray and Sheninger are the perfect guides."

Mark Barnes
Author/Publisher and Creator of the Hack Learning Series

"Present-day America is in the throes of radical disruption of home, community, political, and economic boundaries wrought by the rise of the Smart Machine Age—a historic turning point. *Learning Transformed: 8 Keys to Designing Tomorrow's Schools, Today* offers educators practical insights into processes of educational change essential to ensure learners are ready for a future world that will continue to rapidly evolve in decades to come. In their book, Eric and Tom bring significant disruptive forces into focus and rather than just admiring problems faced by educators caught in this turning point, they offer keys to transform schools and learning so that all learners will be #FutureReady."

Pam Moran
2016 Virginia Superintendent of the Year

∾

"Eric Sheninger and Tom Murray knock it out of the park in *Learning Transformed*. This book will push your thinking and take you, the reader, through an in-depth comprehensive look at today's schools in order to best prepare our students and school communities for lifelong success. The authors share their eight keys for intentionally designing tomorrow's schools that will leave you wanting more. This is a must buy for all educators!"

Jimmy Casas
Senior Fellow, International Center for Leadership in Education

∾

"*Learning Transformed* is an essential read for those looking to empower students, staff, and community as they help create a system that changes the world of education. The combination of evidence-based research with actionable steps to get your district moving is a rare find. Murray and Sheninger not only give you the 'why,' they give you the 'how' and feature districts that are creating incredible environments for students and staff. As a practicing administrator, *Learning Transformed* is definitely the roadmap to give my students and staff an environment where all can thrive."

Joe Sanfelippo
Superintendent, Fall Creek School District (WI)

∾

"Murray and Sheninger call for educators to move away from current 'one-size-fits-all' approaches through intentional redesign of school. Their case for shifting instructional paradigms is grounded firmly in practical, action-oriented expertise and recommendations drawn from the authors' own experiences as school and system leaders, a broad and deep base of cited research, frameworks and tools from other organizations, and Innovative Practices in Action stories told by other administrators across the nation. This book is a rich resource for leaders seeking to bring in new ideas and tools to increase equity, engagement, and effectiveness for today's learners—student and adult—in their schools and districts."

Beth Rabbitt
CEO, The Learning Accelerator

LEARNING TRANSFORMED

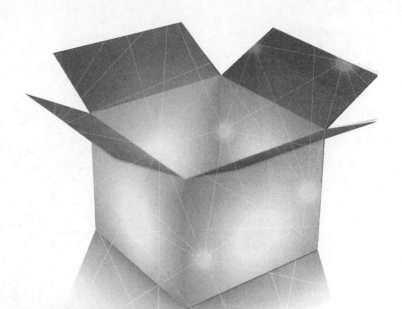

LEARNING TRANSFORMED

8 Keys to Designing Tomorrow's Schools, Today

Eric C. Sheninger | **Thomas C. Murray**

 | Alexandria, VA USA

1703 N. Beauregard St. • Alexandria, VA 22311-1714 USA
Phone: 800-933-2723 or 703-578-9600 • Fax: 703-575-5400
Website: www.ascd.org • E-mail: member@ascd.org
Author guidelines: www.ascd.org/write

Deborah S. Delisle, *Executive Director,* Robert D. Clouse, *Managing Director, Digital Content &*
Publications; Stefani Roth, *Publisher;* Genny Ostertag, *Director, Content Acquisitions;* Allison Scott,
Acquisitions Editor; Julie Houtz, *Director, Book Editing & Production;* Jamie Greene, *Associate Editor;*
Lindsey Smith, *Graphic Designer;* Mike Kalyan, *Director, Production Services;* Kyle Steichen, *Senior*
Production Specialist; Cynthia Stock, *Typesetter*

All web links in this book are correct as of the publication date below but may have become inactive
or otherwise modified since that time. If you notice a deactivated or changed link, please e-mail
books@ascd.org with the words "Link Update" in the subject line. In your message, please specify the
web link, the book title, and the page number on which the link appears.

PAPERBACK ISBN: 978-1-4166-2389-2   ASCD product #117034   n06/17
PDF E-BOOK ISBN: 978-1-4166-2391-5; see Books in Print for other formats.
Quantity discounts: 10–49, 10%; 50+, 15%; 1,000+, special discounts (e-mail programteam@ascd.org or
call 800-933-2723, ext. 5773, or 703-575-5773). For desk copies, go to www.ascd.org/deskcopy.

Library of Congress Cataloging-in-Publication Data

Names: Sheninger, Eric C., author. | Murray, Thomas C., author.
Title: Learning transformed : 8 keys to designing tomorrow's schools, today /
    Eric Sheninger & Thomas C. Murray.
Description: Alexandria, Virginia : ASCD, [2017] | Includes bibliographical
    references and index.
Identifiers: LCCN 2017006914 (print) | LCCN 2017018394 (ebook) | ISBN
    9781416623915 (PDF) | ISBN 9781416623892 (pbk.)
Subjects: LCSH: School improvement programs.
Classification: LCC LB2822.8 (ebook) | LCC LB2822.8 .S53 2017 (print) | DDC
    371.2/07—dc23
LC record available at https://lccn.loc.gov/2017006914

26 25 24 23 22 21 20 19 18   2 3 4 5 6 7 8 9 10 11 12

Eric

To my wife, Melissa.
Your constant support and encouragement make me truly believe that anything is possible. With your love and patience I have learned that dreams can and do become reality. Thanks for lifting me up when I need it the most.

Tom

To my amazing wife, Tammy.
You are my rock and the glue that holds our family together. Thank you for your daily encouragement and support in following my passion. Your unconditional love for our family and unwavering dedication to our children, Paisley and Caden, is beyond measure. Without you, the work that I do isn't possible.

LEARNING TRANSFORMED

8 Keys to Designing Tomorrow's Schools, Today

Acknowledgments

Eric

This book would never have come to be if it had not been for Tom Murray's persistence that we both had a significant story to tell. Once in motion, my family, as always, gave me so much support and inspiration to keep me focused and on task. Thanks to my wife, Melissa, and my children, Nicholas and Isabella, for always believing in me. I can't do what I do without the three of you. Thank you to my parents, Arthur and Jean Sheninger, who taught me at an early age what servant leadership means. Your guidance through all the ups and downs has helped me to become the man I am today. Finally, thank you to the team at the International Center for Leadership and Education. Throughout the past couple of years, you have shown me how, together, we all can make a positive difference in education. Thanks for believing in me!

Both Tom and I are so grateful for the amazing practitioners for providing Innovative Practices in Action. Thank you to Brad Gustafson, Darryl Adams, Suzanne Lacy, Devin Vodicka, Jayne Ellspermann, Robert LiPuma, Bart Rocco, Todd Keruskin, Gail Pletnick, Vince Scheivert, Steve Webb, Feowyn Mackinnon, Samantha Edwards, and Russell W. Booker for sharing your innovative work with us.

Tom

Acknowledging the myriad of people who have influenced my thinking over time is an impossible task. Yet in reflecting on my 17-year career and on life itself, there are those who stand head and shoulders above the rest. It is those people whose shoulders I stand on today. I must start by thanking my amazing team at Future Ready Schools® and the Alliance for Excellent Education. Our mission to serve all kids, particularly those who have been traditionally underserved, has become one of my core values. Specifically, thank you to Governor Bob Wise, the senior leadership team, and my teammates Sara Hall, Lia Dossin, and Kamila Thigpen for putting up with my crazy ideas, keeping me on task, and keeping my perspective broad. Also, thank you to Phillip Lovell, for teaching me the inner workings of federal policy and giving me the confidence and opportunities to work alongside the U.S. Congress.

To my colleagues and teammates in the Quakertown Community School District in Pennsylvania, you shaped my thinking throughout my career in public schools. You've taught me to redefine what's possible, persevere through adversity, and do whatever it takes to meet the needs of kids. A special thank you to my former superintendent Lisa Andrejko. Your vision for teaching, learning, and challenging the status quo constantly pushed my thinking and formed much of the foundation to my beliefs today.

To Scott Godshalk, Jim Moczydlowski, Kathy Winters, Joe Kuzo, Chad Evans, Richard Zinck, Cindy Lapinski, Pat Tannous, Shawn Storm, Dave DiSora, Diane Cressman, Linda Clymer, and the rest of my Strayer, Neidig, and technology department families, thank you for your amazing teamwork, diligence, and collaboration over the years. To my mentors early on—Harry Morgan, Jim Newcomer, Karen Beerer, Jim Scanlon, Bill Gretzula, Joyce Weiss, and especially Mark Wieder—thank you for investing and believing in me and for modeling what our work is all about: loving and caring about kids. To my closest edu-friends, particularly Eric Sheninger, Joe Sanfelippo, Jimmy Casas, Jeff Zoul, Tony Sinanis, Ross Cooper, George Couros, Ben Gilpin, Tom Whitford, Dwight Carter, Rich Kiker, and the #SF17 crew, thank you for always challenging my mindset and for our daily laughs.

To my parents, Tom and Cherie Murray, thank you for your unwavering love and support. You've taught me about helping those in need, leading with integrity, giving freely, putting family first, and living my Christian faith. You've always pushed me to work tirelessly for the things I want and to follow my passion. I will forever work to make you proud. To my grandparents, particularly Grandpa Kroft, thank you for your model to stand up for what was right, no matter the circumstances. I wish you were still here so I could show you your strands of influence throughout this book. To my wife, Tammy, who as an educator has always kept me grounded and as a spouse has given me unparalleled support and encouragement for the early mornings and late nights spent serving others. Finally, to my little loves, Paisley and Caden, thank you for sharing your daddy's time and energy with countless faces that you will never meet.

Together, we would also like to thank the incredible team at ASCD, particularly our acquisitions editor, Allison Scott, and our editor, Jamie

Greene, for working alongside us throughout the book writing process. Your guidance, insight, and support are recognized and appreciated by both of us.

Finally, we would like to thank the thousands of students who have touched both of our lives over the past two decades. It is for you that we work daily. It is for you that we spend countless days per year away from our families. It is you whom we choose to serve. Thank you for teaching us far more than we could ever have learned by ourselves.

Introduction: A Sense of Urgency

The American Education Crisis

Education is simply the soul of a society as it passes from one generation to another.

G.K. Chesterton

Public outcry that the education system is failing and therefore in desperate need of reform may be as old as the United States itself. A review of the nation's history, alongside the trajectory and evolution of its current education system, indicates that education reform has often been at the center of all significant reform struggles throughout the country's history.

Thomas Jefferson and Benjamin Franklin viewed education in the new nation as an extension of democratic principles. Education was seen as a means to an end—a way to solidify colonial independence from Britain—and a tool that would establish and promote the ideals of freedom, liberty, and democracy to ensure a civil society for the years ahead. Formal education was primarily reserved for white males, whereas females (who if they had any opportunity at all) were taught in dame schools, which were often held in the homes of female teachers. Our country's founders advocated for schools that would serve all people of all classes, yet girls were educated in a disorganized, second-tier system and racial motives prevented African Americans from even having the opportunity to go to school. It was an undoubtedly dark time in our nation's history (Gelbrich, 1999).

Although today's public schools hardly resemble the town's dame or private grammar schools of the colonial era, many of today's controversial topics and reform efforts are deeply rooted in our nation's past. Local control of schools, the idea of state-sanctioned standards, and the abhorrent inequities in opportunity for women, students of color, and those from low-income families remain issues that must be addressed today.

In the 1700s, the education system was wrought with significant issues of inequity. Today, more than 300 years later, equity remains one of the largest issues we must tackle as we move forward.

Since the United States was born, its guiding document—the U.S. Constitution—helped shape education policy by omitting any mention of education as a federal responsibility. The Framers purposefully abdicated education decisions to the states, with each state government responsible for setting up its own school-funding formulas, policies, and practice. Today, the issues of state funding, education policies, and desired practice remain front-page news.

By the first half of the 19th century, American society was dealing with unsettling economic and social changes. The rise of factories and the need for workers to perform repetitive, rote tasks became the desired skillset of students leaving the one-room schoolhouse. As towns and cities grew larger, the traditional agrarian work and family structure began to evolve. Simultaneously, the introduction of compulsory schooling brought about the need to manage and educate large numbers of students in a more efficient manner. As the work and school worlds began to collide, skilled workers from small towns were soon replaced by machines capable of doing the work faster and cheaper. Today's machines, through automation and robotics, are replacing workers at an unprecedented pace with the ability to do the work better, faster, and cheaper.

Political changes and the industrialization of our young nation, combined with the growing differences between the North and South over slavery and an awareness of socioeconomic gaps, led to a variety of social reform movements. Land ownership and the rights of women were just two of the areas with which society began to wrestle—and ultimately alter—significantly. The desire to expand educational opportunities, paralleled with the political issues of the time, brought out many key issues during this period, including education for middle- and lower-class boys and girls, access to higher education for women, and a free education for the nation's children of color.

Today, obtaining a high-quality education filled with ample opportunity, access to higher education, and the needs of and opportunities for our children of color remain nationwide issues.

In the early 20th century, educational progressivism, led by the well-known John Dewey, had a significant effect on education. The progressive view that students learn by doing and that students' interests should play a key role in their learning began to grow roots in classroom instruction.

Dewey's progressive style was frequently debated by traditionalists who viewed such notions as communistic and contrary to the American values of that era. As this style of education gained momentum, critics continued to push back and eventually blamed a lack of math and science skills and our failure to keep up with the Soviet Union in the Space Race on the more progressive aspects of the education system.

These same arguments are still being made today.

During the Civil Rights Movement of the 1960s, the U.S. Congress passed its most far-reaching federal education legislation to date with the Elementary and Secondary Education Act (ESEA), which included a federal commitment to support both elementary and secondary school funding, established high standards for accountability, and aimed to close achievement gaps. President Lyndon Johnson believed that our primary national goal should be a full educational opportunity for all students.

The 1980s saw the publication of *A Nation at Risk: The Imperative for Educational Reform* (National Commission on Excellence in Education, 1983). The premise of the charter leading to this report was that our education system was failing to meet the national need of a competitive workforce. The commission was required to "assess the quality of teaching and learning at the primary, secondary, and postsecondary levels" and to "compare American schools and colleges with those of other advanced nations."

Sound familiar? In the report, the commission made 38 recommendations in the following five categories:

- Content
- Standards and Expectations
- Time
- Teaching
- Leadership and Fiscal Support

"Transition to college or work," "performance-based pay," and "meeting the needs of key groups of students such as socioeconomically disadvantaged, minority, and handicapped" were all key aspects of the charter's recommendations outlined in the report. Decades later, "college and career readiness," "merit pay," and "subgroups" remain politically debated topics and headline news.

After an outcry to systemically alter the nation's "failing education system," a bipartisan overhaul of ESEA occurred in 2002 through the introduction of No Child Left Behind (NCLB), which was signed into law by President George W. Bush. NCLB pushed a standards-based education reform—bringing with it a focus on student data, achievement transparency, school accountability, and a new focus on traditionally underserved students—as accountability measures exposed achievement gaps for these students and their peers.

With this new push for accountability, standardized testing—something that had already been relatively common in some capacity for decades—became elevated and a focal point at all levels. The premise was that if high standards were set and measurable goals were implemented, then student achievement would improve. In the process, states were required to develop their own standards while the federal reach was expanded through an emphasis on testing, continued improvement, and teacher qualifications, among other things. The fundamental funding structure shifted in the process; schools deemed to be failing could risk a loss in funding or be forcibly taken over by the state. Terms such as *highly qualified, adequate yearly progress* (AYP), and *data-driven decision making* became commonplace in the vocabulary of educators.

After more than a decade of NCLB, outcries for reform over funding, testing, accountability, and federal power (from all sides of the political spectrum) had grown so strong that a bipartisan Congress stripped away virtually all of the federal power found in NCLB, returning it to states and local districts in a new, bipartisan law known as the Every Student Succeeds Act (ESSA).

Just prior to signing ESSA into law, President Obama declared, "With this bill, we reaffirm that fundamental American ideal—that every child, regardless of race, income, background, the zip code where they live, deserves the chance to make of their lives what they will" (White House, 2015b).

The U.S. Department of Education outlined the following key characteristics of ESSA:

- Holds all students to high academic standards.
- Prepares all students for success in college and career.
- Provides more kids access to high-quality preschool.
- Guarantees steps are taken to help students, and their schools, improve.
- Reduces the burden of testing while maintaining annual information for parents and students.
- Promotes local innovation and invests in what works.

Fast forward to today's American education debate. Are the most recent outcries for education reform valid? Let's look at some published statistics.

Since first being administered in 1969 to measure student achievement nationally, the National Assessment of Educational Progress (NAEP), long known as The Nation's Report Card, has measured the academic achievement of U.S. students in various subject areas. NAEP is the largest continuing and nationally representative assessment taken by students in the United States and is a Congressionally mandated project administered by the National Center for Education Statistics (NCES), within the U.S. Department of Education and the Institute of Education Sciences (IES). Math and reading assessments are administered every two years to a random, representative sample of schools and students in each state. Once results are released, assessment data is analyzed, and policymakers, researchers, and practitioners utilize the results to identify ways they believe educational outcomes can be improved.

The 2015 NAEP Math results indicated the following nationwide (National Center for Educational Statistics, 2015):

- Only two out of five 4th grade (40 percent) and one out of three 8th grade (33 percent) students performed at or above the proficient level.
- In the lowest-performing subgroup—those students identified as black—less than one in five 4th grade (19 percent) and approximately one out of eight (13 percent) 8th grade students performed at or above the proficient level.
- Asian students were the highest-performing subgroup, with 65 percent of students in 4th grade and 61 percent in 8th grade performing at or above the proficient level. This means that the nation's highest-achieving subgroup has more than one out of three students performing below grade-level expectations in math.

The 2015 NAEP Reading results indicated the following nationwide (National Center for Educational Statistics, 2015):

- Just over one in three 4th (36 percent) and 8th (34 percent) grade students performed at or above the proficient level.
- In the lowest-performing subgroup—those students identified as black—less than one in five 4th grade (18 percent) and approximately one out of six (16 percent) 8th grade students performed at or above the proficient level.

- Asian students were the highest performing subgroup, with 57 percent of students in 4th grade and 54 percent in 8th grade performing at or above the proficient level. This means that the nation's highest-achieving subgroup has less than six out of ten students performing at or above grade-level expectations in reading.

In recent years, a slight downward trend has also been seen in SAT scores in each of the three core areas: reading, math, and writing (see Figure 0.1).

FIGURE 0.1

Nationwide SAT Scores (2011–2015)

Year	Reading	Mathematics	Writing
2011	497	514	489
2012	496	514	488
2013	496	514	488
2014	497	513	487
2015	495	511	484

Source: Data from *SAT Program Participation and Performance Statistics,* 2016. Retrieved from research.collegeboard.org/programs/sat/data

When looking at specific subgroups related to SATs, the data are more bleak. In every subgroup, with the exception of Asians, average scores have decreased between 2006–2015. An analysis of the 2015 data makes the gap between subgroups transparent (see Figure 0.2).

FIGURE 0.2

Nationwide SAT Score by Subgroup (2015)

Group	Reading	Mathematics	Writing
American Indian	481	482	460
Asian American	525	598	531
African American	431	428	418
Mexican American	448	457	438
Puerto Rican	456	449	442
Other Hispanic	449	457	439
White	529	534	513

Source: Data from *SAT Program Participation and Performance Statistics,* 2016. Retrieved from research.collegeboard.org/programs/sat/data

In recent years, many colleges and universities have begun removing the SAT requirement on their applications in response to fears that SAT scores seemingly reflect family income, and—on average—Latino and African American students earn significantly lower scores than their white and Asian colleagues do. In addition, trends showed that in each of the SAT's three parts correlated significantly with family income: the lowest average scores were earned by students whose family had less than $20,000 in income, whereas the highest averages belonged to those whose families earned more than $200,000 (FairTest, 2015).

The Programme for International Student Assessment (PISA)—an assessment organized by the Organisation for Economic Co-operation and Development (OECD)—is a "triennial international survey which aims to evaluate education systems worldwide by testing the skills and knowledge of 15-year-old students" (OECD, 2017). First used as a success metric in 2000, governments, policy organizations, and education reformers utilize PISA results to gain insight into the achievement of its nation's students and to compare those results to other countries and education systems around the world.

In 2012, the U.S. PISA report indicated, "Among the 34 OECD countries, the United States performed below average in mathematics in 2012 and is ranked 27th. Performance in reading and science are both close to the OECD average. The United States ranks 17 in reading, and 20th in science. There has been no significant change in these performances over time" (OECD, 2012). Therefore, according to the PISA comparison metric, the U.S. rated average to below average in math and reading when compared to other OECD nations—a sobering statistic for one of the wealthiest countries in the world.

Some will argue, however, that standardized metrics such as PISA create homogenized systems, which promote uniformity and not the creativity needed for future success and that such comparisons shouldn't be used as a systematic success metric. In an interview on the topic, Professor Yong Zhao from the University of Kansas boldly stated, "Countries should 'ignore' the world's most influential education rankings [such as PISA] because they fail to measure what matters" (Seith, 2016). In making the argument that a homogeneous workforce *was not* what the nation needed for future success, Zhao likened competing to reach the top of the PISA tables much like university students competing to see who could drink the most beer, saying, "You're maybe the best drinker, but you've got to think, 'Is it good for you and does it matter?'"

Zhao's premise was that countries needed "creative, entrepreneurial talents able to create value for others"—not uniform workers with identical skillsets (Seith, 2016). At a micro level, recall the decades-old argument regarding whether one is supposed to "teach to the test" or if the test theoretically measures the desired standards. In this case, "teaching to the test" equates to "teaching to the standards" and is thus actually a reliable measurement of desired outcomes. Regardless of where one's viewpoint falls, the nature and quality of the assessments, as well as what transpires from the results, are thrust into the spotlight. Some would argue that we should chase one metric (or set of goals) and ignore another. Others would claim that saying we should ignore metrics that compare academic skills is simply a cover-up and an excuse for a failing system. Yet still others would claim that regardless of what metric is being used or measured, today's K–12 education system is failing on both fronts.

Not all U.S. education statistics are doom and gloom, however. According to the National Center for Education Statistics (2016), nationwide graduation rates increased from 71 percent (during the 1990–91 school year) to 82 percent (in 2013–14), indicating a positive trend upward over the past few decades. In 2002, there were roughly 2,000 schools across the country in which 40 percent or more of their students did not graduate. In 2014, the number of these schools had been reduced to 1,040—a near 50 percent reduction (White House, 2015a). In late 2016, while speaking at a high school in Washington, DC, President Obama announced that graduation rates from 2014–2015 had again increased to the highest rates ever recorded: 83.2 percent (White House, 2016a).

Although the United States may boast its highest graduation rates on record, a Gallup Student Poll (2015) of almost one million U.S. students from 3,300 schools across 46 states indicated a consistent decrease in levels of engagement as students get older, ultimately bottoming out in 11th grade where less than one in three students feels engaged in school. The survey, taken by students in grades 5–12, indicated that only *half of adolescents* report feeling engaged in school, whereas one-fifth were actively disengaged (see Figures 0.3 and 0.4).

Digging deeper, the Gallup poll asked students to evaluate nine engagement related areas, which included the following:

1. At this school, I get to do what I do best every day.
2. I have fun at school.
3. In the last seven days, I have learned something interesting at school.

FIGURE 0.3

Percentage of Students Engaged in School, By Grade

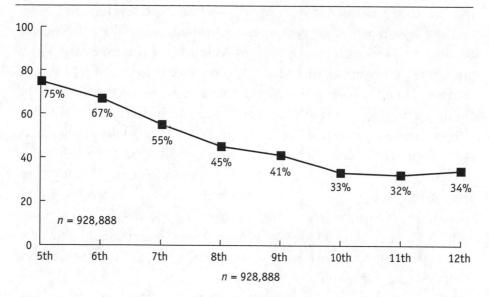

n = 928,888

n = 928,888

Source: Data from "Engaged today: Ready for tomorrow," by the Gallup Student Poll, 2015. Available: www.gallupstudent poll.com/188036/2015-gallup-student-poll-overall-report.aspx

FIGURE 0.4

Percentage of Students Who Strongly Agree, By Grade

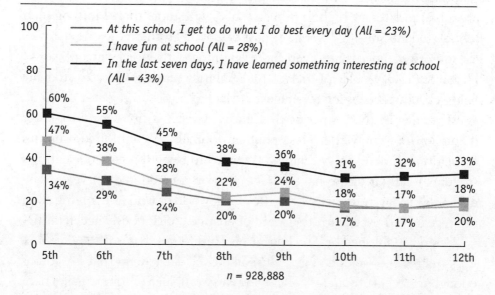

n = 928,888

Source: Data from "Engaged today: Ready for tomorrow," by the Gallup Student Poll, 2015. Available: www.gallupstudent poll.com/188036/2015-gallup-student-poll-overall-report.aspx

Mirroring a similar decline as seen in the self-reported engagement levels of students, the longer students are in the K–12 educational system, the less they feel interested in what they learn, the less fun they have, and the less they feel they get to tap into their own skills and abilities. Student attitudes regarding these areas decline every year from 5th to 11th grade with a tiny uptick in 12th grade, which we believe can probably be attributed to more enjoyable senior year opportunities and the fact that the finish line is in sight. What's also troubling about the survey results is that one of the steepest declines occurs for the item "The adults at my school care about me," decreasing from 67 percent of 5th graders to 23 percent of 11th graders who strongly agreed with the statement. This indicates that many students, particularly at the high school level, don't feel individually known or cared for while at school. This feedback from almost a million children nationwide causes grave concern and should challenge the thinking of us all. We must take responsibility for this student feedback and *transform* the learning experience.

We believe that the freefall in engagement, relevance, and fun—as exhibited in the Gallup survey—is one of the main factors that has led to the issue of chronic absenteeism. An analysis by the U.S. Department of Education (2016) reported that 6 million students (13.1%), nearly one out of every eight students in our nation's schools, missed 15 or more days of school. Correlating with the engagement survey and trend line, chronic absenteeism rates are highest in high school with more than 2 million high school students missing 15 or more days of school. Furthermore, the statistics for minority students are even more alarming with larger percentages of Hispanic (13.3%), black (16.4%), and American Indian (22.2%) students being chronically absent (see Figure 0.5).

The idea of the "American Education Crisis" is not a new topic for discussion or simply the latest political football. As exhibited, outcries for reforming a broken system and the need to better prepare our nation's students for their future have in fact gone on for hundreds of years. The difference today, however, is that the global world of work is evolving at an unprecedented pace, with the speed of change continuously accelerating.

A study published by The Education Trust found that only 8 percent of U.S. high school graduates actually complete a curriculum that is rigorous enough to prepare them for college and the workplace (Bromberg & Theokas, 2016). The study analyzed the transcript data of 23,000 students in the 2009 Federal High School Longitudinal Study, from 9th grade through their

FIGURE 0.5

Chronic Absenteeism in U.S. Schools

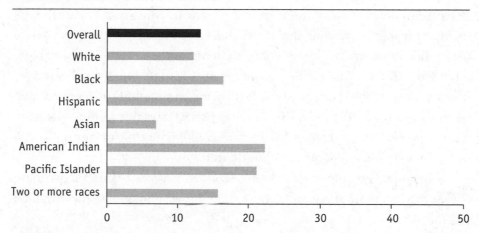

Source: From "Chronic Absenteeism in the Nation's Schools," by the U.S. Department of Education, 2016. Available: www2.ed.gov/datastory/chronicabsenteeism.html

projected graduation year in 2013 and beyond (NCES, 2013). Researchers reviewed the coursework each graduate took and the grades they earned to produce readiness projections. Red flags ensued as evidence suggested a trend that indicated students were "meandering toward graduation" and focused on earning credits instead of building a strong base of knowledge and skills for life after high school. The report's coauthor, Marni Bromberg, believes that the rising graduation rates and higher postsecondary enrollments are a positive development, yet it is important we do not see high school graduation as the end goal. In a post-release interview, Bromberg shared, "Schools might be over-prioritizing what that diploma means [and how results indicated that] schools are really focused on getting students the credits they need to get them across the stage with a diploma in hand as opposed to getting them the knowledge and the skills they need to set them up for success" (Moser, 2016).

As the outcry for education reform continues, the opportunities available for those with only a high school diploma remain in a freefall. In today's global economy, a high school diploma is simply not enough for people to succeed. As corporations move manufacturing jobs overseas, the availability of lower-level positions—those jobs that require low-level skills—moves with them. Simultaneously, the process of automation through technology has made many jobs that were commonplace for decades now completely obsolete.

The continuous dismal achievement of both our low-income students and students of color, and the equity in opportunities for these groups, remains a very real component of the American education crisis. Today's reality mirrors the systemic inequities that have prevailed over time. Since our nation's inception, low-income students and students of color have attended schools with far fewer opportunities; that are typically led by less-qualified, less-experienced educators; and in systems that often receive far less funding. Ultimately, this unfairly perpetuates our nation's struggle with poverty. No longer should one's zip code predict his or her socioeconomic destiny and generational family tree.

Newspaper headlines regarding today's educational issues accentuate the negative on what seems to be a daily basis. Some examples include the following:

- "How Bad are Conditions in Detroit Public Schools? This Appalling" (Strauss, 2016)
- "City to close failing schools for the first time" (Gonen & Campanile, 2015)
- "NYC Public Schools are Still Segregated" (Riazi, 2016)
- "School vs. Society in America's Failing Students" (Porter, 2015)
- "How Troubled Teachers Cheat the System" (Reilly, 2016)

One interesting point to consider regarding today's schools, known by psychologists as the "mere-exposure effect," is the notion that people tend to like things better the more they know and understand them. This notion can be seen when people seem to like things locally but seem more jaded the larger the scale. Research indicates that this also holds true with the nation's perception of schools. The policy journal *Education Next* released its 10th annual large national poll of public opinion in late 2016. Highlighted in that poll is that the opinions of Americans regarding their own local schools has actually risen considerably over the 10 years of polling. In 2016, more than half of those surveyed—55 percent—gave their community school an A or B rating, which rose 10 percent from 43 percent a decade earlier. However, in comparison, public opinion of the nation's schools overall is much lower, with only 25 percent of respondents giving an A or B grade to U.S. schools as a whole (Education Next, 2016).

Showing similar results is a 2016 Gallup poll in which respondents indicated public approval at a low ebb with record rates of political polarization over our nation's schools. However, the survey indicated that three out of four parents approve of their own kids' schools, with 76 percent indicating that they are satisfied with the education their oldest child has received to date (Saad, 2016). These survey results both accentuate the perception gap in understanding our nation's schools, as parents seemingly approve of their community school but overall have serious concerns about the direction of the nation's K–12 education system.

Since the signing of the Declaration of Independence, reform efforts have not reached a consensus as to the single best education system for our nation's children. We believe that they never will. The evolution of the education system has been slow. Providing a top-notch education to every one of the nation's 50 million students in our 100,000 schools and properly training our 3 million teachers is a monumental task. This problem is only amplified when we look at global education. The scale itself is massive, and there is absolutely no silver bullet or simple fix. Moving the needle worldwide is difficult work, but it begins with one school and one district at a time. Regardless of the angle of reform that is taken, all will agree that education plays a foundational role in maintaining a vibrant democracy and free society for our nation's future.

We believe in today's school leaders. They are some of the most dynamic, talented people on the planet, yet "failure" is not an option for the students that we serve. These issues are not isolated to the United States. International security, the success of global economies, and sustainability as a global society depends on the success of our education systems in the years to come.

You are part of the solution.

Industry 4.0: The Next Industrial Revolution

"Never in human history have we seen so many technologies moving at such a pace . . . and everything is being disrupted in the process."

— Salim Ismail (2014)

Today's pace of technological change is staggering, and the speed of current breakthroughs has no historical precedent. Consumers may seem well-versed with the latest personal gadgets, yet growth in artificial intelligence (AI), robotics, autonomous vehicles, the Internet of Things (IoT), and nano-technology remains hardly known except by technology gurus who live and breathe ones and zeros. The coming interplay of such technologies from both physical and virtual worlds will make the once unthinkable, possible.

We believe that we are in the first few days of the next Industrial Revolution and that the coming age will systematically shift the way we live, work, and connect to and with one another. It will affect the very essence of the way humans experience the world. Although the 2000s brought with them significant change in how we utilize technology to interact with the world around us, the coming transformational change will be unlike anything mankind has ever experienced (Schwab, 2016).

The Fourth Industrial Revolution, toward which we are racing as a society, is still in its infancy but growing exponentially. Advances in technology are disrupting almost every industry and in almost every country. No longer do natural or political borders significantly reduce the acceleration of change. Take a moment to consider the digital disruption that has already occurred in the following industries (Goodwin, 2015):

- The largest taxi company owns no (human-driven) taxis. (Uber)
- The largest accommodations provider owns no real estate. (Airbnb)
- The most valuable retailer has no inventory. (Alibaba)
- The most popular media platform creates no content. (Facebook)
- The largest movie house owns no cinemas. (Netflix)
- The largest phone companies own no telecommunications infrastructure. (Skype, WhatsApp, Facebook Messenger)
- The fastest-growing banks actually have no money. (Kickstarter, Zopa, SocietyOne)

In some industries, the number of people needed for the workforce is being reduced—by drastic numbers. According to *The Economic Times* (2015), a Chinese firm specializing in precision technology opened the first unmanned factory at which all processes are operated by computer-controlled robots, machining equipment, unmanned transport trucks, and automated warehouse equipment. Human labor no longer works the long lines in factory. What took 650 people to do a few months prior now requires only three employees to monitor the lines and system control unit. Production reviews indicate that these robots are making far more and far better products than their human counterparts did. Data at the factory show that since the robots had their first day on the job, the defect rate of products has dropped from more than 25 percent to less than 5 percent, and the production capacity has risen from more than 8,000 units per person per month to over 21,000 units.

These robots need no coffee in the morning, no breaks, no paid time off, no vacation time, and they'll never call in sick. These machines will never ask for a raise, and, unlike people, they will get better and cheaper over time. Our traditional system cannot compete under those conditions. As such, companies that have refused to innovate are either on life support or dead.

The First Industrial Revolution began with the transition to new manufacturing processes and lasted from approximately 1760 to sometime in the first half of the 19th century. This revolution included machine production, new steam power, and the development of a complex factory system. During this era, steam engines and railroads were built and sectors such as the textile industry flourished with the ability to mechanize production.

Beginning around 1870 and lasting until the first World War, the Second Industrial Revolution—also known as the Technological Revolution—saw explosions in manufacturing and production technology through the use of railroad networks, plentiful gas and water supplies, new creations with iron and steel, and a significant expansion of the transportation system, which enabled unprecedented globalization. With the rise in availability of electrical power, the opportunity for assembly lines and mass production increased both efficiency and output.

The Digital Revolution, also known as the Third Industrial Revolution, began in the mid-20th century and lasted until around the turn of this century. During that time, information became digital by design, and personal computing, mainframe computers, and the evolution of the Internet came not only to the world of work but also to everyday life. What was once stored in a filing cabinet moved to a computer database. What had previously played on a record player or in a tape deck moved to a portable, digital music device. In a short time, digital music became available for download with the click of a button. Soon after, music stores began to close, since people no longer needed to leave their homes to purchase the music they wanted to hear. Listening to one's favorite album also became cheaper. During this revolution, similar disruptions occurred in the video industry as the thought of driving down the road to rent and return a video became obsolete; movies and television programs began to stream right into our homes—on demand. Anytime, anywhere. Today's children and future generations will have no concept about what it was like to wait a whole week to watch their favorite TV show. On-demand content has already become a way of life.

During the years of the Digital Revolution, the world's information began to grow at an exponential rate. To this day, digital devices continue to get faster, better, and cheaper—a notion that schools must learn to use to their advantage. Computer programs have already rendered certain jobs obsolete as basic tasks can be automated with less cost and reduced error in the process.

Today, we are taking our first steps into the Fourth Industrial Revolution, created by the fusion of technologies that overlap physical, biological, and digital ecosystems. Known to some as Industry 4.0, these possibilities have been defined as "the next phase in the digitization of the manufacturing sector, driven by four disruptions: the astonishing rise in data volumes, computational power, and connectivity, especially new low-power, wide-area networks; the emergence of analytics and business-intelligence capabilities; new forms of human-machine interaction such as touch interfaces and augmented-reality systems; and improvements in transferring digital instructions to the physical world, such as advanced robotics and 3-D printing" (Baur & Wee, 2015). Such systems of automation enable intelligence to monitor the physical world, replicate it virtually, and make decisions about the process moving forward. In essence, machines now have the ability to think, problem solve, and make critical decisions. In this era, the notion of big data and data analytics will drive decision making.

Sound far-fetched? It's not. The time is here, and you're already benefiting from such advances in technology. From AI to self-driving vehicles to automated home systems, the seeds of this new technological revolution are already planted and starting to grow.

Today, a college student can transfer money to and from his or her bank account, listen to music, watch a favorite TV episode, pay bills, book a flight, order pizza, shop at a favorite store, send a message to a friend in the next room, and special order a rare collector's edition item—all while never moving out of his or her seat during an afternoon class. Only a few years ago, those combined tasks would have taken an entire day.

According to the Pew Research Center (2104), 48 percent of experts surveyed believe that robots and other advances in technology will displace a significant number of both blue- and white-collar workers in the coming years. These experts also predicted that robots and "digital agents" will begin to displace more jobs than they create by 2025.

In 2015, a report published by McKinsey & Company indicated that currently demonstrated technologies could automate 45 percent of the activities people are paid to perform, and approximately 60 percent of all occupations could see 30 percent or more of their constituent activities automated (Chui, Manyika, & Miremadi, 2016). These estimates are made with the technologies that are currently available, not those that will be developed in the years ahead. With technology evolving rapidly, we predict that these numbers will only continue to climb.

In the Economic Report of the President (White House, 2016b), White House economists forecasted an 83 percent chance that workers earning less than $20 per hour will eventually lose their current jobs to automation. These economists also estimate that those who earn between $20 and $40 per hour face a 31 percent chance of being replaced, whereas higher-wage earners—those earning more than $40 per hour—have a much smaller chance of replacement, with estimates being as low as 4 percent.

For now.

An all-too-often, prideful, American mindset seems to think "that won't happen to me." This way of thinking is littered with an outright denial or disbelief in the evolving and adapting world in which we live. Validating that notion, the Pew Research Center (2014) also found that 80 percent of Americans think their job will still exist in 50 years, with only 11 percent of today's workforce worried about losing their jobs due to robots or automation. To transfer that mindset to education, those who continuously cling to the mindset of "this is how I've always done things" can only be sheltered for so long as the new revolution not only affects forces outside of our buildings but also the students who are coming in.

The notion of technology replacing people is not a new concept. As early as 1930, long before the first personal device, John Maynard Keynes wrote about "technological unemployment"—the theory that "workers could be displaced due to society's ability to improve labor efficiency at a faster rate than finding new uses of labor" (Keynes, 1930, p. 360). This thought is more relevant today than it was early last century. In a similar light, the notion that we are preparing students for jobs that don't yet exist remains true, but that has always been the case. Nevertheless, in the years ahead, the speed of accelerated change will be unparalleled.

Some continue to believe that these shifts are decades away; others believe that these changes are coming quickly. Noted futurist Ray Kurzweil (2014), Google's director of engineering, believes that AI will equal human intelligence by 2029. Along similar lines, the Future of Jobs report from the World Economic Forum (2016) calculated that by 2020, the technological changes that are underway will likely remove the need for 7.1 million jobs around the world, with only 2.1 million jobs being replaced in the process.

Maybe their calculations are a few years off. But what if they're only half wrong?

Released in 2014 (and revised in 2015), the Employment Projections Program of the Bureau of Labor Statistics (2015a) predicted that by 2024, increases in job growth would occur in positions such as software developers (18.8%), computer systems analysts (20.9%), and market research analysts (18.6%), showing that the ability to utilize data and possess an analytical skillset would be in demand in the coming years. Another area of predicted increase? Healthcare. Occupations with the most projected growth include personal care aides (25.9%), home health aides (38.1%), and medical assistants (23.5%), showing the long-term value in social interactions and relationships.

How are our schools preparing students for the types of jobs that will exist in this future global workforce?

One must wonder what happens to the gaps in already existing inequalities as high-skilled, high-wage earners continue to flourish in the new economy while those who are low skilled become even less employable. How do we avoid a global society filled with technology-induced unemployment, minimal productivity by large masses of the population, and even larger gaps in equity than exist today, resulting in unparalleled poverty in a revolutionized world? Without a high-quality, dynamic education system leading into the future, inequalities will be exacerbated.

What was the key to future work sustainability proposed by the White House in a 2016 report to Congress? Maintaining a "robust training and education agenda" (White House, 2016b). To combat the impending wave of low-skilled job removal, we must develop and empower a generation of innovators who create new industries and companies and also use their genius to find new solutions to tomorrow's world's problems.

As we enter this next Industrial Revolution—Industry 4.0—a robust education, combined with personalized training will be key to one's success and, ultimately, their economic survival. To prepare students for their world of work tomorrow, we must transform their learning today.

You are part of the solution.

Equity: A Moral Imperative

"We are true to our creed when a little girl born into the bleakest poverty knows that she has the same chance to succeed as anybody else."

Barack Obama, Inaugural Address: January 21, 2013

Since the inception of the United States, there has been a great disparity in educational access and opportunity. No Child Left Behind (NCLB), signed into law in 2001, focused a new lens on the achievement gap between low-income and more advantaged students, between students of color—especially African American, Latino, American Indian, and Pacific Islander students—and white students, between English language learners and native speakers of English, and between students with and without disabilities (Darling-Hammond, Zielezinski, & Goldman, 2014). The achievement gaps by both ethnicity and income remain unconscionably large, affecting the quality of life for too many of our nation's children. Fortunately, in recent years, much attention has been brought to these inequities and work is being done to compress the gaps that have existed for far too long.

The challenge of ensuring equity throughout a nation's education system is formidable. Traditional barriers, including inequitable funding systems, undoubtedly impede our progress as a society. According to the U.S. Department of Education, 45 percent of high-poverty schools received less state and local funding when compared with other schools in their district (Heuer & Stullich, 2011). These low-socioeconomic schools are often forced to spend far less per pupil on educational expenditures, affecting student-teacher ratios, access to school counselors, and opportunities for rigorous coursework. Not surprisingly, with fewer opportunities, these traditionally underserved students also attend and complete college at far lower rates than their non-underserved counterparts, further cementing the cycle of poverty for many families.

The School Discipline Data Snapshot from the Office of Civil Rights (2014) at the U.S. Department of Education indicates that minority and low-income students are also suspended, expelled, and drop out at higher rates than their peers. For instance, in preschools nationwide, African American students represent 18 percent of enrollments yet account for 42 percent of suspensions. As these students get older, the picture remains the same. There are disproportionately high rates of suspensions and expulsions of our students of color, disproportionately high rates of suspensions for students with disabilities and English learners, and disproportionately high rates of suspensions for our girls of color (Office of Civil Rights, 2014).

Underserved students are also less likely to have access to a rigorous curriculum taught by highly qualified, certified teachers. It's been found that 81 percent of Asian American and 71 percent of white high school students attend schools where a full caseload of math and science courses are offered, whereas only 57 percent of African American, 67 percent of Latino, 63 percent of students with disabilities, and 65 percent of English language learners had access to these same courses in their schools. What's worse is less than 50 percent of American Indian and Native Alaskan students, living in one of wealthiest nations in the world, have the needed access (Heuer & Stullich, 2011).

In recent years, science, technology, engineering, and math (collectively known as STEM) have received accolades, and a newfound push in these areas has promoted rigorous coursework focused on high-level cognitive thought. In the STEM arena—or STEAM, which includes the arts—computer science is one subject that has come into focus. From Code.org's Hour of Code to President Obama's 2016 Computer Science for All initiative, computer science has helped bring the importance of educational equity to the forefront in an effort to provide opportunities for *all* children. When the Computer Science for All initiative was unveiled, fewer than 15 percent of U.S. high schools offered computer science coursework (Smith, 2016), and only a fraction of those schools offered students the opportunity to learn to code. Consistent with other demographic metrics, in the 10 percent of high schools where computer science courses were available, girls and our students of color were tragically underrepresented; the vast majority of participants were white males.

Girls Who Code, an organization with a mission to "inspire, educate, and equip girls with the computing skills to pursue 21st century opportunities," reports that in 1984, 37 percent of all computer science graduates were female. In recent years, that number has been cut by more than half to only 18 percent. Moreover, in 2013, only 20 percent of AP Computer Science test-takers were female, whereas less than one half of one percent of girls expressed any interest in majoring in the subject after high school (Girls Who Code, 2017).

When students' interest levels in computer science was analyzed over a 40-year period from 1971 to 2011, a wide range in student interest levels was seen (Sax et al., 2015). However, one constant was that females were continuously underrepresented. Two key findings outlined in that study were as follows:

1. Women with artistic or social activist leanings haven't perceived computer science as complementary to their skills.
2. Research indicates girls' deteriorating confidence in their own math abilities.

This generation of girls, our students of color, and all underserved students deserve better. So why does this gap still exist? Although this issue remains complex, we believe there are two prevalent reasons.

1. Sexism still exists in our society and enters the psyche of our little ones at an early age. Walk down the toy aisles of most stores and notice the "pink products" pushing girls to be homemakers and "pretty" while the "blue products" encourage boys to create, design, and take risks.

2. Low expectations for our students of color are still prevalent. A study focused on teachers' expectations of students based on race showed how one's natural bias—a form of racism—affects personal perceptions and expectations and thus classroom instructional practices (Gershenson, Holt, & Papageorge, 2015). With lower expectations, students of color get weeded out of advanced math and science courses at an alarming rate. What's worse, many schools with a high percentage of students in poverty, which often correlates to a high percentage of students of color, often offer little-to-no opportunity for higher-level coursework. Regardless of achievement or ability levels, the opportunity doesn't even exist for these students to take the desired coursework.

A review of College Board data from the 2013 Advanced Placement Computer Science test indicate that only 18.5 percent of testers were female, 3.7 percent were black, and 8.1 percent were Hispanic. Approximately 30,000 students took this exam that year, and in 11 states not a single African American student took the exam; in 8 states, not a single Hispanic student took the exam (Institute for Computing Education at Georgia Tech, 2013).

Zero. In entire *states*.

This represents an epic failure of our current education system and a complete failure in providing equitable opportunity for all of our nation's students. Saying that these unacceptable facts need to change is a gross understatement. Our nation must find ways to engage the amazing talents of our female students and those who are traditionally underserved.

The heart of the conversation around computer science isn't simply about coding. It's not about preparing students to be software engineers or computer programmers. It's about expanding access and opportunity for all students and empowering them to pursue their passions and unleash their genius.

What's interesting is that the data gleaned from the first-ever nationally representative assessment of Technology & Engineering Literacy, which was administered by the National Assessment of Educational Progress (NAEP) in 2014 to over 21,000 students in more than 800 schools to look at STEM-related skills (Nation's Report Card, 2014). For that assessment, 8th grade students were presented with real-world scenarios involving technology and engineering challenges. Students were asked to respond to questions geared toward assessing their knowledge and skill in understanding technology principles, solving technology- and engineering-related problems, and using technology to communicate and collaborate. In an analysis of the results, the following was found:

- A gender gap was evident as girls outperformed boys by an average of three percentage points.
- Students who were not eligible for free and reduced-price lunch scored an average of 28 percent higher than those who qualified.
- Less than half of the students who took the exam (43%) scored proficient or higher. Similar to other national measures, the gap varied widely when comparing scores by ethnicity. Some 56 percent of white and Asian students were proficient on the exam, whereas only 28 percent of Hispanic and 18 percent of African American students who took the exam scored proficient or higher.
- Higher-performing 8th grade students were more likely to engage in technology and engineering activities both in and out of school.

To the last point—and to no one's surprise—those students who engage in technology and engineering activities in and out of school performed better than those that didn't. However, equity in access remains a tremendous disparity in our nation. According to a 2013 report, "Teachers of the lowest income students are the least likely to say their students have sufficient access to the digital tools they need, both in school and at home. In terms of community type, teachers in urban areas are the least likely to say their students have sufficient access to digital tools in school, while rural teachers are the least likely to say their students have sufficient access at home" (Purcell, Heaps, Buchanan, & Friedrich, 2013).

Furthermore, according to a 2014 Pew Research Center analysis of the 2013 American Community Survey, 5 million households with school-age children do not have high-speed Internet access at home. Low-income households, specifically our African American and Hispanic children, make up a disproportionate percentage of the 5 million unconnected families. Compounding the issue for those living in poverty, the Digital

Equity Action Toolkit, released by the Consortium of School Networking, indicated that in 2015, three out of four school districts surveyed did not have any plan for student connectivity once they left the school campus (Consortium of School Networking, 2016).

As two dads of school-age girls, we only want our daughters to be computer scientists if that's their passion. As they get older, we only want them coding if it's what they want to do. We want them to follow their passions and dreams—not what they think the world is telling them, as girls, to do. What we don't want, and what we can't have, is an educational system or a society that pushes the girls of future generations—and our students of color—away from high-octane classes and dynamic opportunities. Our nation needs their gifts and abilities. We need their genius.

You are part of the solution.

The Need for Schools that are Future Ready

The electric light did not come from the continuous improvement of candles.

Oren Harari

The traditional model of schooling in which students are taught to regurgitate information, ultimately preparing them for the industrial model of the past, must dramatically shift to a more personal approach if we are to prepare this generation of students to become successful citizens in a global society. No longer is this notion some idealistic, utopian-esque, desired outcome. We believe that with all that is known about how students learn, the predictions regarding the world they will face upon graduation, and the vast disparities of inequity that have existed for centuries, utilizing a traditional, one-size-fits-all approach to teaching and learning is educational malpractice.

By virtually every metric, too many of today's schools are failing to adequately prepare students for life after graduation. Nearly half of Hispanics, African Americans, and American Indians do not graduate on time with their classmates. *Nearly half*. Nationwide, more than 1 million U.S. high school students drop out each year. That means an American high school student drops out of school every 29 seconds (Watson & Gemin, 2008).

Today's generation of students, regardless of the zip code they call home, deserve and need greater opportunities than the traditional education structure has previously afforded them in the past. This isn't simply an educational issue to debate but an economic issue that will have a lasting impact on generations to come. The future stability of all nations depends on the educational choices their school leaders make today. We must intentionally design our schools and transform the student learning experience.

You are part of the solution.

Organization of the Book

Eight Keys for Intentional Design

This book outlines eight keys to intentionally designing tomorrow's schools so today's learners are prepared for success far beyond earning a high school diploma and are ready to create new industries, find new cures, and solve tomorrow's world problems. Each key, individually dissected in a chapter, serves as a puzzle piece for redesigning our K–12 education system of teaching and learning. The eight keys for designing tomorrow's schools, today, are as follows.

Key #1: Leadership and school culture lay the foundation. School improvement efforts rely heavily on high-quality, collaborative leadership. Educational leaders are tasked with establishing a collective vision for school improvement and initiating change to spur innovation, ensure student learning, and increase achievement. In a world where the acceleration of change continues to grow exponentially, school cultures need to evolve at a faster rate to keep pace with these changes if the ultimate goal is to prepare today's learners for future success. The overarching emphasis is and must be about making a difference in the lives of children. Leading and teaching is challenging work that requires a high level of understanding and patience in order to transform a school's learning culture to one that is valued by students, educators, and other key stakeholders. A new foundation must be established through relationship-oriented, innovative leadership practices in order to create a culture of learning that will prepare students for their future, not our past.

Key #2: The learning experience must be redesigned and made personal. Studies in neuroscience have indicated that students traditionally forget most of the factual information that they 'learned' while in school.

We have all experienced a time when we crammed for a test, earned a passing grade, and promptly forgot the information a few weeks later. These studies indicate that simply shoving factual information into students' brains is ultimately a waste of time and resources. Such practices have led to an engagement crisis, which isn't surprising since students are often told what to learn, when to learn it, and how it should be learned. Very rarely do students have the opportunity to follow their passions, explore their interests, and engage in relevant opportunities that break down traditional classroom silos. Student agency must become the norm, not the exception. Instructional pedagogy must become focused on higher-order skills and problem solving while anytime, anywhere learning must become a realistic possibility for today's "Netflix generation" of students.

Key #3: Decisions must be grounded in evidence and driven by a Return on Instruction. The evolution of the U.S. educational structure has created a generation of students that is hyperfocused on grades, not learning. Students need to be afforded authentic opportunities to use real-world tools to do real-world work that matters. Technology provides educators with the means to allow students to demonstrate conceptual mastery and develop ownership in ways never before imagined. Changing the way and means by which we assess is a step in the right direction, but a more concerted effort to provide evidence that technology is actually affecting learning and achievement is the ultimate goal. School cultures must begin to focus on the Return on Instruction (ROI). When infusing technology, there needs to be an ROI that results in evidence of improved student learning outcomes.

Key #4: Learning spaces must become learner-centered. A shift in pedagogy mandates a shift in learning space design. Such changes are not simply an idea from the latest Pinterest board but one of necessity. Schools and classrooms must transform from an industrial era model with teacher-centric environments and orderly rows of desks and students all facing the same direction to spaces that are learner-centered, more personal in nature, and correlate with research on how space affects learning. Educators who want to build collaboration, problem solving, and higher-order thinking skills yet have spaces that resemble the classrooms of the industrial era are inhibiting innovation and missing the opportunity to unleash student genius. Learning spaces need to be flexible, provide areas for movement, and promote collaboration and inquiry. These types of modern spaces resemble the local Starbucks more than they do a nearby cemetery.

Key #5: Professional learning must be relevant, engaging, ongoing, and made personal. The notion of effective professional learning is something that has been discussed for decades. A comparison of the philosophies of today's school districts yields results that fall across a continuum of who controls and owns the learning. Various studies indicate that the top-down, one-size-fits-all, hours-based, sit-and-get approach to professional learning shows little-to-no impact on student achievement. Nevertheless, many districts continue down this path. We believe that equating seat time with accountability is teetering on negligence. The professional learning that occurs in many districts today must undergo radical reform, as the traditional model is outdated and ineffective. A personal approach to professional learning, where growth is valued more than hours obtained, is needed to shift instructional pedagogy. Who owns the learning is key.

Key #6: Technology must be leveraged and used as an accelerant for student learning. Much of the money spent on technology today has little-to-no impact on student learning. In many classrooms, technology is used simply to digitize outdated practices. Many of today's classrooms have amazing 21st century tools being used in 20th century learning environments. Research also indicates that one of the most common forms of integration—the digital drill-and-kill—has no effect on achievement. Even with stagnant budgets, school districts continue to buy more educational technology than ever before, often with little to show for it. However, when effectively used, technology can amplify great instructional pedagogy, adapt to the individual needs of the learner, and help make learning a more personal, engaging, and rigorous experience. Intentionally designed schools also ensure equity in access and opportunity for *all* students.

Key #7: Community collaboration and engagement must be woven into the fabric of a school's culture. Parents are instrumental in the academic success of children, yet walk into many schools, and the range of parent engagement is all over the map. Some schools work to create a welcoming environment where the community is seen as a tremendous asset. In these schools, you'll see parents working side by side with students, laughing at lunch with a group of students, working in classrooms, and collaborating with staff in various capacities. By contrast, some schools create cultures in which parents hardly feel welcome at all. In these schools, parents are seemingly locked out and left standing at the front door, with the possible exception of a few planned events per year. Every business and university in our country is located within school boundary lines, yet the vast majority have little to no relationship with the schools that line the same streets. From daily collaboration to consistent, relevant communications to supporting home access for students in need, intentionally designed schools are collaborative partners and the hub of the local community.

Key #8: Schools that transform learning are built to last as financial, political, and pedagogical sustainability ensure long-term success. A budget impasse. A political attack. A shift in instructional pedagogy. How will your school district's success stand the test of time? Will one budget cycle or a defeated referendum sink the ship? Will a shift in school board politics undo recent progress? Will instructional growth continue as your teaching staff changes? With the average district superintendent tenure lasting only a handful of years and the pending retirement of a generation of experienced school leaders, long-term sustainability is needed to avoid turmoil that will negatively affect future generations. Is your school built to last?

Toward the end of each chapter, you'll hear from some of the best educational minds working in schools today. These school leaders are breaking through barriers, overcoming obstacles, and helping families break the chains of poverty, all while providing dynamic learning opportunities for all students by fundamentally redesigning the educational landscape in their districts. These vignettes, shared as Innovative Practices in Action and written by the school leaders themselves, relate success stories from districts large and small, from urban to rural, and from some of the most economically challenged communities. Each of these school leaders has intentionally designed his or her way to amazing student success where learning has been transformed.

We can no longer wait. Time is of the essence. It is our obligation to prepare our students for their future and not our past. We must create and lead schools that are relevant for the world our students live in—not the world our staff grew up in. We must do this . . . starting today.

You are part of the solution.

1 Creating a Culture of Innovation

 Leadership and school culture lay the foundation.

The Role of Leadership

Management is about persuading people to do things they do not want to do, while leadership is about inspiring people to do things they never thought they could.

Steve Jobs

The influence of leadership is second only to the influence of the classroom teacher in determining student success. The effect of leadership is also greatest in schools with the highest levels of need (Leithwood, Louis, Anderson, & Wahlstrom, 2004; Marzano, Waters, & McNulty, 2005).

So what is true leadership?

When people come across the word *leader*, it often precedes the word *follower*. Leadership is not about attracting others to follow. This notion conveys a sense of power, authority, and control that might serve one well in the short term (by getting others to fall into line through conformity), but it doesn't create the innovative conditions necessary for sustainable change. The definition and resulting perception of *leader* needs a makeover.

Great leaders don't tell people what to do but instead take them to where they need to be. There is no agenda to create a harem of followers or disciples. True leaders know that their success is intimately tied to the work of the collective. As such, they encourage risk taking and create a culture of innovation and trust. One person doesn't win a war, an election,

29

or a football game. The pinnacle of success comes from a dynamic team approach where each person knows that he or she has an important role to play—that the work has meaning. We can also say with certainty that one person doesn't singlehandedly build a successful business. This same principle undoubtedly applies to schools and districts, as school leaders must be creative and forward thinking in obtaining streams of human talent and capital resources required to sustain their success.

The following acronym has been developed to add context to the evolving role of leadership in schools today. The best leaders do the following on a consistent basis:

Learn
Empower
Adapt
Delegate
Engage
Reflect
Serve

Learn

Learning is the heart of the work. Great leaders are committed to professional growth since they know there is no perfection in any position—just daily improvement. Leaders engage in both formal and informal experiences to improve their practice, which will ultimately have a positive effect on student learning (Leithwood et al., 2004). Leaders make the time to learn and get better on a daily basis and, in turn, make their learning visible as an inspiration to others. Leaders who love their work are always learning.

Empower

A key element of effective leadership is the ability to empower others to take risks, remove the fear of failure, and grant autonomy to innovate. A recent study that surveyed 1,500 workers from six different countries showed that humility is one of four critical leadership factors for creating such an environment (Prime & Salib, 2014). People who are empowered find greater value in the work they are engaged in. Empowerment leads to respect and trust, which builds powerful relationships focused on attaining a clearly articulated vision.

Adapt

Continuous change is inevitable. As such, leaders must embrace a sense of flexibility and openness to change when the need arises. In fact, the best leaders will be proactive and "create change" before external influences force it. Research has shown that the ability to adapt to an array of situations, challenges, and pressures is pivotal to accomplishing one's goals (Yuki & Mahsud, 2010). The research illustrates that leaders need to have mental models that facilitate understanding about the complex effects of their behaviors on multiple objectives and that stress the importance of balancing competing values. Leaders need to appreciate and take advantage of opportunities to increase their self-awareness of relevant traits, skills, and behaviors, and they need to develop necessary skills *before* they are needed. In addition, they are comfortable navigating unclear situations while blazing an unexplored trail. The research also shows the need to recognize responsibility for helping others develop and use the skills and behaviors required for flexible and adaptive leadership (Yuki & Mahsud, 2010). Success in life is intertwined with our ability to adapt in order to survive. Such evolution through adaptation creates better leaders.

Delegate

Delegation is an essential aspect of distributive and collaborative leadership; no leader can do everything by himself or herself. Research has shown that extending leadership responsibilities beyond the teacher is an important lever for developing effective professional learning communities in schools (Morrisey, 2000). Building greater capacity in staff through purposeful delegation is also an important means of sustaining improvement (Fullan, 2001). The decisiveness to delegate certain tasks and responsibilities is not a weakness. On the contrary, it enables leaders to apply sharper focus to areas of greater importance. Collaborative leadership also builds confidence in others' ability as coleaders of an organization—even when they don't have a fancy title or letters after their name.

Engage

In today's global, sharing economy, access to relevant, up-to-date information is vital. Leaders understand this fact and develop strategies to authentically engage with their stakeholders through multidimensional communication and by taking control of public relations, developing a positive brand presence, and establishing an effective feedback loop

(Sheninger, 2014). One of the greatest challenges for today's school leaders is the ability to create an environment that cultivates each person's intrinsic motivation. An ecosystem of engagement flourishes when leaders understand the foundational drivers of human engagement—the need for trust, a sense of belonging, the need for hope, and the need to feel invested in the work. Increased engagement results when leaders meet stakeholders where they are, encourage two-way communication, and become the "storyteller-in-chief."

Reflect

It is difficult to find a great leader who does not regularly reflect on his or her own work and effectiveness. Reflection, which can be defined as the process of critically thinking about your behaviors, attitudes, beliefs, and values, has been identified by numerous researchers as an important part of any formal or informal learning process (Schon, 1983; Kolb, 1984; Mezirow, 1998). Leadership is learning, and learning is leadership—at both the individual and group levels. The ability to reflect, however, is not necessarily an inherent attribute; it must be cultivated over time. Unless one is actively engaged in the practice of reflection, it is doubtful that this capability will develop on its own (Roberts, 2008). In a digital world, reflection can take many forms and results in greater transparency. It's not how one chooses to reflect but an emphasis on consistently integrating the process that defines a great leader.

Serve

Beyond the notion of titles and power, leadership is about serving others. The best leaders work diligently to meet the needs of others, as they realize it's not about them; it's about obtaining the organizational vision; and for schools, that's doing whatever it takes to serve the community and all of its children. Leaders must model the behaviors they seek, empower people to expand their personal capacity, and put the needs of the organization above themselves. Leaders flourish through their influence—not because of a fancy title. Serving others taps into one's heart and soul as these leaders are driven by far more than a position of power or a paycheck. In a study done by Sipe and Frick (2009), it was found that "servant leadership" was the predominant factor in an organization's level of success. Ultimately, the best leaders don't add more followers; they develop and empower more leaders.

Model Your Vision; It Starts with You

The secret of leadership is simple: Do what you believe in. Paint a
picture of the future. Go there. People will follow.

Seth Godin

I (Eric) remember back to my days as an elementary school student. Boy
did I have a warped sense of what leadership really was. Back then, recess
leaders (that is, on the playground) were perceived as those who had the
most athletic ability. These individuals were always in a position to select
the kickball teams or control the organization of literally every activity.
This was not only accepted but also embraced by every kid. Herein lies the
problem. Social hierarchy determined how the teams would be organized.
One by one, kids were selected based on how well he or she could kick a
ball. This always left a feeling of dread among those kids who were picked
last every time. In this example, I, like many of my fellow classmates, made
the conscious decision not to step up and lead.

Maybe this example is not the best one to articulate my view of leadership, but then again, maybe it can get the point across. Reflection of
those days at recess has taught me a great deal about what leadership is
and—most importantly—what it isn't.

We first have to look at the underlying methodologies of how society
determines or anoints leaders. There are many assumptions when it comes
to leadership. One that is regularly portrayed is that leadership is some-
how an inherent trait that is either passed down from prior generations or
something that is bestowed upon someone. Although DNA influences our
personalities, leadership skills are developed over time. Throughout history
and in many cultures, there have been people who were born into a leadership role, but for the most part, monarchies have become a thing of the
past. Another prevalent assumption is that leaders are granted power and
influence through their titles, positions, or abbreviations. In some cases,
they might have decision-making power but be ineffective, detrimental
leaders. This begs the question as to whether having power is really a
characteristic of our most effective and influential leaders.

We need to move past preconceived notions about who qualifies to
be a leader. There is no ownership right of dynamic leadership. Effective

leadership has very little to do with titles and positions, especially in the context of leading and intentionally designing schools. During the countless conversations we have had, a common theme is prevalent among many educators who seem to believe that real change can only come from adults who have a specific title (such as a board of education member, superintendent, central office administrator, principal, or supervisor). These conversations often continue with stories of many so-called leaders, anointed by title, who did anything but lead.

Ineffective leadership squanders opportunities to transform organizations in positive ways. Leaders by title (LBT) often exhibit many defining characteristics such as egos, power trips, taking credit for the work of others, handing down mandates/directives, invisibility (i.e., they're never seen or around when needed), ruling by fear, and insecurity when their ideas are challenged in the open. They commonly tell others what to do without having done it themselves or assisting in the process. LBTs work to convince or mandate others to do something instead of modeling the way.

Changes that are implemented by LBTs are never sustained. What scares us the most about LBTs is that they have the ability and designated power to inhibit the changes that are so desperately needed. The perception of what a leader is needs to change, and it begins with you.

As is evident with LBTs, titles don't create effective leadership. Simon Sinek has said that great leaders don't wear the titles they have. Dynamic leadership is composed of a mix of behaviors, mindsets, and skills, which are all used to empower people to be at their best and operate at full capacity—far more than they thought possible. Such vision is a relentless force—a critical anchor that propels decisions—and it determines actions. In the case of schools, great leaders help others see the value of change by clearly articulating a compelling *why* and working to build support through consensus. As such, a laser-focused vision is a foundational prerequisite for any organization's success. An effective leader also has the courage to step in and make the difficult decisions that need to be made, since they previously calculated the risk-reward ratio. These leaders also stand by and own their decisions in the face of adversity, and they leverage their human capital to continuously refine and march toward the vision.

In our opinion, the best leaders have one thing in common: they do, as opposed to just talk. Leadership is about action, not position or chatter. Some of the best leaders we have seen during our years in education have never held any sort of administrative title. They had the tenacity to act on a bold vision for change to improve learning for kids and the overall school culture. These people are often overlooked and may not be considered "school leaders" because they don't possess the necessary title or degree that is used to describe a leader in the traditional sense. Nevertheless, the effect these leaders can have on an organization is much greater than an LBT. We need more leaders by action (LBA). Make no mistake about the fact that you are surrounded by these people each day. They are teachers, students, parents, support staff members, and administrators who have taken action to initiate meaningful change in their classrooms or schools. These leaders don't just talk the talk; they also walk the walk. They lead by example in what might be the most effective way possible: by modeling. They don't expect others to do what they aren't willing to do. It doesn't take a title or a new position for these leaders to be agents of change. LBAs drive sustainable change and make the transformation of learning possible.

Never underestimate your own unique talents and abilities; they have the power to shape the future of our schools and create a better learning culture that our students need and deserve. Everyone has the ability to lead in some capacity, and our schools—and the kids who are being shaped inside them—need more educators to embrace this challenge. Great leaders work to build capacity in these people and empower them to lead change.

Let's not accept the notion that all leaders are born or appointed to a position of power. Leadership is a choice and something that Stephen Covey (2009) has written about extensively.

> Most of the great cultural shifts—the ones that have built great organizations that sustain long-term growth, prosperity, and con-tribution to the world—started with the choice of one person. Regardless of their position, these people first changed themselves from the inside out. Their character, competence, initiative, and positive energy—in short, their moral authority—inspired and lifted others. They possessed an anchored sense of identity, discovered their strengths and talents, and used them to meet needs and pro-duce results. People noticed. They were given more responsibility. They magnified the new responsibility and again produced results. More and more people sat up and noticed. Top people wanted to learn of their ideas—how they accomplished so much. The culture was drawn to their vision and to them.

The most influential and effective leaders are those who

- Model expectations.
- Talk less and do more.
- Create a shared vision and implement it.
- Believe in taking calculated risks.
- Do not fear failure and learn to 'fail forward.'
- Work tirelessly to build positive relationships with others.
- Collaborate for the greater common good.
- Constantly learn and reflect.
- Help others see the value in change.
- Focus on solutions as opposed to excuses.

Intentionally designed schools are led by high-octane leaders who model the way, build capacity in others, and create cultures of innovation. These leaders create the vision and make it happen. In their schools, learning is being transformed.

From Vision to Action

Vision without action is merely a dream. Action without vision just passes the time. Vision with action can change the world.

Joel A. Barker

There is often a great deal of emphasis on establishing a vision when beginning the change process, and rightfully so. Effective leaders understand the importance of a shared vision and the need to articulate lofty goals and expected outcomes. A clear, well-articulated vision sets the stage for the time and effort required to follow through on what might be a long, arduous journey (Sheninger, 2015b). These leaders are forward thinking, and in order to effectively lead change, a shared vision must be created. "The only visions that take hold are shared visions—and you will create them only when you listen very, very closely to others, appreciate their hopes, and attend to their needs. The best leaders are able to bring their people into the future because they engage in the oldest form of research: They observe the human condition" (Kouzes & Posner, 2009).

John Ryan (2009) elaborates on how leadership success always starts with a clear vision:

> Great leaders give real thought to the values, ideas, and activities they're most passionate about—and those are the things they pursue, rather than money or prestige or options forced on them by someone else. The visions these leaders have can be—and, in fact, should be—challenging to put into action. They realize them only by setting realistic, demanding goals and then going after them relentlessly, with the help of other talented men and women who are equally committed and engaged.

Ryan states that compelling visions can truly change the world, but staying invested in them can be extremely difficult when hard times arrive. The real work and testament to great leadership is moving past the visioning process by developing a strategic plan to turn vision into reality. We all have been a part of, or witnessed, one too many visioning exercises that focused on the formation of a mission statement. The result, for the most part, is a hollow vision, created by hours of debate and born out of a handful of statements, that ultimately is not supported by action. Many, including us, would consider this type of exercise a waste of time. We would even go so far as to say that getting people in a room for countless hours to develop a jargon-filled paragraph is more indicative of an LBT than an effective school leader. Mission statements do not lead to sustainable change or intentionally designed schools. Forward-thinking visionaries who persistently strive to implement a vision through actions do.

Developing a shared vision is an attribute linked to all great leaders, but the best leaders ensure that a strategic plan is developed and then meticulously implemented. A vision has to result in a systematic plan that provides a focus for the change initiative. The plan must then be monitored and evaluated if the desired outcome is sustainable change that will lead to transformation. The real work comes after a vision has been established.

David Taylor (2014) outlines 10 crucial elements to successfully move from vision to actionable change:

1. **Make it a priority.** Make innovation a priority for the organization.
2. **Strategize strategic success.** Understand how the vision aligns with the strategic goals of the organization.

3. **Communicate a new reality.** Communicate to the organization what achieving the vision will mean.

4. **Inspire the team.** The leaders must inspire the organization to move from where they are to the promise that the vision brings.

5. **Embrace the vision.** The vision should be discussed and supported at all levels of the organization.

6. **Be loud and proud.** Speak about the new changes whenever possible.

7. **Spread the word.** Communicate the vision at every opportunity.

8. **Own it and live it.** Leaders must live the vision and not just pay lip service to it.

9. **Drive the train; don't watch the parade.** Leaders must get their hands dirty and get involved with the details.

10. **Don't just delegate everything.** Leaders model desired practice.

Great leaders are never satisfied with simply developing a shared vision. They work tirelessly to model expectations during the planning and implementation phases of the change process while empowering others to embrace the needed change. It is easy to talk the talk. Great leaders walk the walk while helping others experience greatness and success along the way. Great visions can, and will, lead to the development of a legacy. Your legacy will be defined by how well you positively affect the lives of others.

Developing a "Culture of Yes"

If we create a culture where every teacher believes they need to improve, not because they are not good enough but because they can be even better, there is no limit to what we can achieve.

Dylan Wiliam

One key to change is developing a "culture of yes." This does not and will never occur through an onslaught of directives, mandates, top-down demands, or micromanagement techniques—nor is it a pass for low quality. As our good friend Jimmy Casas shares, "You can't build capacity if people are always asking you for permission." As educational leaders evolve, they must begin to rethink the change process by creating school cultures focused on embracing change as opposed to buy-in (Sheninger, 2014). If educators understand and value why a particular change is being implemented, then they are more prone to support and promote it. This is at the heart of successful change leadership. When people understand the value of change, they are more intrinsically motivated to embrace it, which results in sustainability and ultimately leads to transformation.

Change in any organization is often an arduous task, especially during the initial implementation stage. The onset of the process is typically fraught with challenges, such as overcoming the status quo, a mentality of "if it isn't broke why fix it," fear, a leadership void in the school hierarchy, lack of knowledge on how to initiate change, no clear vision, too many concurrent initiatives, naysayers/antagonists, and a one-size-fits-all approach. We must realize that change is difficult and that a commitment to see the process through is vital if the end goal is cultural transformation that sticks.

Success also lies in a leader's ability to make difficult decisions. Leadership is not a popularity contest. True leaders make tough decisions instead of trying to please everyone. I (Eric) fell victim to the allure of putting popularity first early in my career as a young principal. After realizing the school was stuck in a rut, it took some self-reflection to get myself on track and do the job I was hired to do. Personal reflection led to a mindset shift, and from that point on, several sustained change initiatives resulted in a culture that worked better for our students and staff and ultimately improved student learning outcomes and achievement (Sheninger, 2015b). Leaders are defined by the examples they set.

You must develop a mindset for change in order to create a culture of yes. This process begins with a reflection of why change is so hard and an assessment of why previous change has failed in your school or district. Every school and district has its own culture and unique set of potential roadblocks. Pinpoint areas of difficulty that could morph into challenges or excuses: time, lack of collaboration, finances, limited support, poor professional learning, resistance, mandates/directives, and a history of frivolous purchases. Once the challenges and potential obstacles are visible, begin to develop a roadmap for change by using the following questions:

1. Where should we begin?
2. What are the school factors that influence student learning and achievement?
3. How do we change culture and move past the status quo?
4. How do we get educators and school systems to embrace change instead of always fighting for buy-in?

It is important for leaders to examine and seek answers for each of these driving questions. The questions themselves focus on a leader's ability to initiate change. Utilizing this lens, a culture of yes can be cultivated through the following drivers: strategic thinking, communication, meaningful work, key stakeholders, and a commitment to learning. Effective leaders develop a shared vision with input from all stakeholders, including students. They then craft and implement a plan for action that supports the purpose for the change. The glue that holds the entire process together is a leader's passion for how the change will positively affect students and staff.

Strategic Thinking: After developing a shared vision, a plan for action must be developed. The plan identifies the purpose and focus for the change, and it provides methods to monitor successful implementation and sustainability. The best school leaders model the expectations they set for others. (For a systemic model of strategic thinking for action planning, see Appendix A.)

Communication: The most effective leaders are effective communicators. The art of communication allows them to accomplish tasks and get things done, disseminate important information, acquire new information, develop a shared vision, reach decisions through consensus, build relationships, and motivate and empower people to embrace change. In today's digital age, effective leaders also leverage available technology to transform communication.

Meaningful Work: With any change initiative, you must ensure that a solid foundation aligned to teaching, learning, and leadership is in place. The work should be grounded in evidence and be aligned to the latest research and best practices. As successes occur, it's important to celebrate with staff and students. Showing people how proud you are of their hard work helps expedite the change process and assists in motivating others to embrace the change effort.

Key Stakeholders: Successful change initiatives ultimately depend on moving the masses, but this can best be accomplished by building positive relationships at the individual level. Empower staff to embrace change by putting them in a position to experience the value for themselves. Provide autonomy to those who are already on board while focusing more time and effort on supporting staff who are not yet willing to change.

A Commitment to Learning: The best and most effective leaders never stop learning; they understand that there will always be work to do, no matter how much success is encountered. As Antoni Cimolino states,

"There is something to be learned every day, both by looking in the mirror at yourself and by looking at the people around you" (Seijts, 2013).

Today's leaders have a great advantage over their predecessors when it comes to learning—social media. The ability to learn anything, anytime, anywhere, and from anyone through Personal Learning Networks (PLNs)—something we'll discuss in more detail in Chapter 5—is a game-changing resource to build effective leadership skills.

A great deal of time and effort (and a large number of difficult decisions) embody every successful change effort. With that said, it is imperative that the changes you implement actually stick and don't become short-term blips on the radar. Hargreaves and Fink (2004) provide some key points on sustaining change that will enable you to develop a clear focus during the visioning and planning process. Change needs to focus on

- Improvement that fosters learning, not merely change that alters schooling.
- Improvement that endures over time.
- Improvement that can be supported by available or obtainable resources.
- Improvement that does not negatively affect the surrounding environment (i.e., other schools and systems).
- Improvement that promotes ecological diversity and capacity throughout the educational and community environment.

A culture of yes thrives when improvement is seen as the result of a collective effort to improve learning for all kids.

Empower Your People

Great leaders don't succeed because they are great. They succeed because they bring out greatness in others.

Jon Gordon

Effective leadership is a continuous choice, and empowering your people is vital to intentionally designing schools. So how can school leaders empower their team?

Adapt when needed. A great leader knows that his or her respective leadership style will never work for everyone. Being able to successfully navigate different personalities and situations requires flexibility and a willingness to change course on the fly.

Love the work. Enjoying the work provides the resolve to persevere when challenges arise. Most of all, great leaders have fun and do what it takes to ensure others have fun as well.

Show appreciation. Sir Richard Branson has been known to say "Train people well enough so they can leave. Treat them well enough so they don't want to" (Branson, 2014). Great leaders know that success is not isolated to one person in an organization. Leadership is a collective effort wherein everyone plays a role. Great leaders go out of their way to put others—not themselves—on a pedestal while consistently praising deserving efforts both in public and private.

Eliminate excuses. Challenges and obstacles will always be prevalent in any organization, especially schools, and they often morph into excuses about why certain initiatives can't be accomplished. As such, school leaders often "no" themselves right out of innovative ideas. Great leaders clear the way for their staff by removing obstacles and challenges through empowerment and autonomy. If it is important enough, a solution will be found. If not, an excuse will be made.

Establish a focus through vision. A clear vision provides guidance not only to the goals at hand but also for how to accomplish them. Great leaders work with stakeholders to develop a shared vision and resulting action plan that keeps everyone focused on a goal of improved student learning. Great leaders also know that vision alone is not enough.

Model expectations. A great leader never asks anyone to do what he or she isn't willing to at least try. Setting an example by putting yourself in others' shoes provides the inspiration and motivation for staff to embrace change.

Start small. Great leaders don't set out to radically change school culture in one fell swoop. They understand that success is the culmination of numerous small wins that build momentum for larger changes.

Know when to delegate. Common sense dictates that no one can do it alone. Great leaders exhibit trust in others when certain tasks are passed along. This in itself works to develop more leaders throughout an organization. The process of delegation also allows for more of a focus on the larger issues at hand.

Provide meaningful feedback. There is a big difference between meaningful feedback and criticism. Great leaders articulate where their staff excel and highlight specific areas of growth. Meaningful feedback is the fuel for improvement.

Communicate effectively. You won't find a great leader who is not also a master communicator. Great leaders understand that listening, facilitating dialogue, asking questions, creating an open environment, and clearly getting to the point are essential skills. They also understand the importance of a multifaceted approach to increase stakeholder engagement.

Change Agents Build Relationships: A Key to Culture

Leadership is not about being in charge. Leadership is about taking care of those in your charge.

Simon Sinek

As mentioned, *change* is a word that is spoken about in education circles more and more each day. But herein lies the problem: talk and opinions get us nowhere. The fact of the matter is that education has to change dramatically, but how this is initiated should no longer be a contentious topic for discussion or debate. The best leaders don't just talk about change. They make it happen. It is relatively agreed upon that the structure and function of most schools around the world no longer meet the needs of today's learners. There is a quiet revolution gaining steam as more educators and students push back against the traditional policies and mandates that have been forced upon them. Leaders need to decide if it is worth it to conform or to forge their own path and provide students with the education and learning experiences they deserve.

Meaningful change has and always will begin at the individual level. It is at this level where change is sustained to the point that it becomes an embedded component of school or district culture. The hardest, but most gratifying, work in which a leader might ever engage is empowering colleagues to change. School leaders need to remove barriers to the change process, eradicate the fear of failure, provide autonomy, and empower teachers to drive change at the classroom level. Dynamic relationships propel this change to happen.

Consider trying the following strategies to help your colleagues begin the process of changing their professional practice.

- Lead by example even when (initially) it might be a lonely place. Real change comes from colleagues modeling expectations for one another.
- Share current research and practices that support the change you are championing.
- Encourage colleagues who might be resistant to change to attend professional learning opportunities with you. Get them involved in high-quality professional learning related to the change effort. At the very least, make sure you share your experiences during a faculty meeting or in personal conversations.
- Tackle fears head on to alleviate concerns.
- Help others see the value of the change on their own.
- Clearly articulate how the change will improve professional practice and result in improved student learning and achievement outcomes.
- Be patient. Like you would your students, treat your colleagues with respect and remember how satisfying and rewarding it is when you help students succeed. Adult success offers tremendous rewards as well.
- Get your students involved. There is no better way, in our opinion, to convince educators to change than when they can see firsthand the impact it has on kids.
- Work on building better relationships. This could lead the way to embracing change that otherwise might have been resisted.

Successes can then be promoted within the school and district to serve as a catalyst for cultural transformation. The same holds true for both teachers and administrators when it comes to students, who are our primary stakeholder group. Schools should be designed to meet the needs of students, but if they are not given a seat at the table or allowed to be a focal point of change efforts that ultimately affect them, then a golden opportunity is missed. Never underestimate the power you have to make your school, district, and entire education system better—regardless of the position you hold. Be the change you wish to see in education, and others will follow.

There is some debate about the difference between school culture and school climate, but both affect the operational functionality of the inner workings of the school. School climate reflects how members of the school community experience the school, including interpersonal relationships, teacher and other staff practices, and organizational arrangements. It includes factors that serve as conditions for learning and that support physical and emotional safety, connection and support, and engagement. A positive school climate reflects an attention to social and physical safety; support that enables students and staff to realize high behavioral and academic standards; and the encouragement and maintenance of respectful, trusting, and caring relationships throughout the school community. The U.S. Department of Education (2016) indicates that students learn best when they are in environments in which they feel safe, supported, challenged, and accepted.

We'd make the case that teachers are also at their best in such environments. A positive school climate fosters trust, respect, communication, and cooperation among students, staff, parents, and the school community. By improving school climate, schools lay the foundation for improving student achievement and building vital positive relationships with staff.

The role of a change agent is to provide relevancy, meaning, and authenticity in the teaching and learning process. It hinges upon your ability to provide an environment and activities that unleash students' passion for learning and allows them to demonstrate conceptual mastery by creating artifacts with the tools of their choice. Additionally, it relies on a bold vision to grant students and educators the autonomy to take risks, learn from failure, and adapt as needed. We need to realize that sometimes it's our own lens that gets in the way. It's our own mindset that can inhibit our ability to see things differently and ultimately redefine what's possible. Meaningful change—transformed learning—will happen only if we give up control and establish a culture built on trust and respect.

If our goal is to prepare the next generation of thinkers, doers, inventors, and change agents, then we must abdicate some control, trust students and educators, and work to develop a better system that will produce these desired outcomes. Educators must acknowledge the real challenges with which they are faced each day and work to develop solutions to overcome them. Challenges should not be seen as insurmountable obstacles to change but rather opportunities to do things differently and better. There must also be a desire to embrace new thinking and strategies that not only address higher standards but also prepare students for the world they will face upon graduation. The end result will be the proliferation of uncommon learning strategies that, in time, will become common.

Shift the Paradigm

If you want something you never had, you must be willing to do something you've never done.

Unknown

The world continues to evolve and progress as a result of technological advances. Only a few years ago, it would have been impossible to predict some of the foundational shifts that have become embedded in our daily lives. As we outlined in the Introduction, the speed at which such changes have taken place continues to grow exponentially. For example, in 2003, the idea of a smartphone began with Blackberry, only to be eclipsed by Apple and the release of the first iPhone in 2007. Disruptive innovations, such as Netflix, Uber, and Airbnb, have begun to dramatically alter consumer behaviors—in many cases for the better. These innovations have completely overhauled entire sectors of the economy. Make no mistake about it, technology is shaping the world in ways that we could never have imagined only a few years ago. The types of disruption we are seeing are improving effectiveness, efficiency, and results for people who are now globally connected. As such, competition has flourished, and there's been an exponential growth in innovation. We must either adapt and evolve or risk becoming obsolete and extinct.

Therefore, it's incredibly perplexing, to say the least, to see so many schools (really, education as a whole) remain static when it comes to change. Walk into the average neighborhood school and, for the most part, you will see the same structure and function that has dominated education for the past 100 years. The pressure to conform to a world that equates school success to standardized metrics is, for all intents and purposes, one of the main reasons we are not seeing disruptive innovation in today's classrooms. However, if schools and leaders do not learn from history and the effect of disruptive innovation, then it's only a matter of time before they suffer the same fate of obsolescence, which would be catastrophic to our economy and the world as we know it.

As Thomas Kuhn (1970) argued, scientific advancement is not evolutionary but rather a "series of peaceful interludes punctuated by intellectually violent revolutions," and in those revolutions "one conceptual world view is replaced by another" (p. 10). Thus, a paradigm shift constitutes a change from one way of thinking to another—a mindset shift—which spurs a revolution that transforms learning and professional practice. This sounds great in theory, but as time has proven, it doesn't happen on its own. For a paradigm shift to occur and be sustained over time, it must be driven by change agents (in classrooms, schools, districts, and other educational organizations) who are willing to disrupt the status quo.

In a world where people use technology in almost every aspect of their lives, it is incumbent upon leaders, regardless of their position, to replace the conceptual view of school with a more meaningful one. This is where the concept of digital leadership really comes into play. By carefully analyzing current components of professional practice, educators can begin to make the necessary paradigm shifts to replace existing practices with more effective and relevant ones. The following are some specific ideas in relation to the Pillars of Digital Leadership (Sheninger, 2014).

Student Engagement, Learning, and Achievement: We can ill afford to teach and lead in the same ways we were taught and led. It is important to sift through the fluffy ideas that abound (and set aside the allure of new tools) and begin to integrate technology with purpose. Success is contingent upon sound instructional design, high-quality assessments, and an improved feedback loop. When implemented correctly, digital tools can transform education.

Learning Spaces and Environments: Desks in rows, LCD projectors used as glorified overhead projectors, uncomfortable furniture, poor lighting, and inflexible arrangements can no longer be the acceptable norm. In order for students to think and solve problems in the real world and beyond, they need to learn in spaces and environments that emulate today's reality. Research on learning spaces has shown that redesign can empower learners and affect student learning (Barrett, Zhang, Moffat, & Kobbacy, 2013), a topic we will discuss at length in Chapter 4.

Professional Growth: As we will discuss in Chapter 5, traditional forms of professional learning such as "sit and get," one-size-fits-all, and training that lacks accountability all lead to a significant waste of time and money. Technology enables professional learning to take place anytime, anywhere, and with anyone around the world. No longer are time and location the barriers to growth they once were. Combining improved professional learning experiences with the power of a PLN sets the stage for meaningful improvement that can be transformational.

Communications: Most schools still heavily rely on traditional means of communication (e.g., email, newsletters, phone calls). The shift here is to begin to meet stakeholders where they are and engage them in two-way, real-time communication. As we highlight in Chapter 7, this blended approach will result in more transparency, exposure, and amplification of the vision.

Public Relations: If you don't tell your school's story, someone else will. Do you really want to roll the dice and take a chance with that? Everyone has access to the same video, image, and text tools and has the ability to become a storyteller-in-chief. There is a considerable amount of power in stories that focus on students' successes and staff members' accomplishments. No longer does any educator have to rely on the media alone to share the daily awesomeness that occurs in classrooms and schools.

Branding: Communications + public relations = branding. This is not a business-minded concept focused on selling; instead, it's a method of telling stories and consistently sharing a positive narrative about what happens in your district each and every day. This results in greater support and appreciation for the whole child approach that many schools are now focused on.

Opportunity: As the saying goes, if opportunity doesn't knock, then build a door. The digital world allows us to build and open doors like never before. The paradigm shift here will naturally result with a sustained focus on the other six pillars.

It is evident that a paradigm shift in learning, teaching, and leadership is needed to improve our education system. Opinions, talk, and ideas alone will not do the trick. To intentionally design schools, and ultimately transform learning, it is imperative that we raise the bar so holistic improvement becomes the norm—not an exception.

You are part of the solution.

Innovative Practices in Action

Coachella Valley Unified School District, California
Dr. Darryl Adams, Retired Superintendent

Recognized by the White House in 2014 as one of the Top 100 Innovative Superintendents

I believe that the three main components of managing change in an organization, business, or institution are trust, relationship building, and effective communication.

Trust: Without some level of trust, constituents, team members, customers, teachers, and staff will not believe you or believe in you!

Relationship Building: Just as important is the need to cultivate positive relationships. As you establish trust, you build positive relationships, and you build positive relationships by getting to know people and letting them get to know you.

Effective Communication: People will trust you and be willing to build a relationship with you only if you are willing to make them feel important, look them in the eye, and speak plain truths in a personable, engaging way.

If you are trustworthy and authentic, and if you are willing to share your strengths and weaknesses, then you lay the foundation for managing the change needed in your school, organization, or business.

Establishing Trust

Establishing trust is essential in managing cultural change. People will support you and trust you if they are congruent with and can identify with what you stand for and with what you value. One way to establish trust is always to be open, honest, and ethical. As a role model for your organization, people will watch you and analyze your every move and decision. People will also watch what you allow, and if it is not in line with your values, you will begin to lose trust. Members in the organization will also scrutinize how you make decisions and who is included in the decision-making process. Just as there is no *I* in *team*, there is no leader without followers and no change without trust! Leaders who manage change effectively should not work in isolation but in concert with their team and with constituents, board members, upper management, union leadership, and so on. These interactions help establish and maintain trust; remember that you are being watched, so handle your business honestly and ethically.

Cultivating Positive Relationships

Building relationships is another key component of effectively managing change. Team members, customers, and constituents want to trust you, but they also want to know you. Do not be afraid to share parts of your life that are applicable to who you are and what you stand for. Until I shared my upbringing of being born and raised in a poor section of Memphis, Tennessee, most of the people in my school community thought I was from a privileged background. But after sharing stories of trial and tribulation and how those experiences shaped my life, we all realized we had much more in common than not. I was also open and honest about failures and disappointments in my life and how they helped me become a better person and leader. As I opened up, team members opened up and we all began to build empathy toward each other and a camaraderie that insulates us from apathy and negativity.

Effective and Personable Communication

Effectively communicating the vision, mission, and goals to a school community, business, or organization helps promote a change in culture. When I came to my district, I quickly realized that a change in culture was necessary. I sought to find the one common denominator that we all would look at and say that needed to be changed. I began to speak about the one data point that raised concern, and I knew it would also raise concern in our school community. And that data point was this: approximately 30 percent of our graduating students went on to college but only 16.5 percent graduated from college.

By using this information, I was able to show the community that something needed to change in our culture and in our expectations. I spoke about how that statistic was unacceptable, especially since I had students coming back to me and complaining about being placed in remedial English and math classes in their freshman year in college. It was quite clear to me and to everyone that something needed to change academically and culturally. Effectively communicating the need to transform our entire system of educating, our way of thinking, and our expectations led to a change in culture that has seen our graduation rate go from the mid-60-percent level to the 80-plus-percent level. Our college-going rate has increased to 50 percent, and our college graduation rate has also increased. Our culture now and our primary reason to exist is known to everyone, and that culture expects "All students will graduate prepared for college, career, and citizenship!" This change in culture is shared by the entire school community as a whole.

In conclusion, managing change to change culture is possible if one can establish trust while building positive and productive relationships and communicating in a personable and engaging way. The more these principles can permeate throughout your school, organization, or institution, the more successful you will be in serving those who rely on your products or your service.

(Dr. Darryl S. Adams was selected by the White House and the U.S. Department of Education as one of the Top 100 Innovative Superintendents in America and was praised by President Obama for the district's 1-to-1 iPad initiative and innovative Wifi-on-Wheels program, which ensures equity and access to technology and the Internet. Dr. Adams was also named by the Center for Digital Education as one of the Top 30 Technologists, Transformers, and Trailblazers.)

Greenwood Elementary School, Minnesota
Dr. Brad Gustafson, Principal
2016 Minnesota Distinguished Principal of the Year

I believe all students deserve innovative schools. I also believe that teachers are the true difference makers in delivering on the promises of the digital age. They are the ones who champion relationships, relevant learning, and connectedness. In order for a culture of innovative learning to emerge, teachers need to feel supported and experience the power of connecting in a digital sense firsthand.

This is precisely why we, as school leaders, need to pull our "learning weight" by modeling, providing tangible support to staff, and practicing connectedness ourselves. When a school's culture says "yes" to connectedness—one of the single greatest drivers of innovation—it is ultimately our students who will win. Over the course of the past several years, I have observed students' innovation increase more than I ever thought possible.

A few short years ago, I never would have imagined our students assembling a 3D printer on their own, creating codable mini-golf courses for robotic droids, or producing cross-state collaborative podcasts with kids across the country. The learning our students have led does not stop there. They are creating innovative challenges using quadcopters (drones), presenting to people in other states (in person and via Google Hangouts), and inventing creative contraptions using a fleet of mobile MakerSpaces. Truth be told, I was largely unaware that many of these learning opportunities ever existed prior to becoming connected in a digital sense.

In order to create world-class experiences for kids campuswide, educators must be connected to new ideas, emerging research, cutting-edge tools, and one another. My doctoral research findings showed that when school leaders model connected learning, innovation is incubated like no other leadership behavior (Gustafson, 2015). Most schools have pockets of innovation, but what separates good schools from world-class learning institutions is the nature of the learning that's occurring.

The nature of learning is a derivative of pedagogy. Teaching and learning that is purposeful and connected is oftentimes more innovative than what traditional leadership practices produce. Moving from the practices that served students well the better part of the previous decade requires intentionality. When I reflect back on our team's journey, I can identify several milestones we've accomplished together. Each step along the way propelled us toward a more relevant and student-centered learning paradigm.

First, our early-adopters modeled what it meant to be "connected learners." We took risks and began practicing "connectedness" by sharing the work students and staff were immersed in beyond the walls of our school. Next, we sought ideas and additional perspectives from educators using the professional learning networks we were developing. During this time, our team created a space on Twitter marked by a simple hashtag (#GWgreats) where the school community could celebrate learning, exchange ideas, and share professional resources.

Flat-screen televisions were installed in the entryway and office area to livestream staff tweets. This made everyone's learning that much more visible. Teachers who stopped by the office could also virtually visit their colleagues' classrooms by checking out the livestreamed tweets. Now students stop by the televisions to check out photographs of their classmates' learning. By displaying some of the digital collaboration our team was involved in, we were also modeling digital leadership for students, but the learning did not stop there.

Next, we planned a series of professional learning sessions that delved into why and how learning can be transformed when it is connected. During this time of professional learning (which has spanned several years), parents were also part of the process. Annual parent seminars about social media provided additional support to parents who sought to navigate a new and connected landscape. These meetings were recorded and/or livestreamed to increase accessibility for those families unable to attend in person. In addition to the parent seminars, a social media support booth was staffed each fall during open house.

I'm convinced that social media can be learning media when it is leveraged to make learning visible. In fact, we've seen our school demonstrate how connectedness can enhance collaboration by transcending traditional barriers like time and proximity. This powerful understanding has even manifested in our school's youngest learners. For example, when a kindergarten class was discussing coding using a Bee-Bot with their teacher, one student suggested that the class "Ask Twitter" for help with a question she had about the Bee-Bot. (When the 5- and 6-year-olds in a school begin to recognize the potential value in connecting beyond their walls, you know the teachers have done an incredible job modeling!)

Our team has made a habit of saying "yes" to relevant tools and pedagogy. We refuse to limit learning based upon what we don't know. Instead, we model a true growth mindset by looking beyond our own limitations and connecting with others to grow . . . and occasionally contribute. Learning that is grounded in a connected pedagogy has the potential to unleash innovation and ignite an insatiable curiosity in kids . . . and that's exactly what digital-age students deserve!

(Dr. Brad Gustafson is an elementary school principal and author of Renegade Leadership. *He is passionate about creating innovative schools that serve today's students. Brad is a Digital Innovation in Learning Award winner and was also recognized as Minnesota's 2016 National Distinguished Principal.)*

2 | Redesigning the Learning Experience

⚲ The learning experience must be redesigned and made personal.

The Need for Personal and Authentic Learning

The difficulty lies not so much in developing new ideas as in escaping from old ones.

John Maynard Keynes

Studies in neuroscience have indicated that students traditionally forget most of the information they were taught while in school. These studies have consistently demonstrated that only a small fraction of the content that is taught in the classroom is actually retained a year or more later (Lieberman, 2012). We have all experienced a time when we crammed for a test, earned a passing grade, and then promptly forgot the information a short time later. These studies indicate that simply shoving factual information into our students' brains is a long-term waste of time and resources. Most often, students are told what to learn, when to learn it, and how it should be learned, which we believe has ultimately led to an engagement crisis. Very rarely do students have the opportunity to follow their passions, explore their interests, and engage in personal and authentic learning opportunities. Therefore, massive disengagement has become a natural byproduct of a traditional education experience. Typically speaking, the longer students are with us, the less engaged they become. It's evident that we often school the love of learning right out of children by the time they graduate. As such, the learning experience must be transformed.

Intentionally designed schools not only break from the traditional one-size-fits-all lock-step progression of teaching and learning but also redesign the learning experience to one that is personal and authentic for students. To be globally competitive in the years ahead, students must be given the opportunity to exercise more agency and ownership over their learning. This can only be accomplished through intentional design.

Ultimately, personal learning is about tailoring instructional strategies needed by the learner while leveraging students' unique interests and passions and building on their strengths. Intentionally designed schools develop and implement various adaptive and dynamic interventions to meet individual needs and see student agency (voice, choice, advocacy) as a valuable component of the instructional process. Making student learning personal and authentic is no longer an option; it's a necessity. It's the exact type of learning that students experience outside of school when consuming and creating content—they choose what they will learn, from whom they will learn it, and how it will occur. If we want to reengage students and reignite their passion for learning, we have no choice but to give them various opportunities to choose what they are learning, how they will learn, and ultimately, how they can show mastery of their learning.

Some will argue differences between *personal learning* and *personalized learning* and the role technology plays in the definition of each. Regardless of which side of the argument you are on or which term you prefer, student learning should not occur in isolation or lead to students working independently behind laptops for hours at a time. What's key is that the learning experience adapts to the needs and interests of the student, is at times created by the student, and ultimately leads to powerful, shared experiences that motivate the student to engage more and dive deeper—both independently and collaboratively with others.

Learning that is personal represents a movement from the "what" to the "who" as a means to facilitate student ownership of the learning process. A more personal approach to learning can result in increased relevance and value for students, leading to better outcomes and results. Advances in technology now empower educators through both blended and virtual pathways and provide various methods and tools to support the learning process. When implemented well, these changes can undoubtedly enhance and improve the learning experience for many students.

As districts have worked to redesign student learning experiences, a variety of methods have begun to empower more personal, engaging, authentic experiences. Some full schools have formed around these methods, whereas in other places, strands, courses, or entire grade levels have begun to move the needle and shift mindsets and practices. What are some of these more personal practices? (It's important to note that there is overlap between many of these, as well as variation within each practice.)

STEM and STEAM

STEM integrates four general areas—science, technology, engineering, and math—into a cohesive, real-world learning paradigm rather than siloing each area into separate and discrete instructional content areas (as is traditionally done). Schools have begun this trend in response to the predicted job growth in these areas, and many have worked diligently to ensure the inclusion of traditionally underrepresented students of color and females in STEM disciplines. Schools leveraging a STEAM approach include arts and design as part of the process.

Deeper Learning

The premise of deeper learning is that through hands-on, real-world experiences, students can effectively master rigorous academic content, improve communication, and enhance problem-solving and collaboration skills. Strategies leveraged focus on the skills students will need to be successful in the future and are often supported by business leaders, college personnel, and employers. The ultimate goal of deeper learning is for students to be able to transfer what they learn in school to solve real-world problems, while becoming more engaged, confident, and self-directed as a result of the experience.

Linked Learning

Known often as an approach to high school redesign, linked learning integrates rigorous academics that meet college-ready standards, career-based learning while in the classroom, work-based learning, and a variety of student supports. For students in these schools or pathways, education is organized around industry-sector themes. Woven together, these pathways provide hands-on, relevant learning experiences for students with high academic standards and provide simultaneous opportunities to learn real-life skills from employers.

Project-based Learning (PBL)

A dynamic classroom approach in which students actively explore real-world problems and challenges while acquiring a deeper knowledge (i.e., project-based learning) is based on the premise that students learn best by experiencing and solving real-world problems. In a PBL approach, students tackle realistic problems while teachers act as coaches and facilitators of student inquiry and reflection. Students have increased control over their learning and usually work collaboratively to solve a complex task. Some form of culminating presentation, product, or artifact is created to help exhibit students' growth and understanding.

Blended Learning

A blended learning approach is one in which students learn partially through online learning, partially in a supervised brick-and-mortar location. It is a learner-centered methodology designed to provide students control of time, place, path, and/or pace through the purposeful alignment of traditional teaching practices and technology-enabled learning opportunities. Blended learning creates opportunities for teachers to reimagine the learning environment in support of relevant learning practices and increased engagement. This technique results in an amalgamation of digital content, tools, and best practices that allows for personalized instruction so all students are able to achieve mastery. Blending a classroom provides educators with the reach, efficiency, and individualized information necessary to personalize learning.

Competency-based Learning (CBL)

Competency-based learning is an approach that puts the focus on student mastery of desired learning outcomes. In CBL, students progress through curricula at their own pace and depth, and they do so when the expected competencies are mastered. CBL transitions away from seat time and instead empowers students through a variety of strategies, some of which may include online and blended learning, dual enrollment, early college high schools, and credit recovery. In a CBL model, the content is relevant and tailored to the individual need of each student.

Social Emotional Learning (SEL)

The process by which humans acquire the knowledge, attitudes, and skills needed to manage what's been coined Emotional Intelligence (EI) is referred to as social emotional learning. EI is the ability of an individual to recognize emotions—both in themselves and in others—discriminate between feelings, use the collected information to guide thinking and behavior, and adapt to their environment. Although SEL itself is not typically referred to as a program per se, various programs do provide instruction and opportunities to practice and apply SEL-related skills. These skills are fundamental to child development and to the mental health and overall well-being of an individual.

The area of SEL is often overlooked in schools. We believe that supporting the emotional well-being while in school and giving students skills and strategies for the long term is *one of the most important things* school leaders can do. Social emotional skills affect relationships with others, the workplace, family members, and sense of self. Intentionally designed schools recognize this value and work to support social emotional learning in various ways.

Career and Technical Education (CTE)

For decades, career and technical education schools and programs have given students dynamic opportunities to learn real-world skills that were personal, relevant, and aligned to their interests. However, due to a lack of funding and in some places a stigma against old-school "vo-tech," high-quality CTE is not available for many students. From programs in business, agriculture, family and consumer sciences, automobile repair, cosmetology, and computer science, CTE can provide students with dynamic, personal skills for their future. One study by the Fordham Institute found that students with greater exposure to CTE were more likely to graduate from high school, enroll in college, be employed, and earn higher wages. The study also found the greatest boost for males and students from low-income families (Dougherty, 2016).

As school leaders work to create their plan for the future, finding ways for students to have personal and authentic learning experiences is key to redesigning the learning experience. Intentionally designed schools are purposeful in their programing, coursework, and lesson design so that personal learning experiences are the norm, not the exception, and available for *all* students.

Teaching the "Netflix Generation"

If we teach today's students as we taught yesterday's, we rob them of tomorrow.

John Dewey

The availability of content and the multitude of distribution platforms have grown exponentially in recent years. The explosion of social media, combined with the ability to stream content to virtually all types of devices, both at home and while on the go, has radically altered the way in which people interact with media. No longer does one have to wait until a scheduled time to watch their favorite television show. It's available when and where they want it, often on various platforms and in multiple formats, with the click of a button. Users can even remove or ignore the media they don't want, such as commercials. This "Netflix generation" of students (and all future generations) has no basis for understanding information that isn't readily and immediately available. These students have come to expect high-quality content—on demand, anytime, and anywhere. This mindset puts our schools in an interesting position.

In classrooms where teachers view themselves as the key disseminators of information, content is primarily derived from a static textbook, and information isn't meant to be consumed until a particular point during a larger scope and sequence. This model has become obsolete to the current Netflix generation. Such a learning environment is seen as completely irrelevant and unrelated to the world students experience outside the classroom walls. To avoid this, and in an effort to remain relevant in a digital world, many school leaders have been purchasing vast amounts of technology with the hopes that it'll move instructional practices into the current century. Remaining relevant to a generation of students who consume and create digital content daily obliterates the perceived effectiveness of a traditional stand-and-deliver, regurgitation-based methodology. If your mindset is that a teacher's main job is content delivery, then they've just been outsourced by Netflix and YouTube.

Fortunately, a recent survey indicates that schools are evolving in these areas to adapt to the Netflix generation. Project Tomorrow, an organization that studies trends in this area, produces the yearly Speak Up Survey and analyzed feedback from almost half a million students, parents, and educators from over 2,000 districts throughout the United States in 2015. Some of the key findings from this survey were the following (Project Tomorrow, 2016):

- Over three-quarters of middle school students (78 percent) are tapping into online videos, and 6 out of 10 (61 percent) are playing online games, all in service of various types of self-directed learning goals.
- School principals (84 percent) are almost unanimous in their belief that the effective use of technology within instruction is important for student success. However, they do acknowledge challenges or barriers to meeting the expectations of effective technology usage.
- Five out of ten administrators note that the implementation of digital content resources, such as videos, simulations, and animations, was already generating positive student outcomes.
- Almost 60 percent of technology leaders say that one-quarter of instructional materials in their schools today are digital—not paper-based—and 26 percent say that their level of paperlessness is 50 percent.
- The top subject areas in which students in grades 6–12 watch videos to support their homework, research projects, or studies are science (66 percent), math (59 percent), social studies/history (53 percent), and English/language arts (45 percent).

School curricula and experiences are evolving, yet on the whole, the speed of transformation remains slow. As school leaders spark this evolution, they often rely on massive amounts of technology to "fix" traditional issues, which we believe has led to the current "educational technology fallacy."

The Educational Technology Fallacy

The technology itself is not transformative. It's the school, the pedagogy, that is transformative.

Tanya Byron

In recent decades, school leaders have grown to understand the evolving work world students will face upon graduation—and technology's role in the acceleration of that change. Simultaneously, an explosion in the availability of educational technology, in part due to an infusion of venture capital funding, has created more tools and "ed-tech solutions" than ever before. Seemingly at every turn, people are promising silver bullets to fix school and district issues or selling schools on a need they didn't realize they had. In feeling the need to keep up, school leaders have found themselves buying more educational technology than ever before, deploying vast amounts of devices, and left to wonder what impact, if any, those purchases have had.

During the final budget meeting in my (Tom) last year as a technology director in Pennsylvania, the school board president publically asked me, "Tom, if we are going to spend an additional [dollar amount] on technology, will student achievement increase next year?" If put on the spot, how would you answer such a question?

My response? "Well, Mr. President, it depends. We are purchasing tools that can make new high-level learning experiences possible, yet it is in the hands of our great teachers to make that impact." Though uncomfortable, that question, from the person responsible for signing the check for the purchase, was an excellent one. Districts need to be able to confidently answer this type of question before any large technology purchase.

Simply buying devices and deploying them in mass will in itself not improve student achievement. Educational technology is not, and never will be, a silver bullet to prepare students for their future.

To this point, research on educational technology indicates that access to devices alone is simply not enough to shift the learning paradigm. A 2015 report released by the Organisation for Economic Co-operation and Development (OECD), examined how students' access to and use of information and communication technology (ICT) devices has evolved in recent years. It also explored how education systems and schools have been integrating ICT into students' learning experiences. The report sent shockwaves through the educational technology community. In summary, the OECD report

> Provides a first-of-its-kind internationally comparative analysis of the digital skills that students have acquired and of the learning environments designed to develop these skills. This analysis shows that the reality in our schools lags considerably behind the promise of technology. In 2012, 96 percent of 15-year-old students in OECD

countries reported that they have a computer at home, but only 72 percent reported that they use a desktop, laptop, or tablet computer at school, and in some countries fewer than one in two students reported doing so. And even where computers are used in the classroom, their impact on student performance is mixed at best. Students who use computers moderately at school tend to have somewhat better learning outcomes than students who use computers rarely. But students who use computers very frequently at school do a lot worse in most learning outcomes, even after accounting for social background and student demographics.

Wait, what? The report goes on.

The results also show no appreciable improvements in student achievement in reading, mathematics, or science in countries that had invested heavily in ICT for education. And perhaps the most disappointing finding of the report is that technology is of little help in bridging the skills divide between advantaged and disadvantaged students.

But how can this be? "Put simply, ensuring that every child attains a baseline level of proficiency in reading and mathematics seems to do more to create equal opportunities in a digital world than can be achieved by expanding or subsidizing access to high-tech devices and services" (Schleicher, 2016, p. 63).

We believe the findings of the OECD report are indicative of the types of technology use prevalent in many, if not most, schools. Low-level, drill-and-kill technology infusion, which is probably the most implemented technology-based practice, simply leads to low-level learning. Compounded over time, technology integration that is focused on low-level skills will most certainly have a negative effect on student achievement.

Professor Mark Warschauer (2007) compiled research showing that access alone isn't enough to raise the bar, particularly for underserved students. He writes, "Overall, students who are black, Hispanic, or low-income are more likely to use computers for drill-and-practice, whereas students who are white or high-income are more likely to use computers for simulations or authentic applications" (p. 148). The evidence in these studies indicates that student income and race correlate strongly with the type of computer use in which they engage. In low-income schools, digital tools are often used for remediation purposes and implemented through low-quality digital drill-and-kill pedagogical practices. On the other hand, in primarily white, higher-income schools, technology is more often used for interactive learning and authentic applications. In both learning environments, the physical access was the same. How the technology was used and, thus, the opportunities provided to students, though, were drastically different.

Furthermore, a mountain of evidence, combined with the experience of many school leaders, affirms that transforming instructional pedagogy has been painfully slow, despite the influx of new technology into their schools. Decades later, the "ideal" student-centered, personalized instruction model oversold and promised by ed-tech companies still remains the exception, not the norm.

As with many initiatives, early adopters embrace new changes, a majority makes minimal changes, and some people flat out resist changing at all. In schools, factors such as educators' mindset about what constitutes high-quality teaching; a lack of personal experience with technology; and sporadic, one-size-fits-all, low-level professional learning has had a negative effect on teachers and administrators alike. At scale, teachers most often domesticate technologies by trying to layer their use on top of existing (teacher-centric) instructional practices. Today's "latest and greatest" technology might simply be a digital storage hub, with no pedagogical difference from a folder full of worksheets from decades past. However, the same technology can also be leveraged to create dynamic learning opportunities and unleash student genius. *The teacher*, not the technology, is the key variable to this equation.

With the rapid growth of online testing, schools have also rushed to buy educational technology that supports these assessments. Since some states require online assessments, districts have essentially been forced to add large numbers of devices. So far, the emphasis of this type of technological integration has overwhelmingly been on the assessment side, and the instructional side has gotten lost in the process. This has led to devices in schools being spread out somewhat randomly—tossed around with little precision yet done with the hope that it'll enrich current growth far and wide. In many cases, the devices become simplistic instructional add-ons or gap fillers for time, yielding little to no instructional benefit.

We must also question the pedagogical practice of teaching and learning in a traditional format and then assessing digitally. We believe that such assessments require an additional skill set. In cases where assessments are fully digital but are rarely used during the learning process, students are likely to perform at a lower level.

The research is clear. Technology by itself does not, and will not, transform teaching and learning. In fact, like any tool, when used poorly, it can have negative consequences. We believe that

- Simply adding the latest technology to traditional learning environments can have a negative effect on teaching and learning.
- Technology can accelerate great teaching practices, which can in turn support equity and create greater opportunities for all students.
- Technology can amplify poor teaching practices and increase the amount of time students spend on low-level learning tasks.
- Assessing students in an online format but consistently using traditional instructional methods during the learning process can yield lower results. Online assessments require a digital skill set and comfort level that may not be present for students who have learned in a very different fashion.

A 2014 report by the Stanford Center for Opportunity Policy in Education and the Alliance for Excellent Education set out to study the effective use of technology, particularly with students who are most at risk (Darling-Hammond et al., 2014). The report verified that early versions of technology-based instruction that were structured like "electronic workbooks," where students passively moved through a digital curriculum, showed little effect on achievement. The report cited one particular study that evaluated the impact of math and reading software products in 132 schools across 33 districts, which found no significant difference on student test scores between classrooms that used the software and classrooms that didn't (Dynarski et al., 2007). The report also cited another large study that evaluated the effectiveness of students' exposure to a phonics-based computer program, which also found no effect in terms of gains on reading comprehension tests (Borman, Benson, & Overman, 2009). Time and again, the "digital drill and kill" or use of technology as an electronic workbook shows little to no effect on student learning.

So what does the effective use of technology actually look like? What *is* worth the investment of time and money? There are three important variables for the successful infusion of technology, particularly with at-risk students who are learning new skills.

Interactive Learning: The interactive use of technology can enhance student learning and, ultimately, achievement by providing multiple ways for learners to grasp traditionally difficult concepts. Interactive learning opportunities have become more robust as adaptive content and systems have evolved in recent years. In these systems, the content levels up and down based on a student's ability; in other words, it adapts to a student's level of need. When leveraged for interactive learning, students become active users—not passive consumers of content.

Use of Technology to Explore and Create: When students are given the opportunity to leverage technology to explore and create, new learning can be accelerated. When this is the case, students are able to create and develop new content rather than absorb content passively. When empowered to explore and create, students also demonstrate higher levels of engagement, more positive attitudes toward school, higher levels of skill development, and self-efficacy.

Right Blend of Teachers and Technology: When students have ubiquitous access, particularly in environments with 1:1 student-to-device ratios, digital experiences can be blended into the learning environment to extrapolate concepts and maximize learning opportunities. In these environments, students can access the "right blend" of direct instruction and technology-accelerated learning. Student voice and choice play an important role while the teacher gives the needed level of direct support.

Technology use is most productive when experiences combine the "structured learning of information with collaborative discussions and project-based activities that allow students to use the information to solve meaningful problems or create their own products, both individually and collectively" (Darling-Hammond et al., 2014, p. 15).

Displaying lesson notes on an interactive whiteboard, answering multiple-choice questions in an online platform, typing documents that are saved to the cloud, reading a textbook on a mobile device, or looking up facts online may make certain tasks more efficient, but they do nothing to challenge or redefine an outdated pedagogy. Leveraging technology to create a more teacher-centric environment is detrimental to student learning and undoubtedly fails to create the personal and authentic learning opportunities students need. Intentionally designed schools refuse to utilize technology for technology's sake. These schools purposefully use technology as the right tool, at the right time, to create the needed access and opportunity.

Rigor and Relevance to Reboot Pedagogy

Productive learning is the learning process which engenders and reinforces wanting to learn more.

Seymour Sarason

Learning must always be relevant, meaningful, and applicable. Student engagement on high-level tasks is a bedrock necessity of attentive and deeper learning (Sheninger, 2015b). When students are excited about their academic growth or in their creativity, originality, design, or adaptation, they can think and act critically to curate content and apply information to address a range of cross-disciplinary tasks that are both creative and original. This could include collaborating with others via social media, networking, or reviewing, which requires students to select, organize, and present content through relevant digital tools and with multiple solutions. Technology provides many opportunities to engage learners like never before, yet it is imperative that this engagement also leads to high levels of learning in which students create a variety of artifacts that demonstrate conceptual mastery. Being engaged on low-level, menial tasks leads to low-level learning. As such, when using technology as a tool, the focus must be on sound instructional design principles composed of authentic-based learning activities that are meaningful and relevant to the learner.

In many cases, there seems to be a tendency to water down expectations when it comes to integrating technology. During a recent presentation on digital pedagogy for deeper learning, I (Eric) asked attendees to discuss and then share out (through the backchannel we were using) how they were effectively integrating technology in their classroom, school, or district. There was an emphasis on describing in detail what the effective use of technology meant to them. As the results poured in, there were a few consistent responses that stood out. Most attendees flat out stated that they or their schools/districts were not effectively integrating technology. Others confessed that they weren't sure what effective use constituted. Many of the remaining responses were simply a list of digital tools that were being used as a measure of effectiveness.

The question about effective use provides a great opportunity for all of us to critically reflect upon the current role technology plays in education. There is a great deal of potential in the plethora of tools now available to support or enhance learning, but we must be mindful of how any tool is being used. Take a tool such as Kahoot, for example. This tool is used in many classrooms around the world to get students more engaged and add a level of fun and excitement to the learning process. However, most of the time, the questions that students are asked to answer in Kahoot are focused on the lowest cognitive domains and are typically in a multiple choice format. We have nothing against Kahoot and think it is a great tool that has a great deal of promise. Simply put, it's not the tool's fault how it is used. Our issue in this case is how this particular tool, and many others, are often utilized in the classroom.

The burden of responsibility here lies with both teachers and administrators. In many cases, the engagement factor is emphasized over learning outcomes and actual evidence of improvement aligned to standards. High levels of engagement on very low-level tasks will yield very low-level learning.

Enter the Rigor/Relevance Framework as a means to ensure that technology is integrated effectively. The Rigor/Relevance Framework is a tool developed by the International Center for Leadership in Education to examine curriculum, instruction, and assessment. It is based on combining two continua focused on critical thinking (rigor) and application (relevance) and made possible by strong relationships among students, teachers, parents, and beyond.

The framework's continuum of knowledge describes the increasingly complex ways in which we think (see Figure 2.1). This knowledge taxonomy is based on the six levels of critical thinking, also known as the revised Bloom's Taxonomy:

6. Creating
5. Evaluating
4. Analyzing
3. Applying
2. Understanding
1. Remembering

The low end of this continuum involves acquiring knowledge and being able to recall or locate that knowledge in a simple manner. The higher end of the continuum targets more complex ways in which individuals use knowledge. At the highest level, knowledge is fully integrated into one's mind, and individuals can do much more than locate information—they can take several pieces of knowledge and combine them in both logical and creative ways. At this level, students can solve multistep problems, create unique work, and devise solutions.

FIGURE 2.1

Rigor/Relevance Framework

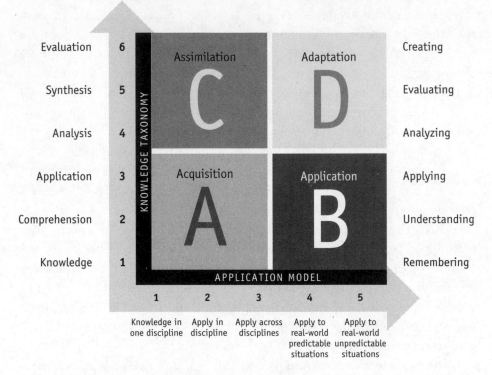

Source: From "The Rigor Relevance Framework®," by the International Center for Leadership in Education, 2016. Copyright 2016 by Houghton Mifflin Harcourt. Reprinted with permission. Available: http://www.leadered.com/our-philosophy/rigor-relevance-framework.php

The second continuum is known as the Application Model. The Application Model describes putting knowledge to use. Whereas the low end is knowledge acquired for its own sake, the high end signifies action—use of that knowledge to solve complex real-world problems and create projects, designs, and other works for use in real-world situations. The five levels of this action continuum are as follows:

1. Knowledge in one discipline.
2. Apply in discipline.
3. Apply across disciplines.
4. Apply to real-world predictable situations.
5. Apply to real-world unpredictable situations.

The Rigor/Relevance Framework has four quadrants. **Quadrant A** (Acquisition) represents simple recall and basic understanding of knowledge for its own sake. Relevant skills provide basic knowledge of digital and social media. Examples include knowing that the world is round and that Shakespeare wrote *Hamlet*.

Quadrant B (Application) represents low rigor with high degrees of application. It includes knowing how to use math skills to make purchases and count change. These skills show a student's ability to apply his or her acquired knowledge in digital and social media, for example at the remembering and understanding levels of critical thinking. When solving more complex problems or designing solutions, this is best described by Quadrant B.

Quadrant C (Assimilation) embraces higher levels of knowledge, such as knowing how the U.S. political system works and analyzing the benefits and challenges of international cultural diversity. In a digital sense, students are able to use a variety of tools to master the applicable skills.

Quadrant D (Adaptation) requires students to think and work at high levels of rigor and relevance. Students are challenged to analyze, synthesize, and evaluate their knowledge to new and unpredictable real-world situations. The ability to access information in wide-area network systems and gather knowledge from a variety of sources to solve a complex problem in the workplace are best described by Quadrant D.

Each of these four quadrants can also be labeled with a term that characterizes the learning outcome or student performance (Figure 2.2). The Rigor/Relevance Framework provides a comprehensive platform through which we can synthesize teaching, learning, and technology to ensure purposeful integration.

Technology should be integrated in a way that increases engagement through relevance. As students are utilizing technology, are they just applying it in one discipline? We are not saying this is a bad thing, but we must eventually move beyond this typical comfort zone when it comes to the use of digital tools. When integrating technology, does the task allow students

- to make connections across various disciplines and content areas?
- to solve real-world predictable problems?
- to solve real-world unpredictable problems?

The other aspect of this framework is the most important. Are students working, thinking, or both? Successful technology integration is dependent on the level of the task at hand. Sound pedagogy always trumps technology.

Think about the formative and summative assessments you either use or see in your respective role. Are students demonstrating high levels of cognitive thought? How do you know whether students have learned or

FIGURE 2.2

Rigor/Relevance Outcomes

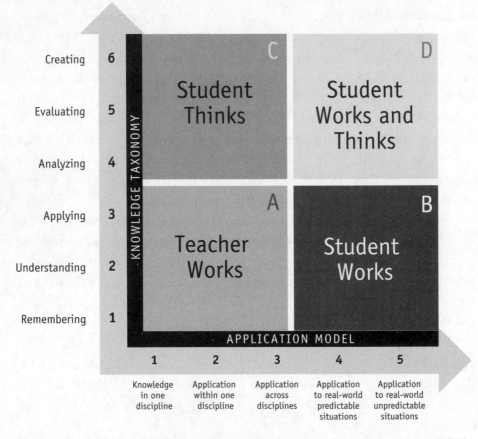

Source: From "The Rigor Relevance Framework®," by the International Center for Leadership in Education, 2016. Copyright 2016 by Houghton Mifflin Harcourt. Reprinted with permission. Available: http://www.leadered.com/our-philosophy/rigor-relevance-framework.php

not when integrating technology? What does the feedback loop look like? These types of questions are extremely important to ask as a teacher or administrator to determine the level of effectiveness and—ultimately—the impact on student learning.

Let's pretend that you are an elementary school math teacher addressing the following content standard. Here's what a progression from Quadrant A to D might look like.

Standard: Determine the order of operations to correctly solve problems with more than two numbers.

Quadrant A—Acquisition: Students gather and store bits of knowledge and information. They are primarily expected to remember or understand this acquired knowledge, and they receive an assignment in a learning management system (LMS), such as Google Classroom, Edmodo, or Schoology. They open the assignment to reveal a video tutorial from the teacher. During the video, the teacher teaches a mnemonic for the order of operations (e.g., Please Excuse My Dear Aunt Sally) along with several tips for completion. Students close the video and use the information to complete and submit several sample problems in the LMS. The teacher provides small-group and individual remediation as necessary.

Quadrant B—Application: Students strive to apply appropriate knowledge to new and unpredictable situations. With that in mind, they are shown the video tutorial and asked to create their own mnemonics for the order of operations using a tool such as Google Slides or Microsoft PowerPoint. They are also asked to create a sample math problem that includes parentheses/brackets, multiplication/division, and addition/subtraction whose answer reveals an interesting fact about their respective community. Students submit their sample problems and mnemonics via the LMS. The teacher provides small-group and individual remediation as necessary.

Quadrant C—Assimilation: Students extend and refine their acquired knowledge to automatically and routinely analyze and solve problems and create unique solutions. Prior to the start of the lesson, the teacher identifies key academic vocabulary and leverages Google Search along with direct instruction, questioning, and feedback to provide foundational clarity. Students are shown the video tutorial and asked to create their own mnemonics for the order of operations in Google Slides or PowerPoint. They are also asked to create a sample math problem that includes parenthesis/brackets, multiplication/division, and addition/subtraction whose answer reveals an interesting fact about them. Students then post their mnemonics and sample problems via Google+. Peers can vote for the most creative mnemonic by providing comments. Finally, students will select four of their peers' problems to solve and submit their solutions and mnemonics via the LMS. The teacher will provide small-group and individual remediation as necessary.

Quadrant D—Adaptation: Students collaborate in groups according to proficiency levels to create video tutorials that explain the order of operations and provide creative new mnemonics. Students are also provided time to do a gallery walk and review their peers' videos. Each student will also create a sample problem that includes parenthesis/brackets, multiplication/division, and addition/subtraction whose answer reveals an interesting fact about them. Students will solve four of their peers' problems and submit their video tutorials and solved sample problems via the LMS. The teacher will provide small-group and individual remediation as necessary.

The Rigor/Relevance Framework and the use of the quadrants can help maximize the effective use of instructional tools such as G Suite (formerly Google Apps for Education) or Office 365. Digital tools are not extraneous elements we can haphazardly plug into the learning environment. The reality that teachers face necessitates an intentional design process that accounts for a strong standards focus in conjunction with a commitment to research-based best practices for creation, design, exploration, and interactive learning. As such, we must develop methodologies for lesson design and student-centered learning experiences.

Here is an example of what is possible when teachers take the task of summarization, which is among the nine most effective teaching strategies (Marzano, 2003), and leverage a tool such as G Suite in conjunction with the four quadrants to integrate high-quality instructional practices.

Standard: Determine the central idea of a text. Provide an objective summary.

Quadrant A—Acquisition: Students access a text via Google Classroom, type responses to short answer comprehension questions, name the file, and submit it to the teacher.

Quadrant B—Application: Students work in teams via Google Docs to create collaborative Cornell Notes to summarize a text. Teams peer review and provide feedback via the commenting feature in Google Docs.

Quadrant C—Assimilation: Students use Google Slides to storyboard essential elements from a text. Slides include photo and video elements collected via Google Search to support the students' assertions and conclusions.

Quadrant D—Adaptation: Students use a video communication tool such as Google Hangouts to debate text assertions with peers in other regions. Summaries, prompts, and essential questions are created by students prior to the activity and then provided to everyone via Google Classroom.

When integrating technology, whether it's with G Suite or another instructional tool like Apple Classroom, the Rigor/ Relevance Framework can be used as a guide to reflect on the quality of learning that's occurring. When infused well, technology *can be* an amazing tool for teachers and leaders to support a systemwide approach to rigorous learning. Ultimately, with dynamic technology integration grounded in best practices, learning opportunities become limitless, and students can take their learning to new heights—thereby creating Quadrant D learning experiences (Figure 2.3).

Categorizing technology use by the four quadrants is a support tool for creating and analyzing rigorous and relevant learning experiences. Verbs and examples of technology use can be combined to create a learning experience for each quadrant. Figure 2.3 illustrates and categorizes examples of learning tasks that integrate technology into quadrants of the Rigor/ Relevance Framework. It is important to note that tools can vary from quadrant to quadrant based on how they are used. For example, a Google Doc could be used in both a Quad A or D activity. The key is ensuring technology is integrated in purposeful and meaningful ways to support high-level learning and relevance.

With robust and reliable digital tools in hand, students grow to develop their own learning tasks—such as podcasting, blogging, or digitally storytelling—that stretch their creativity, originality, design, or adaptation. These students think and apply knowledge critically to curate content and apply information to address a range of cross-disciplinary tasks that are both creative and original (Sheninger, 2015b). This could include collaborating with others using social media, networking, or reviewing. Their work requires an ability to select, organize, and present content through relevant digital tools, which provide multiple solutions.

The overall goal when integrating technology should be to provide opportunities for students to work and think. Another key strategy for successful integration is to use technology when appropriate. Technology will not improve every lesson or project, thus a focus on pedagogy first, technology second will help ensure success. Many aspects of the Rigor/Relevance Framework can be used to guide you in developing better questions as part of good pedagogy including the following steps:

- Anticipatory set/do-now
- Review of prior learning
- Checking for understanding (formative and summative)
- Closure

The most important aspects of pedagogy are assessment and feedback. If technology (and innovation in general) is going to have a positive impact on learning, let's ensure these areas are improved first. Then, going forward, always lend a critical eye to how technology is being used to address standards and inform instruction.

The Rigor/Relevance Framework provides educators with a common language, constitutes the lens through which we can examine all aspects of a learning culture (curriculum, instruction, assessment), and helps create a culture around a common vision. It ensures technology is integrated in a purposeful fashion so that ultimately, students can take more ownership over their own learning.

FIGURE 2.3

Rigor/Relevance Framework with Technology

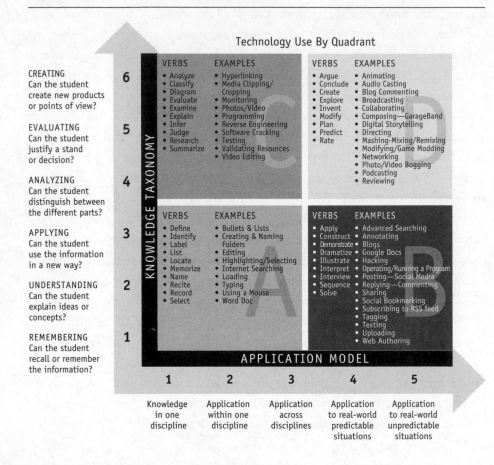

Source: From "The Rigor Relevance Framework®," by the International Center for Leadership in Education, 2016. Copyright 2016 by Houghton Mifflin Harcourt. Reprinted with permission. Available: http://www.leadered.com/our-philosophy/rigor-relevance-framework.php

Moving from Passive to Active Use: The Digital Use Divide

There are two types of schools: Those that prepare kids for the future, and those that allow adults to live comfortably in the past.

Weston Kieschnick

Traditionally, the term *digital divide* has been used to describe unequal access to digital technologies, and it refers to places where access to devices and Internet connectivity are either unavailable or unaffordable. It has often served as a main discussion point in conversations about connectivity in rural areas or for those living in poverty. Closing the digital divide has been a core mission of a number of organizations and policy decisions over the past few decades at the federal, state, and local levels. Many schools have worked diligently to get connected and support student access, and programs such as eRate (which we discuss in Chapter 6), have financially supported such connectivity efforts in schools. Although much work remains to be done in closing this gap, great progress has been made in providing connectivity and device access.

FIGURE 2.4
Digital Use Divide

While essential, closing the digital divde alone will not transform learning.
We must also close the digital **use** divide by ensuring all students understand
how to use technology as a tool to engage in creative, productive,
life-long learning rather than simply consuming passive content.

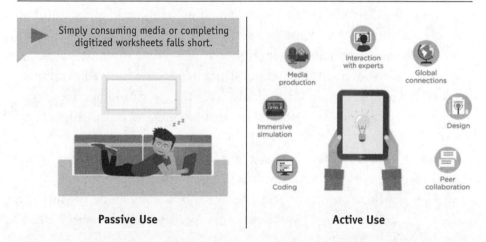

Source: From "Section 1: Engaging and Empowering Learning Through Technology," by the U.S. Department of Education, Office of Educational Technology, 2015. Available: http://tech.ed.gov/netp/learning

The 2016 National Education Technology Plan coined the term *digital use divide*, which is defined as "the disparity between students who use technology to create, design, build, explore, and collaborate and those who simply use technology to consume media passively" (Office of Educational Technology, 2016, p. 18). This notion has been obvious to school leaders since technology first began finding its way into classrooms, and it's a far larger issue than the digital divide. Walk down the hallway in many schools, and dramatic differences can be seen between one classroom and another one across the hall, even though they may have identical devices, programs, and infrastructure.

The digital use divide contrasts the difference between *passive use*, where technology is used to consume media content, and *active use*, where technology is used to explore, design, and create (see Figure 2.4). School leaders who intentionally design schools are cognizant of this divide, and they work to ensure technology is used actively. As schools rush to buy devices to support a transformed learning experience, they must be cognizant of the research-backed effective uses of technology. They must also give thoughtful attention to ensuring active use of technology and support classroom instruction and learning design that moves from consumption to creation.

Building Student Agency

For schools to transform learning, student agency must be a core component and value of all involved. *Agency* is defined as "the capacity, condition, or state of acting or of exerting power." Therefore, we can define student agency as students' capacity to act or exert themselves into their learning. Compliance-driven, traditional school structures do anything but facilitate the development of agency. Historically, with the exception of choosing a few elective courses, adults—not the student—typically control all aspects of schooling.

Student agency is about empowering kids to own their learning (and school) through greater autonomy. It is driven by choice, voice, and advocacy. As schools transform to meet the needs of today's modern learners, student agency is a natural byproduct of the process, but the design must be intentional in nature.

How can school leaders make student agency a reality in their schools?

- Develop pedagogically sound learning activities with standards-aligned assessments, and enable students to select the right tool for the task to demonstrate conceptual mastery.
- Empower students to co-create rules and expectations.

- Provide avenues for students to provide honest feedback on school culture. Tools that create a backchannel for communication can also be used to gather perception data from students.
- Implement portfolios as a means of authentic assessment.
- When hiring new teachers and administrators, have students sit on the interview committee.
- As policies that affect students are created or updated, provide a forum for them to give feedback.
- Integrate personalized and personal learning pathways (e.g., blended and virtual).
- Have protocols established for students to suggest new courses and extracurricular activities.
- Implement academies or smaller learning communities.
- Let students select books for independent reading based on their interests and reading level.

The issues seen in today's society, along with those that will soon take on worldwide relevance, are difficult. No one person will be able to solve global issues on his or her own. As such, we must support a generation that can work with others yet is receptive to critical feedback and reflective of their own practices. Our students will enter a world where their ideas—their genius—will only matter if they have the agency to develop and share them. Helping students become their own biggest advocates is key.

Modern learners with agency make things happen through their actions. They can adapt to changing times and are reflective in their own growth and self-development, yet building these skills does not occur in teacher-centric learning environments. To build these skills, learners must have the opportunity to make meaningful choices about their learning and find their voice while advocating for their own growth. Intentionally designed schools recognize that student voice and choice help create student agency and lead to the development of students who can solve tomorrow's problems.

Redesigning the learning experience is not a simple feat, nor does such transformation occur overnight. School leaders who are transforming learning to be personal and authentic are grounding student experiences in research-based evidence, utilizing a high-level framework to support dynamic student-learning opportunities, and leveraging student agency to develop students with the necessary skill sets to thrive long into the future.

You are part of the solution.

Innovative Practices in Action

Vista Unified School District, California
Dr. Devin Vodicka, Superintendent

2016 AASA California Superintendent of the Year

Irrelevant. This was the word that was most frequently used by the students in our district when I asked for input to inform the development of our strategic plan to help us achieve our vision to become the model of educational excellence and innovation. Other students bemoaned the passive experience at schools and asked for more of an active role. It was clear that our approach was not resonating with students as intended. We needed to redesign the learning experience.

These comments reinforced the districtwide data that kept me awake at night. At that time, our graduation rates hovered around 80 percent, which meant that about one in five students were not completing high school. It was clear to me that student disengagement was a fundamental problem that we needed to address.

In response to this challenge, our approach was to shift to personal learning. The initial version of our strategic plan detailed many specific actions to begin the process. When we shared the plan with our community, we received strong feedback about anxiety regarding the proposed changes. We listened to the concerns and made significant revisions to the plan. As such, we spent an entire year bringing teams together to help us create a common definition of *personal learning*. We partnered with researchers and industry experts to assist in the process. The result was the formation of a one-page graphic that highlighted the major components of our desired personal learning model: a holistic student profile, robust technology infrastructure, personalized learning pathways, adaptive learning environments, and competency-based systems.

After its creation, teams went on a "road show" to school sites to share the proposed model and to solicit volunteers to implement the approach. We found five schools that were willing to be early adopters, which we then identified as "Personal Learning Challenge Schools." Fortunately, these five sites included a mix of elementary, middle, and high school locations. These early adopters took the lead and explored ways to adapt practices,

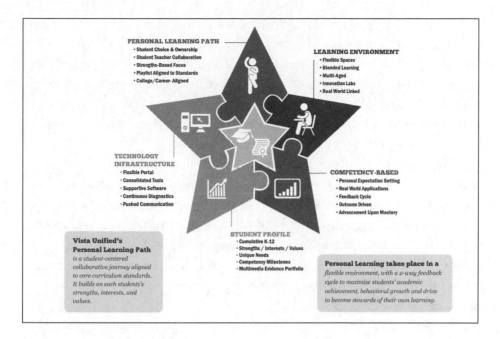

coming together to share lessons learned through regular convenings of a personal learning steering committee.

Most practitioners found that a natural entry point for personal learning was to focus on the strengths, interests, and values of each student. Various tools and assessments were field tested, and we collected feedback from students to inform our next steps. Building on our robust technology infrastructure, a number of software platforms were piloted to promote student choice and "playlist" experiences for students. We also provided some seed money for the challenge schools to purchase furniture and equipment that would transform the learning environment. Donations from partners such as Qualcomm helped accelerate changes to more flexible spaces that would promote personal learning experiences.

After one year of implementing the personal learning model at the five challenge schools, both qualitative and quantitative data indicated that there was great promise with this approach. Student feedback was overwhelmingly favorable as they expressed much greater interest in their studies. At Vista High School, we had 50 percent fewer absences and a 99 percent reduction in discipline incidents among the students who participated in the Personal Learning Academy. Almost two-thirds of the students increased their grade point averages by a full point or more. One of the students said that she used to fall asleep at school and now she remained awake and was energized by her learning. This is the type of feedback that we wanted to hear.

About three-quarters of middle school students in the personal learning interventions at Rancho Minerva Middle School and Vista Innovation and Design Academy improved math achievement grade equivalency by one year in six months time. Average growth in reading and math for all students at Casita Elementary was over one year after just six months. At Temple Heights Elementary, 3rd grade students improved from 36 percent to 47 percent proficiency on reading assessments.

These are very encouraging results that reflect well on the concerted and courageous efforts of numerous leaders, teachers, staff members, families, partners, and students in our community. Positive news about this effort has spread organically at both the local and national level, and we are thrilled to be able to share that next year we will have a total of 14 personal learning challenge schools—representing almost half of our total schools—and our goal is to continue to scale best practices until we can reach every one of our students.

We still have a great deal to learn as we seek to transform the student experience into a meaningful, student-centered journey that builds on the unique strengths of every learner. Much work remains to be done, particularly with respect to competency-based approaches, but I am very optimistic that our personal learning model holds great promise for the future.

(Devin Vodicka, Ed.D, is the superintendent of the Vista Unified School District in San Diego County, California. He has been recognized as the California Superintendent of the Year by both the Association of California School Administrators in 2015 and by the American Association of School Administrators in 2016. Vista High School was selected as one of the first XQ Super Schools in 2016, resulting in an award of $10 million to expand the Personal Learning Academy to a schoolwide model.)

Talladega County School District, Alabama
Suzanne Lacey, Superintendent

Innovation and Change Award Winner,
National Principals Leadership Institute

Talladega County Schools' story is much like other high-poverty districts throughout the nation marked by average to below-average student performance scores. Nearly 73 percent of students qualify for free and reduced-price lunch and have specific material needs that often create additional barriers for learning. With 17 schools, the delivery of instruction was traditional and often boring and uninviting for students now living in the 21st century. School leaders wanted more, knew a change was needed, and began to study other schools that were providing meaningful work fueled by technology. In 2008, Talladega County Schools began an aggressive campaign to redefine learning for the district's 7,700 students. Guided by the system's strategic goals to increase student engagement, integrate technology to support instruction, and train teachers in innovative practices, district stakeholders researched and visited successful schools across the nation.

Project-based learning (PBL), integrated with a 1:1 student-to-digital-device initiative, proved to be an effective model for increasing student engagement and meaningful work. The goals of the PBL model powered by technology were to prepare students for rigorous higher-education coursework, career challenges, and demands for skills beyond content knowledge—in particular, communication, collaboration, creativity, and critical thinking, which are all skills addressed within the College and Career Ready Standards. Visits to other schools across the nation that were already implementing the PBL model were impressive and gave teachers the needed confidence to go back to their own schools and share their excitement about strategies and technology tools that were stimulating student learning in powerful ways.

Further, the model required stakeholders to go beyond the traditional methodology of instruction to one that engaged students, increased rigor, increased attendance, and better prepared students for both college and careers. Since 2008, the district has reached unprecedented success under this aggressive change model by increasing the graduation rate to 94 percent for all seven high schools. Since that time, two high schools have received the Innovation and Change Award presented by the National Principals Leadership Institute. The award given to Winterboro High School in 2012 marked a four-year journey of extraordinary change that now serves as a model for other schools' thinking about remaking learning. Winterboro hosts thousands of visitors each year and continues to serve as the cornerstone for exemplary teaching and job-embedded staff development for the district. In 2016, Childersburg High School also received the prestigious Innovation and Change Award. Much like Winterboro, Childersburg's success has been rooted in an emphasis on PBL, advanced placement courses, and collaborative leadership development.

The district's goal of empowering both students and teachers to "own" their learning has affected each school culture significantly. Unlike the past, students are now expected to share their learning through interactive leadership notebooks, portfolios, and projects. Teachers have become the "experts down the hall," often providing professional learning for their colleagues based on authentic field experience in a nontraditional classroom environment. Throughout the transition, each school developed student leadership teams that worked collaboratively with teachers and administrators to redefine the purpose of their school and to move toward the concept of a professional work environment. Students shared their ideas openly and offered opinions to better support the change process. A culture of respect quickly emerged that allowed both students and teachers the opportunity to reflect and work toward higher expectations. Disciplinary infractions were reduced and attendance rates soared because school was more purposeful and, finally, more personal.

#LeadingtheWay symbolizes the reputation that Talladega County Schools has achieved not only locally but also across the state and nation. This initiative has inspired a progressive and uniform vision for all schools in our rural district to provide access to information technologies and high-quality learning opportunities for all students. Today, the district opens its doors to representatives from educational institutions, businesses, and nonprofit organizations to observe the PBL model in action. The district was selected for membership in the League of Innovative Schools, which is quite an accomplishment for a rural district that just eight years ago was by all metrics traditional and below average. Not anymore. Our students need and deserve these types of transformed learning experiences.

(*Dr. Suzanne Lacey was appointed superintendent of Talladega County Schools in 2008. Since that time, Dr. Lacey's leadership has been recognized at both the regional and national levels. In 2014, she was selected to attend President Obama's ConnectEd Initiative in Washington, DC, as part of 100 outstanding superintendents from across the nation. That same year, Talladega was featured as one of three districts highlighted on Digital Learning Day for its systemic transformation.*)

3 Ensuring a Return on Instruction

> 🔑 Decisions must be grounded in evidence and driven by the Return on Instruction (ROI).

The role of the teacher is to create the conditions for invention rather than provide ready-made knowledge.

Seymour Papert

Grounded in Evidence

In a world that is, for better or worse, consumed by technology, it should not come as any surprise that schools are jumping on this bandwagon. As discussed in Chapter 2, there are many ways that technology, when integrated with purpose to accelerate best instructional practices, can help students learn and demonstrate conceptual mastery at an accelerated rate. This synopsis makes for a great sound bite, but school leaders must begin thinking beyond the next technology fad if the goal is to systemically improve learning outcomes.

In the United States alone, schools spend billions of dollars a year on technology purchases. Therefore, it is more than appropriate to assume that schools around the world are spending an inordinate amount of money on educational technologies. If this is the case, then we must be able to answer this question: *What evidence do we have that our ed-tech expenditures have actually improved teaching and learning?* Our guess is that many school leaders may cringe while reading and reflecting on that question, and that is okay. A major step in intentionally designing schools is to begin to critically analyze technology initiatives and align them to clear results. If such an analysis can't be made, then there is no sense in continuing down a path of blindly spending money. School leaders can begin by reflecting on this simple yet imperative question.

For educational technology to be fully embraced as a powerful teaching and learning tool, there must be a focus on substance over assumptions and generalizations. Saying that technology and innovative practices are "transforming education" for the better is a lot different than showing results-based evidence of it actually occurring. It is important to move past the broad claims, one-time emotional keynotes, and drive-by workshops focused on the latest technology tools. This is not the type of change that schools need and deserve when it comes to technology and innovation.

There is a great deal of evidence to make educators reflect on their use of technology. One of the most glaring is the 2015 OECD report. Let's review this excerpt from the report:

> Schools have yet to take advantage of the potential of technology in the classroom to tackle the digital divide and give every student the skills they need in today's connected world, according to the first OECD PISA assessment of digital skills. Even countries which have invested heavily in information and communication technologies (ICT) for education have seen no noticeable improvement in their performances in PISA results for reading, mathematics, or science (OECD, 2015).

The OECD report points to an issue that cannot be ignored in a world where skill levels in reading, mathematics, and science matter more than ever. A strong foundation in these areas and a focus on critical thinking, problem solving, and creativity are needed to prepare students for their future—not ours. There is a need for balance in a high-stakes world, but the potential merits of technology are being rebuked in some circles due to a lack of clear results and evidence of sustained improvement. Thus, the sentiments of many educators are aligned with the OECD findings. Larry Ferlazzo (2016) penned a piece that asks educators to provide their response to why educational technology has over-promised and under-delivered:

> Good teaching is not about where or what to click. Good teaching is about building quality relationships with students, helping students make connections to the real world, building students individual cognitive networks, and having our students enjoy learning for the sake of learning. Technology will never solve all the ills of

education! Nor should it! So what is the biggest problem in Edtech? The biggest problem is that we have been teaching teachers and students how to use technology without giving them the *why* of technology. We have mistakenly believed that giving teachers and students new software or a new box will help fix education.

Most ed-tech–related professional learning, a topic we'll examine in Chapter 5, focuses on low-level, how-to tool use. Although not inherently bad as a starting point, it is our opinion that only a small percentage of technology-based professional learning opportunities focus on instructional pedagogy. Instead, these opportunities often focus on the "how-tos" of a tool—a tool that will inevitably evolve over time. Click here, add this picture, and save this document are all examples of very basic skills of a technology-based workshop, yet if we don't move past these types of trainings, a return on instruction will never occur, and low-level technology infusion will continue to reign supreme.

Return on Instruction (ROI)

For decades, school leaders have discussed "the need" to integrate technology. The problem with these conversations has been a lack of focus on the why and how technology can support a learning transformation. The greatest technology in the world will not garner hypothesized improvement if a concerted effort to *change pedagogy* isn't the foundation. As alluded to in the OECD report, the problem isn't the technology itself per se but the lack of high-quality pedagogy, which stems from a lack of high-quality professional learning to support educators with effective implementation. There is a need not only to better prepare teachers and administrators with the skills and mindset to usher in needed change but also to study and showcase powerful examples of success. Showing teachers what "high-quality" *actually looks like* is key. Professional learning must help educators do what they already do—better. It can't be hypothetical, especially when focused on technology and innovation. Practices, skills, and techniques need to be real, be proven, and leave educators with a sense that they can implement them to improve learning outcomes.

Constant hoopla around technology in education has resulted in an arms race of sorts where the use of the latest flashy tool trumps effective, meaningful long-term use. The same can be said about fluffy, pie-in-the-sky ideas that do not take into account the real challenges that many districts and schools face. The good news here is that high-quality digital transformation can and has succeeded in many schools around the world. For such transformation to occur, there needs to be an emphasis on instructional design, digital pedagogical techniques, and the development of better assessments aligned to higher standards. This might not be flashy or newsworthy, yet it is nonetheless crucial in establishing systemic change that can be scaled beyond isolated pockets of excellence in any given school. It is important to note that this dilemma is not only specific to technology but also to innovation. There must be a concerted focus on the why, the how, *and* deep evidence of results.

In addition to professional learning, we must also be more critical of what we see and hear when engaged in the ed-tech debate. For technology to be taken seriously as a tool to support and enhance teaching and learning, we must no longer accept assumptions and generalizations as to what it actually does. A primary goal of education should be to have students empowered to own their learning, create artifacts that demonstrate conceptual mastery, use their voice, be responsible in online spaces, and connect with the world in meaningful and authentic ways. Both of us have served in various teaching and leadership roles, and we want teachers and administrators to utilize technology and innovative practices to improve teaching, learning, and leadership. However, the school leader in each of us also understands the need to balance this with clear, evidence-based results. This is a reality for every teacher and administrator that cannot be ignored. It is important to show how students apply what they have learned in relevant ways that are aligned to the highest levels of knowledge taxonomy. Listening to someone share how a particular tool has "transformed education" simply doesn't cut it anymore.

The next step is to connect practices to results that prove—beyond assumptions and generalizations—that technology positively affects teaching and learning. It is important to remember that if teaching, learning, and leadership don't evolve, technology and innovation will never have the type of impact we expect and that are possible. It is not a matter of if but when key stakeholders and decision makers will ask for indicators of evidence that illustrate positive effects on student learning outcomes, elements of school culture, and community engagement. Let's face it, they should be asking these questions already. The stakes are too high, and we need to develop students who not only are divergent thinkers prepared for college and careers but also possess the confidence and drive to follow their interests and passions.

Evidence in the form of data, observations/evaluations, artifacts, portfolios, and case studies can effectively craft a narrative that reflects a Return on Instruction (ROI). Simply put, when integrating technology, there needs to be an ROI that results in evidence of improved student learning outcomes.

Success Metrics: The Utilization of Data

Defining success is typically easier than quantifying it. Regardless of what anyone claims, quantitative and qualitative data are essential and need to be part of the intentional design process. This, of course, is only one metric of success. The key to measuring an ROI in ed-tech is to be able to align various data sources to technology use. Standardized test scores, because of their widespread use and publicity, have the greatest ability to illustrate to stakeholders (who might not be as knowledgeable about innovative pedagogical techniques) how technology is positively affecting learning and achievement. This fact is tough to ignore, regardless of how you feel about the issue, since many industries throughout the world rely on standardized data as a primary metric of success. We can't be naive and completely ignore these data, yet keeping them in perspective and in the proper context is essential.

One excellent example comes from a study of Lockport City Schools in New York (conducted by the University of Buffalo). This particular case study illustrates how students in a 1:1 iPad environment exhibited significant achievement gains when compared to students in classes without devices.

Lockport City School District, New York
Robert LiPuma, Director of Assessment and Technology

The Lockport City School District, in cooperation with the University of Buffalo, is reporting on the second year of a three-year longitudinal study that is currently in its final year, so we will continue to study the impact of iPads in the classroom and specifically on academic performance. The data show that iPads used in a 1:1 setting are supporting an instructional shift and, in turn, making a dramatic impact on student performance on the New York State Assessments.

The Study and Results

It is our belief that traditional public education has to evolve into something more effective for our children today. The iPad has made it possible for a small city school district such as Lockport, with a poverty rate over 50 percent, to set up a learning environment for students that was simply not possible before without spending more money than was available. State budget cuts had drastic consequences for school districts such as Lockport, resulting in school closures and staff reductions. However, creative and innovative strategies with our use of technology increased without increasing our spending. As you can see, the results are very promising. Let me explain briefly why I believe the results we are seeing are so positive.

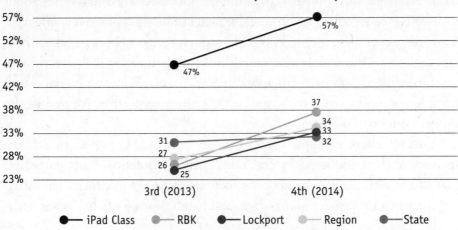

English Language Arts (ELA)
New York State Assessments % Proficient (Scored a 3 or 4)—2 Year Results

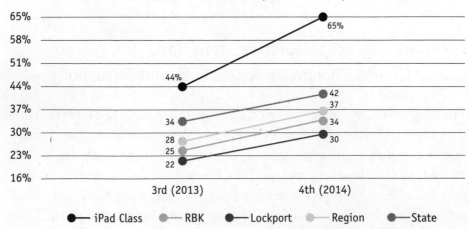

Mathematics
New York State Assessments % Proficient (Scored a 3 or 4)—2 Year Results

Our district leadership has a shared vision. We have proceeded with this initiative with an end goal in mind and patiently executed a dynamic plan that was supported from our board of education, superintendent, building leadership, technology staff, teachers, and students.

Collaborative leadership at the district and building levels has kept the project moving forward successfully. Working together with a trust that all leaders would do their part toward the same end goal gives everyone ownership and credit for the accomplishments.

Allowing people to step up to the challenges in a distributive leadership model has helped change the culture regarding our use of technology and the way we manage a district, building, or classroom. We have no shortage of qualified individuals willing to work hard to make a difference for our students, and we have capitalized on their leadership.

The final piece of the puzzle is a broad technology focus. We maintain a broad use of technology in our buildings and across the district. We work to provide teachers with the tools that help students become more successful. We encourage the use of technology and measure the effectiveness in academic results. The data are clear, and teachers respond positively when they are empowered to try different things and, ultimately, see the results for themselves. We continue to expose our students to various forms of technology, such as iPads, Macs, PCs, desktops, and laptops, because we believe that a dynamic public education includes many tools, not just one.

Some Conclusions

It might be easy to believe, based on these data, that iPads are the golden ticket to academic success for this generation of learners. This is not the case. I would like to introduce one more piece of data that the University of Buffalo presented to us during our first years of using the devices. For two years, the University of Buffalo observed our classrooms—both the classrooms that used iPads and those that did not. They found that after one year of using the iPads, the focus of class time had changed from traditional instruction (lecture) 67 percent of the time to less than 21 percent of the time, and that students working on task and engaged in learning went from 15 percent to more than 75 percent of the time. Thus, *the instructional pedagogy shifted in the process.*

For Lockport, the iPad has been a tool to help engage students, and their enthusiasm for the use of the device has not decreased after five years. When visiting our classrooms with iPads, the engagement and enthusiasm students have for using the tool for learning is obvious. Disciplinary problems have almost gone away, and with all of the qualitative data seen in the classroom, it is easy to see that something special is happening. Students are excited about what they are doing and learning. After the first two years, the big question that remained was "Is this pilot with the iPads making a difference on student achievement, and can we collect the needed data as proof?"

We strongly believe that leveraging these tools is making a positive effect on our students and that using the devices in authentic ways has the potential to engage learners in differentiated learning activities that are more personal in nature. We believe that any strategy that engages learners on higher-level learning tasks for the majority of class time will have a positive effect on academic results. For Lockport, the iPad is helping engage our students on the desired learning tasks, and the data are showing very positive results.

It is important to note that the device itself didn't result in increases in engagement levels and higher levels of student achievement. The success was tied to the changes in pedagogy combined with the purposeful use of the device to support and enhance a more personal approach to learning. The Lockport case study undoubtedly shows a positive Return on Instruction. Another study out of Michigan State University examined the impact of 1:1 laptop programs and also found significant results. The researchers conducted a synthesis of results from 96 published global studies on 1:1 programs in K–12 schools from 2001–2015. They identified 10 rigorously designed studies and examined the relationship among these programs and academic achievement, and they found significant benefits (Zheng, Warschauer, Lin, & Chang, 2016). In addition to test score increases in math, science, reading, writing, and English, the researchers also discovered numerous other student benefits. Students

- Increased writing across a wider variety of genres.
- Received more feedback on writing.
- Edited and revised written work more.
- Routinely published work more.

The study also found an increase in autonomous work focused on the synthesis and critical application of knowledge. Other studies support this important outcome as well. Mouza (2008) found that elementary students in a 1:1 environment routinely created and published stories electronically. It has also been found that students who were allowed to use laptops to solve problems exhibited higher-level problem-solving skills than those in a comparison group (Lowther, Ross, & Morrison, 2003). Over time, we believe that more research will be conducted that shows the positive effects of technology infusion—but this will only happen when there is a firm commitment to improving instructional design and pedagogy.

When ensuring a ROI, school leaders should include other data sources, such as graduation rates, acceptances to four-year colleges or rigorous vocation programs, attendance rates, discipline referrals, and levels of authentic student engagement. When discussing "engagement," we must make sure that what is being discussed is actually leading to high levels of learning and students aren't simply engaged in low-level tasks. When studying ROI, school leaders should use various sources of evidence and ensure a holistic view. Focusing on just one metric will lead to a myopic understanding.

Redefining Supervision: Meaningful Observations, Evaluations, and Walkthroughs

---

Be wise enough not to be reckless, but brave enough to take great risks.

Frank Warren

I (Eric) still vividly remember my early years as an assistant principal and principal. Instructional leadership was a routine part of the job, along with the budget, master schedule, curriculum development, meetings, emails, phone calls, and many other duties. With the evolution of social media, yet another responsibility was added to my plate in the form of digital leadership. With so many facets of the work, being a school administrator requires me to be a jack-of-all-trades. School leaders are forced to balance two hemispheres: one focused on managerial tasks and one focused on leadership and pursuing the vision. With a seemingly unending list of managerial responsibilities, the latter hemisphere is where many leaders fail to live up to the most important aspect of the position—instructional leadership. School leaders who intentionally design their schools ensure that instructional leadership is their top priority.

Even though I tried, the frequency with which I observed teachers rarely extended beyond the minimal expectations. I simply wasn't in classrooms enough, and the level of feedback provided through the lens of a narrative report did very little to improve teaching and learning both in and out of the classroom. If improvement is the ultimate goal, then we as leaders need to put the most focus on elements of our job that affect student learning. Instructional leaders understand that management is a necessary evil associated with the position, but it's not something that should come at the expense of improving the learning culture and increasing achievement.

Let's be honest. The above scenario is common and one to which many, if not most, school leaders can relate. We believe that the traditional evaluation system for educators is broken and in desperate need of repair. Consider, for example, how teacher observations typically play out. More often than not, it is a scripted process that results in a dog-and-pony show only a few times per year. There is often a preconference meeting to discuss what will happen during the lesson, and the lesson then takes place soon after with the administrator in attendance. Sometimes, the observer will stay the entire time, but in many cases this is not the case. The process often concludes with a postconference meeting to discuss what has been observed.

Sound familiar?

Let's run some numbers and use a traditional example in which a tenured teacher is formally observed one time per year. Let's also assume that the teacher has five instructional periods per day and a contracted school year made up of the 180 school days. Over that school year, the teacher will teach 900 instructional periods ($5 \times 180 = 900$). Observing this teacher once a year gives the observer a 0.11 percent—just over one-tenth of 1 percent ($1/900 = 0.11$)—of a snapshot of that teacher's instructional practice. Under these assumptions, nine full-period observations would only yield a 1 percent snapshot. There's not a statistician in the world who would argue that this type of supervision or evaluation model is even remotely statistically significant, much less accurate.

To understand if the transformation of teaching, learning, and leading is truly occurring, school leaders must spend significant time in classrooms, and *instructional leadership must be the top priority*. It's essential that leaders remove the dog-and-pony-show supervision model, which will go a long way to increasing accountability and establishing a culture that expects instructional excellence every day—and not simply during a scheduled instructional period. If we are serious about raising the bar and ensuring that technology is being leveraged as an accelerant for authentic learning, then we must make a concerted effort to improve a supervision process that has little relevance or effectiveness. Just like with students, high-quality, timely feedback is essential to growth and sustained improvement. This is amplified when technology is added to the picture. Leaders must not only be knowledgeable of these pedagogical shifts but also be in a position to provide excellent, meaningful feedback.

The more time that leaders spend in the classroom, the more qualitative evidence they will gather that supports a shift in teaching and learning is actually occurring. As a high school principal, my (Eric) teachers had a combination of five formal evaluations of instruction and a myriad of informal observations. The process consisted of a minimum of three unannounced observations, a mid-year evaluation, an end-of-year evaluation, and many instructional conversations in between. In addition, my entire leadership team and I each conducted five nonevaluative walkthroughs *per day* to ensure that we understood what was happening in the classrooms and where we needed to place our focus. This type of support, from the district office to the building level, is important since we shouldn't forget that building leaders need just as much support as teachers do, and they must be held to the same high standard. Today's school leaders are in desperate need of more high-quality feedback relative to their role in digital implementations. Only a collaborative leadership style makes this support possible.

Leveraging Opportunity: Artifacts, Portfolios, and Evidence-based Growth

Artifacts

Artifacts provide qualitative evidence of the methodologies and pedagogical techniques implemented in school. Examples include digital lessons, projects, assessments (formative, summative, rubrics, etc.), curricula, and student work that align to higher standards. Blog posts are a great way for leaders to showcase and publically highlight dynamic examples of these artifacts. Included in Appendix B is an example of a teacher using Instagram and a rubric aligned to the Common Core State Standards. A focus on sharing artifacts through social media can also help ease stakeholder concerns about the level at which students are meeting more rigorous standards through innovative practices.

While at New Milford High School, my (Eric) teachers aligned artifacts to their observations to support not only what happened during the observed lesson but also what happened before and after. All of these artifacts were aligned to standards found in the McREL tool we used. Many other evaluation tools that are currently used by various school districts allow for the uploading of artifacts that support how well teachers and administrators are meeting the expected professional standards. By the end of the year, all observation comments and artifacts were gathered in each teacher's final evaluation—giving me, their supervisor, a body of evidence that clearly articulated whether teaching and learning was actually changing. The end result was a comprehensive evaluation and portfolio loaded with relevant evidence, making a ROI evaluation possible.

Portfolios

The creation, curation, and sharing of artifacts naturally lends itself to the process of portfolios. Through these reflective tools, educators (teachers and administrators) and students can demonstrate evidence of growth and improvement over time in relation to personal learning goals. In essence, this form of evidence tells a learning story over time and can further demonstrate how technology is being integrated with purpose to support learning in both personal and professional outcomes. Many educators seem to discuss portfolios quite often, but we rarely see examples that are aligned to student and professional standards.

While at New Milford, I remember a meeting with teacher leaders that was a tipping point that ultimately changed the direction of professional learning at my school. During this conversation, I was passionately sharing my experiences as a connected learner. As social media was not even a blip on the radar at the time, these teacher leaders were skeptical about the alleged benefits I described, and they were protective of any time they may have had available. Undeterred, I continued to talk about the concept of a Personal Learning Network (PLN) and what it had done for my own professional growth. I shared how it's simplistic nature, built on conversations with educators all around the world, led to new knowledge development, resource acquisition, exposure to innovative ideas and strategies, support, feedback, friendships, and spirited discussion, ultimately leading to growth. Best of all, at least in my mind, was the newfound ability to learn anytime, from anywhere, with anyone in the world—completely for free. Little did I know that this conversation set the stage for one of the most significant learning shifts we would ever experience.

Evidence-based Growth

Once I got off my soapbox to finally catch my breath, one of my teachers shared that the concept was great but questioned the amount of time that teachers had to engage in meaningful learning on social media. With the many state mandates and district-directed professional learning hours, as well as time after school devoted to grading and lesson planning, time just didn't seem to be readily available. Who was I to disagree? She spoke the truth. My teacher leaders went on to propose a job-embedded growth model, and although that sounded great in theory, it was certainly going to be difficult to implement.

As the instructional leader in the building, I wanted to try really hard to honor their request and at least attempt to find a way to implement a consistent pathway to learning during the school day. Then it came to me—much to the chagrin of my assistant principal. The inspiration came from Google's 80/20 Innovation Model (Mediratta & Bick, 2007).

The premise of this model was that for a period of time, Google employees had to spend 80 percent of their time on their assigned job duties, but the other 20 percent could be spent working on anything they were passionate about—so long as it improved Google's bottom line. As we reflected on this idea and how it could be implemented at a high school, we seized an opportunity embedded in the eight-period schedule. In the end, we developed and created our own 80/20 model to empower teachers to grow in areas they were passionate about.

By contract at New Milford, all teachers were required to teach five instructional periods. In addition, each teacher had a lunch, prep, and duty period, all of which were 48 minutes in length. Knowing the effectiveness of noninstructional duties (e.g., cafeteria, hall, in-school suspension), we had to alter those times. By cutting the noninstructional duties in half, we were able to free up each teacher two to three periods per week, empowering them to engage in activities related to professional growth. This was the birth of the Professional Growth Period (PGP). In order to fully free up our teachers, our administrative team assumed the duties that were cut since we couldn't sacrifice student supervision entirely (Sheninger, 2014, 2015b). It's easy to see why my assistant principal was not happy with the idea at first. Once in place, the school's culture and ownership over learning continued to shift. The improved school culture did not warrant so much attention to—and supervision—of, those duties, which eventually made the new model more feasible for everyone.

The PGP became a dedicated time for staff to grow as educators and learners. Depending on the semester, each teacher had two or three duty periods every week to engage in professional learning opportunities. They were encouraged to find their passion and work to define their purpose. PGP time was not a free for all, since it had to be spent learning, innovating, and pursuing ways to become a master educator. Think of it as a personal learning opportunity that catered to each staff member's specific needs and interests. Sample activities had to be aligned to New Jersey's professional educator standards and included

- Becoming a connected educator by developing and engaging in a Personal Learning Network.
- Researching best practices.
- Developing innovative learning activities.
- Creating interdisciplinary lessons.
- Engaging in face-to-face professional learning.
- Learning to use new technologies.
- Earning a digital badge using the in-house platform we created.
- Collaborating on projects with colleagues.

PGP time met the need for what teachers desperately wanted and needed to improve their craft, built on innovative thoughts and ideas they wanted to pursue, and empowered them to acquire new knowledge. It was stressed that this time was not to be used to make copies, leave the building to get coffee/food, or socialize in the faculty room. It was all about evidence-based learning.

During our end-of-year evaluations, the expectation was that each staff member would submit a personal learning portfolio that demonstrated how PGP time was used to improve his or her professional practice. Accountability for the ownership of the learning was high. The learning portfolio could be created in any way that fit the creative nature of the staff member, but it should clearly identify what was done to

- Improve instruction.
- Integrate technology effectively.
- Engage students in high-level learning activities.
- Address the Common Core State Standards.
- Increase student achievement.

The PGP learning portfolio had to clearly articulate what they learned and how they integrated that new knowledge into professional practice to improve student learning. Adding depth to the PGP process and portfolio was the digital badge platform (created by our media specialist), which acknowledged the informal learning teachers achieved. Teachers would access the Worlds of Learning platform (www.worlds-of-learning-nmhs.com) developed by media specialist Laura Fleming. They would select and watch a screencast modeling how to use a particular tool. After watching the screencast, they had to show evidence of how they learned the tool and create a standards-aligned task for students to complete. Laura then vetted the tasks and awarded a digital badge if completed successfully. The end results were teachers who had been empowered to take ownership of their learning through autonomy and a proliferation of innovative practices, all of which led to a strong ROI.

Driving Evidence-based Instructional Leadership

Success is no accident. It is hard work, perseverance, learning, studying, sacrifice, and most of all, love of what you are doing or learning to do.

Pele

It's easy to simply say how we should improve instructional leadership. However, actually doing the work is no small feat. To leverage a true Return on Instruction, we offer the following suggestions.

Be Present in Classrooms Regularly

This seems so simple yet is a constant struggle due to managerial demands. Begin by increasing the number of formal observations conducted each year and commit to a schedule to make it happen. Schedule time on your calendar. Daily. Another successful strategy is to develop an informal walkthrough schedule with your leadership team. At New Milford, we used a color-coded shared document to keep track of which classrooms we visited—as well as the specific feedback provided to each teacher. This created a collaborative leadership approach where we were consistently visible and present.

Streamline Expectations and Eliminate Ineffective Practices

Begin by establishing a common vision and expectations for all teachers. Using the Rigor/Relevance Framework (as presented in Chapter 2) can support this process. This will provide all teachers with consistent, concrete elements to focus on when developing lessons. Developing and utilizing a common language for these conversations is key. Get rid of the dog-and-pony-show ritual of announced observations. If lesson plans are still collected, ask for them to demonstrate what will occur in future learning to ensure connections. Consider less of a focus on lesson plans and more on relevant and formative assessment and feedback.

Improve Feedback

Provide at least one suggestion for instructional improvement, no matter how great the observation is, to promote a growth mindset. Simply put, there is no perfect lesson. Suggestions for improvement should always contain clear, practical examples and strategies that a teacher can begin to implement immediately. Supervisors should also celebrate the positives they see, particularly if they are areas of growth for the particular teacher. Just like with students, timely, relevant feedback is essential.

Be a Scholar

Being a scholar not only helps a leader improve professional practice but also puts the leader in a position to have higher-quality conversations with teachers and their colleagues about their own improvement. This adds a new level of credibility to instructional conversations. School leaders should also make a point of aligning constructive feedback to current research. We encourage leaders, as they come across research that supports the types of effective pedagogical practices that they yearn to see in their classrooms, to archive the research in an easily referenced document that can be used while providing feedback. Leaders should invest time over the summer to read, research, curate, and adapt these instructional feedback techniques for use throughout the school year. It not only saved us time when providing observational feedback but also greatly improved our relationships with our teams as instructional leaders. (We encourage school leaders to begin with the dozens of research studies cited throughout this book, all of which can be found in the References section at the end.)

Model

The best school leaders don't ask their teachers to do anything they are not willing to do themselves. This is extremely important when modeling technology integration and reflecting on your own professional learning to improve practice. If a teacher is struggling with his or her assessments, simply stating that he or she needs to work on building better ones offers no support—only criticism. Leaders should either provide a high-quality example for reflection or cocreate an assessment with the teacher to model growth.

Teach a Class

This can be accomplished regularly during the year or by coteaching with both struggling and distinguished teachers. Unfortunately, some teacher contracts prohibit what is, in our opinion, a very effective practice. During my (Eric) first couple of years as an administrator, I was able to teach a section of high school biology. This gave me the opportunity to lead by example. Such modeling also provides a better context for the evolving role of the teacher in the digital age. An instructional leader who walks the walk builds better relationships with staff and in turn will be in a much better position to engage staff in conversations about instructional improvements.

Grow Professionally

School leaders should attend a variety of conferences or workshops each year that are aligned to a major initiative or focus area in their school or district. They should also try to read at least one education book and another nonfiction book related to a different field such as leadership, self-help, or business. Many powerful lessons and ideas can be gleaned if we venture outside the education silo. To complement traditional means of professional learning, work to create or further develop a Personal Learning Network. Social media provides a 24-7 pathway to ideas, strategies, feedback, resources, and support that every educator has the opportunity to leverage.

Write in Order to Reflect

As it has for many other connected educators, writing has really enabled both of us to process our thinking, which has resulted in a more critical reflection of our work in relation to teaching, learning, and leadership. Our reflections not only assist us with our own growth but also act as catalysts for our staff and others to reflect on their own practice. Having teachers write a brief reflection prior to the postconference is a great strategy to promote a conversation on improvement that isn't one-sided. Such metacognitive practices can lead to deeper reflections.

Integrate Portfolios

As previously mentioned, when leveraged as a reflective tool, portfolios can support instructional growth. These tools can provide additional clarity and instructional detail over a long period of time. Portfolios can include learning activities, assessments, unit plans, examples of student work, and other forms of evidence to improve instructional effectiveness. They can also be used to validate, model, and celebrate great practices.

Co-observe

At times, the instructional feedback from various school leaders serving on the same team is all over the map. Without a collaborative, consistent approach utilizing a common language—built on a common vision—teachers can be left confused, leading to instructional anxiety. We believe that instructional leaders, particularly while working in teams, should co-observe lessons and privately discuss the feedback they want to give. Think of it as an interrater reliability of sorts that helps ensure consistent communication to teachers.

The 10 strategies presented here can be implemented immediately to improve your instructional leadership skills and ability. For school leaders, there is nothing more important than ensuring that rigor and relevant teaching and learning, built on high-quality relationships, are consistently taking place in your classrooms. Having conclusions that ensure a return on instruction and are grounded in evidence is essential.

You are part of the solution.

Innovative Practices in Action

West Port High School, Marion County Public Schools, Florida
Jayne Ellspermann, Principal
2015 NASSP Principal of the Year

When I was transferred to West Port High School, I knew there would be challenges. The public perception of the school was not good. My friends would tell me, "Jayne, I love you, you were my child's best principal. We live in West Port's attendance area, but I will not send my child to your new school."

West Port's population was poor and diverse. Few students took AP or honors courses. Most bright students transferred to schools that offered International Baccalaureate (IB) and Advanced International Certificate of Education (AICE) programs. Teachers were writing hundreds of discipline referrals a day, and school surveys indicated both students and staff did not feel safe at school. To no surprise, West Port was one of the lowest-performing high schools in the school district.

The first order of business was to address a demoralized school culture. The first two days of school became procedure- and relationship-building days. Schoolwide procedures were introduced and time was used creatively to meet the needs of students and staff. An emphasis was placed on sharing what makes West Port a great place to work and learn. Facebook and Twitter were used to communicate our school's accomplishments; auto calls, our school's website, and weekly talking points also shared our successes.

We carved out 30 minutes every Thursday and Friday for a schoolwide character development or a school spirit building activity like a pep rally, student performance, or a student versus staff activity. Students who struggled with making good decisions were assigned four days in our Character Development Academy where they reflected on their choices and completed their academic work. Within the first year, the number of discipline referrals was cut in half. Today, we go days without a single referral.

A focus on academic rigor resulted in an increase in available AP courses from 8 to 23, and most importantly, they are open to all students. West Port became accredited as a campus of our local college and in 2015–2016, over 6,500 college credits were earned on our campus with 87 students graduating with an associate's degree a month before they graduated and earned their high school diploma. West Port was the only high school in our district to earn a state grade of A for five years in a row and has been the highest-performing high school in our district for the past five years.

This was accomplished due to a deliberate focus on instructional pedagogy and a desire to challenge every student. To make this possible, our staff embrace data to ground decisions in evidence. Teachers meet every Tuesday for collaborative planning to review data on attendance, discipline, and academic performance, and they work on alignment of curriculum and instruction and on individual student needs. A problem-solving team meets each week to look at schoolwide trends in attendance, discipline referrals, and academic performance. Personal calls and home visits are made to reengage students in school when needed. A data room has pictures of at-risk students highlighting what they need to be successful, and teachers take ownership and "adopt" these students. Every Friday, the staff gathers for an intense, energized 30 minutes at Friday Faculty Focus to share positives, look at current data, generate solutions, and participate in book studies and professional learning on instruction.

Power Hour was a result of faculty collaboration. With its creation, students were given an hour to eat lunch, work on academics, and participate in school activities. Teachers have time for lunch and 30 minutes of "office hours" where they can offer extra help or sponsor a club or activity. The empowerment of students to control a minimum of one hour of their day has resulted in transformational academic improvement. Student course failure dropped from 37 percent to 3 percent. With students getting the support they need and an improvement in course success, our graduation rate rose to 92 percent.

Furthermore, students who are not successful academically during the first grading period are invited to a Student Success Chat where they meet with their teacher and an administrator to develop a personal plan for success. These conversations often reveal situations outside school that need to be addressed and often supported. These targeted and specific interventions allow us to provide students with the support they need in order to be successful in school.

With our transformation, West Port High School has become a school of choice for our community. Enrollment has exceeded our building capacity, growing from 1,400 to more than 2,600 students, yet our demographics have not changed. We still have over 65 percent of our students living in poverty and over 60 percent of our students are ethnically and racially diverse. What has changed is a culture focused on continually improving instruction and empowering students to own their learning. Setting high expectations and creating positive relationships with students and teachers are at the heart of our success. The change is a result of embracing data, intentionally focusing on instruction, challenging students, and creating an environment where all students can succeed. The conversation has changed since my first year, and the sentiments of my friends are much different than when I first arrived. Parents now ask, "What can I do to get my child into West Port High School?" This is where we want to be.

(During her 12 years as principal of West Port High School in Ocala, Florida, Ellspermann took a low-performing, high-poverty, highly diverse school and ushered in a pervasive college-going culture built on personalization, which resulted in improved academic performance, a positive school climate, and a 92 percent graduation rate. Her personal mission is to create an environment where her students and staff can exceed their perceived potential. Bringing college courses to high school and initiating Power Hour were key factors in West Port's success. Ellspermann has a bachelor's degree in psychology from the University of Georgia and a master's degree from the University of Florida.)

4 | Designing Learner-Centered Spaces

 Learning spaces must become learner-centered.

Ninety-nine percent of teaching spaces were anticipated either in an image of an ancient Syrian palace school 4,000 years ago or in the Greek amphitheater: rows or rings of seats meant to focus the attention of the many on the one. But education is not about transferring information from one to many; it is about learning within the student. When printed books were new, transferring information was vital, but today, information is ubiquitous and readily available, and students can pick it up when and where they want. Instead, the classroom ought to focus on assimilation and application of knowledge to new contexts. The teacher becomes the guide on the side, instead of the sage on the stage, requiring wholly new learning spaces and teaching techniques.

Eric Mazur

Design Empowers Learning

The United States is home to nearly 100,000 public K–12 schools, which cover about 7.5 billion total square feet and 2 million acres of land (Bendici, n.d.). Approximately $2 trillion of net worth is invested in these school facilities, making this investment the largest educational investment in the nation. With the average age of schools in most districts between 30 and 50 years old, a large portion of this investment is now at risk due to age and lack of adequate maintenance (Nair, 2014). In the United States alone, in addition to the routine maintenance which totals hundreds of millions of dollars each year, more than $12 billion is spent annually to renovate and build new schools (Abramson, 2012).

With their average age in mind, most of today's learning spaces were originally designed and built for teacher-centric learning environments, coined by Alfie Kohn (1999) as the "cells and bells" model. In this analogy, students occupy cells until the bell rings and then move down the hall to another cell to do the same. The process repeats until freedom is granted at a particular time.

Sound familiar?

School buildings, the nation's largest educational investment, are traditionally built for this "cells and bells" model. This type of design, however, is in direct contrast to what we know about how students learn, how tomorrow's teachers will need to teach, and all that we understand from educational research about the impact of learning space design.

All you have to do is look around and see the amazing changes that are taking place in workspaces around the world. Many people have become enamored with what places such as Google and Pixar have done to improve working conditions for their employees—and these companies have exhibited great success while their workplaces are very unconventional. These types of workplaces have embraced the mantra that a creative work environment motivates and inspires innovation. These types of changes are both exciting and innovative. To get better results, they *intentionally* incorporated elements that foster creativity, collaboration, flexibility, and communication. This is more than a great concept that has become a reality in the workplace; we believe it should be common sense as well. Who wants to go to a job all day and sit in a hard chair at a desk in a creatively stifling cubicle, while being rained on by effervescing light? No one. That's certainly not our idea of an ideal workspace, and we would wager that most school leaders feel the same way. As expectations related to producing better outcomes change, businesses have capitalized on a design trend that has led to improved results.

But what about schools? What about the work we do? If we know that we as leaders wouldn't want to work in these types of spaces, then how can we possibly ask our kids to do so? Leaders who intentionally design schools understand that *design empowers learning*. For learning to be transformed, our traditional spaces must be as well.

A Look at the Research

As instructional models have begun to shift, the impact of the learning space—the physical environment in which teaching and learning takes place—has come into focus. As the learning space has been studied, considerable evidence indicates an explicit relationship between the physical makeup of the environment and educational outcomes (Barrett & Zhang, 2009). In studying various pieces of literature on the effect of design, Barrett and Zhang began with the understanding that a "bright, warm, quiet, safe, clean, comfortable, and healthy environment is an important component of successful teaching and learning" (p. 2), and they worked to identify the complexities behind the effect of each. Some aspects of the environment had significant effects, whereas other aspects were inconclusive. They went on to explore the effect of learning environments on student achievement, engagement, affective stage, attendance, and overall well-being. Their research, which we'll explore further later in this chapter, suggested direct connections between the learning space and sensory stimuli among students. The evidence of such connections came from the medical understanding of how human sensory perception affects cognitive calculations. As such, Barrett and Zang (2009) identify three key design principles:

1. **Naturalness:** Hardwired into our brains, humans have the basic need for light, air, and safety. In this area, the impact of lighting, sound, temperature, and air quality are prevalent.
2. **Individualization:** As individuals, each of our brains is uniquely organized and, we perceive the world in different ways. Because of this, different people respond to environmental stimuli in various ways. Therefore, the opportunity for some level of choice affects success.
3. **Appropriate Level of Stimulation:** The learning space can offer the "silent curriculum" that affects student engagement levels. When designing the space, it's important for educators not to overstimulate and thus detract students' ability to focus but to provide enough stimuli to enhance the learning experience.

Supporting this notion, a research study out of the University of Salford Manchester (UK), followed 3,766 students in 153 elementary classrooms from 27 different schools over a three-year period, analyzing classroom design elements along the way. The report indicates clear evidence that "well-designed primary schools boost children's academic performance in reading, writing, and math" (Barrett, Zhang, Davies, & Barrett, 2015, p. 3). The study found a *16 percent variation* in learning progress due to the physical characteristics of the classroom. Additionally, the study indicated that whole-school factors (e.g., size, play facilities, hallways) do not nearly have the level of impact as the individual classroom.

School leaders will often write off the notion of redesigning learning spaces due to financial constraints. However, research indicates that schools don't need to spend vast amounts of money to make instructional improvements. In fact, changes can be made that have little to no cost yet make a significant difference. Examples include altering the classroom layout, designing classroom displays differently, and choosing new wall colors (Barrett et al., 2015). These research-based factors are minimal financial commitments that can help boost student outcomes.

The effect of learning spaces on various behaviors—territoriality, crowding, situational and personal space—has been the focus of some sociological and environment behavioral research. The consensus of this research is that the space itself has physical, social, and psychological effects. One study measured the impact of classroom design on 12 active learning practices, including collaboration, focus, opportunity to engage, physical movement, and stimulation (Scott-Webber, Strickland, & Kapitula, 2014). The research indicated that intentionally designing spaces provides for more effective teaching and learning. In this particular study, all of the major findings supported a highly positive and statistically significant effect of active learning classrooms on student engagement.

There's little disagreement over the fact that physical activity is linked to higher academic performance and improved behavior. From the oxygen that flows to the brain to the physical health of students, an environment that promotes movement and interactivity promotes student learning. It's also understood that even short bouts of physical activity in a classroom can improve students' on-task behavior, thereby boosting engagement.

In a research study on the link between standing desks and academic engagement, researchers observed nearly 300 children in 2nd through 4th grade over the course of a school year (Dornhecker, Blake, Benden, Zhao, & Wendel, 2015). The study found that students who used standing desks, more formally known as stand-biased desks, exhibited higher rates of engagement in the classroom than did their counterparts seated in traditional desks. Standing desks are raised desks that have stools nearby, enabling students to choose whether to sit or stand during class. The initial studies showed 12 percent greater on-task engagement in classrooms with standing desks, which equated to an extra seven minutes per hour, on average, of engaged instruction time. Engagement in this study was measured by on-task behaviors such as answering a question, raising a hand, or participating in active discussion. Overall, the results indicated that standing desks help combat childhood obesity and increase energy expenditure without negatively affecting academic engagement.

As a follow-up to this study, one of the lead researchers, Mark Benden, shared the following conclusion: "Standing workstations reduce disruptive behavior problems and increase students' attention or academic behavioral engagement by providing students with a different method for completing academic tasks (like standing) that breaks up the monotony of seated work." Benden went on to say that "Considerable research indicates that academic behavioral engagement is the most important contributor to student achievement. Simply put, we think better on our feet than in our seat" (Davis, 2015).

In a similar light, many researchers believe that active, standing experiences in elementary school should be the norm rather than the exception. One team spent two years studying 193 students across three elementary schools in Texas (Wilson, 2016). Some students were observed in classes that had traditional desks, whereas some were in classes that had standing desks. Other students had one year of traditional desks and one year of standing desks. After adjusting for grade, race/ethnicity, and gender, the study found that students who used the standing desks had a 5.24 percent decrease in Body Mass Index (BMI) percentile compared to the kids who sat. The only altered variable in the study was the desk itself, showing the impact of the space on something as personal as physical health.

There's little disagreement that creating flexible spaces for physical activity positively supports student learning outcomes. However, it's important to note that it's not simply the physical layout of the room that affects achievement. Research also indicates that teachers, particularly those in the early elementary grades where young children have an immature ability to regulate focused attention, must also consider visual stimuli. One particular study investigated whether classroom displays that were irrelevant to ongoing instruction could affect students' ability to maintain focused attention during instruction and learn the lesson content. Researchers placed kindergarten children in a controlled classroom space for six introductory science lessons, and then they experimentally manipulated the visual environment in the room. The findings indicated that the students were more distracted when the walls were highly decorated and, in turn, spent more time off task. In these environments, students demonstrated smaller learning gains than in cases where the decorations were removed (Fisher, Godwin, & Seltman, 2014).

In addition to the physical and visual makeup of the learning space, a building's structural facilities profoundly influence learning. Extraneous noise, inadequate lighting, low air quality, and deficient heating in the learning space are significantly related to lower levels of student achievement (Cheryan, Ziegler, Plaut, & Meltzoff, 2014). According to data from the National Center for Education Statistics, more than half of U.S. public schools in 2012–2013 reported the need to upgrade structural facilities including plumbing, air quality, and temperature regulation. Additionally, according to statistics, students of color and lower-income students are more likely to attend schools with inadequate structural facilities, yielding another level of educational inequity (Alexander & Lewis, 2014).

The tradition of learning space planning that utilizes a seats-per-square-foot mindset may be an efficient process for traditional calculations, yet it is ultimately a disservice to the academic desires of 21st century teaching and learning. Evaluating learning spaces based solely on the assumption that all seat time is created equal is counterintuitive to what we know about high-quality teaching and learning. Redesigning traditional learning spaces isn't simply a notion that should take place as school districts build new buildings and renovate outdated ones. Understanding how the learning space itself can affect the way students learn is essential. Part of the issue facing school leaders today is that quite often the decision about learning space design is made by those without recent (or any) experience teaching or by those with little knowledge of classroom design. If learning is going to be transformed, then the spaces in which that learning takes place must also be transformed.

Avoiding the "Cemetery Effect"

While driving the backroads of Pennsylvania one summer, I (Tom) came across a carefully laid-out cemetery. It grabbed my attention, so I pulled over for a closer look. As I perused the scenery, I noticed that all of the tombstones were equidistant from one another. The rows were impeccably aligned; each faced the same direction. Outlined by a stone wall, the plot of land was a perfect rectangle. With the exception of some updated landscaping, the space remained seemingly untouched for a number of decades.

My heart sank when I thought about how this space—a cemetery—resembled the classroom space I designed for my very first class of 4th graders. The learning space I created early on as a teacher would have looked almost identical to this cemetery if drawn as a map. Add an oversized wooden desk in the corner and an interactive whiteboard and U.S. flag on the front wall and you have not only the first classroom environment I created but also an environment that resembles many of today's learning spaces.

These classrooms are suffering from what we'll coin the "Cemetery Effect." Side-by-side images of classrooms from the early 1900s and ones from today yield eerie similarities, even after more than 100 years of research and innovation. During the industrial era, when students were essentially trained to work in factories, "career readiness" meant preparing for jobs in which a worker would spend hours a day performing the same routine task, often even spending his or her entire career at the same company. In the one-size-fits-all, sit-and-get instructional model, an ability to regurgitate information was the key to success and a sufficient paradigm for that world of work.

But that world of work no longer exists in the United States.

The need to redesign our students' learning environments is not simply an idea from the latest Pinterest board; it's one of necessity. There are certainly times when students should work independently and quietly in their own spaces, yet for far too long, that's been the main model of instruction in many classrooms. Learning cannot be personal and authentic if every student is an island in the space. Schools and classrooms must transform from an industrial era model to one that is learner-centered, is personalized, and leverages the power of technology.

Designing Learner-Centered Spaces

Many learning environments have remained relatively static over time. Walk into one of these spaces today, and you will often see a 900-square-foot classroom, desks in rows, students facing forward, and most of the action taking place in the front quarter of the room by the teacher. To this day, these spaces are often created with the interest and convenience of teachers—*not learning*—in mind. Although there is certainly a time and place for the teacher to be front and center, many learning spaces remain almost completely teacher-centric, with little to no thought given to brain research or learning theories that point to how students learn best.

In the 1930s, Lev Vygotsky's research became the foundation for social development theory—the understanding that social interaction plays a foundational role in the development of cognition (McLeod, 2014). Vygotsky strongly believed that community plays a central role in the process of making meaning. This notion is something that many early elementary teachers have mastered for years. As students get older and rise in grade levels, the notion that teachers transmit knowledge for students to remember becomes more prevalent, and the role of play and interaction often becomes minimal.

Since the 1960s, constructivism, the idea that people construct their own understanding and knowledge through experience and reflection, has been foundational in many introductory college education courses. Previous educational philosophies placed little to no value on a number of core constructivist ideas, including the importance of play and exploration. The idea that play is an important part of students' cognitive development and the concept that "to understand is to invent" are both foundational to today's Maker movement, which empowers students to construct their own understanding and engage in authentic, meaningful learning. According to Jean Piaget, "Education, for most people, means trying to lead the child to resemble the typical adult of his society . . . but for me and no one else, education means making creators. . . . You have to make inventors, innovators—not conformists" (quoted in Bringuier, 1980, p. 132).

According to Nancy Van Note Chism (2002), learning spaces intentionally designed for a constructivist approach should not be limited to the classroom but instead should spill into corridors, across campus, and throughout the interconnected digital web. These types of spaces include

- Small-group meeting spaces.
- Spaces for projects.
- Spaces for whole-class conversations.
- Spaces where technology is easily accessible.
- Spaces for display of ideas and working documents.
- Spaces that can easily accommodate movement and noise.

Next-generation spaces pull from the current generation's social development and constructivist philosophies to provide all students with a community that has opportunities to create, invent, and tinker. This allows students to learn in authentic and meaningful ways.

Shifting Spaces for Shifting Pedagogy

If you are going to focus on changing how students learn, then you have to ensure the learning space accommodates that learning.

Justin Tarte

Today's educational paradigm is no longer one of knowledge transfer but one of knowledge creation and curation. The "cells and bells" model has been prevalent for more than a century, but it is no longer relevant for today's learners. As educators work to shift to instructional pedagogies that are relational, authentic, dynamic, and—at times—chaotic in their schools, learning spaces must be reevaluated and adapted as necessary. Pedagogical innovation requires an innovation in the space where learning takes place. Simply put, if the space doesn't match the desired learning pedagogy, then it will hinder student learning outcomes.

Innovative learning spaces reach beyond classroom walls to every corner of the school. If we desire creativity, collaboration, ingenuity, authenticity, and multifaceted approaches to learning, then the spaces in which these experiences occur must be relative. Although schools have been slow to match research with practice in this area, the concept can be well demonstrated in the workplaces of some of today's most innovative companies. From small tech startups to market dominators, leaders in these companies work diligently to design spaces for collaboration, inquiry, and active learning. In order to promote such innovative practices, our schools must do the same by intentionally designing spaces for the type of learning that tomorrow's leaders need.

Designing for Collaboration

If we are truly going to ensure that students become college and career ready or—more importantly—life ready, then we must help develop students who can work together, engage in respectful discourse, problem solve, and collaborate in both physical and virtual spaces. Learning spaces designed for collaboration have flexible seating arrangements, boast comfortable furniture, and are agile enough to be reworked in a short time period. Collaborative groups may go from only a handful of students to larger groups in a short time period. These types of spaces also harness the collaborative nature of technology.

Designing for Self-Directed Learning

Although collaboration is key, there are undoubtedly times when students will want—and need—to work independently and in their own space. Whether they are plugged in wearing headphones or taking a deep dive into literature in a quiet place, the opportunity and choice to work independently is important. Having various learning spaces for different types of learning maximizes student opportunity and choice.

Designing for Inquiry, Exploration, and Creation

Inquiry can be variously defined as "a request for information," "an official effort to collect and examine information about something," or "the act of asking question in order to gather or collect information." The process begins with collecting information through our senses—seeing, hearing, smelling, touching, and tasting—and then linking that information together to make sense of the world around us. Learning spaces designed for inquiry do not emphasize a demarcation between teacher and student spaces; have no set "front of the room"; create Makerspace-type areas for students to create, tinker, and design, and employ instructional pedagogies that push students to ask questions and seek understanding—not listen to information and regurgitate. The problems of tomorrow will be solved by those students who have such opportunities today.

Designing for Active Learning

The traditional "sit-and-get" mindset and educational model in which pedagogy is driven by teachers passing on their knowledge to students—not by students gaining knowledge through experience—yields learning spaces with little movement and minimal active learning. All too often, we erroneously assume that a weekly physical education class or (ever-diminishing) recess time satisfies the human need for movement. We know there's a connection between motor movement and brain development, yet traditional learning spaces often aren't designed for motor skill–development activities. Students need to be able to move, jump, and shake during activities; stretch or run in place for a short period of time; or dance for expression. Doing so yields brain-based learning experiences that gets blood flowing and provides additional oxygen to the brain—thus enabling higher levels of learning.

Designing for Relationship Building

Learning spaces that promote socially catalytic interactions, where students can engage in social skills and relationship building, connect classroom spaces to common areas where students and staff can meet informally. During a class period, these spaces may be used for small-group instruction and interactions. Before school, between classes, and after school, these spaces provide areas where class discussions continue, social skills are built, and informal interactions occur.

Northfield Middle School is located in Atlantic County, New Jersey— an area that had the highest percentages of home foreclosures and unemployment in the nation during parts of 2014 and 2015. Former Principal Glenn Robbins and his team renamed their hallways "Idea Street" and intentionally designed informal meeting spaces throughout these transitional spaces. Complete with surfboards mounted on the walls to capture the culture of the beach community, these spaces have whiteboards, flexible and comfortable seating, a LEGO creation board, exercise bikes, and custom branded charging stations for students and staff to use at all times of day. When asked about the creation of Idea Street, Robbins shared the following:

> Statistically speaking, traditional "battleship blue" painted hallways in a school building make up to 30 percent or more of unused space. The focus of Idea Street was to build an experience for all that walk into our building that we are a creative culture of learners/makers who understand that learning takes place anywhere and at any time. Why should we continue to believe that all learning takes place in the four walls of the classroom? Ultimately, our goal is to resemble Silicon Valley tech companies or Ron Clark's schools instead of placing students in school environments that we knew growing up." (personal communication, July 27, 2016)

Intentionally designing spaces for relationship building is founded on the premise that every space can be a learning space.

Designing for Ownership

Do your students feel like they belong in the space, or does the space feel sterile? The need to feel belonging has long been documented and is a main concept of study in foundational education and psychology coursework. Learning-centered spaces that are more personal promote temporary student ownership over the space. This ownership may only last a single class period, but the need to feel ownership over space correlates with one's "hierarchy of needs" (Maslow, 1943).

Designing for Sustainability

Environmental care and economic longevity are both important lessons for students and priorities for long-term sustainability. As new spaces are designed, or as older spaces are revitalized, an environmentally friendly design can be cost effective and benefit learners. According to the U.S. Department of Energy, schools that adopt readily available high-performance design principles and technologies can reduce utility bills by up to 25 percent. On top of increased energy savings and lowered water costs, teacher retention can be improved and healthcare costs lowered (Plympton, Brown & Stevens, 2004). Improved conditions also lead to reduced student absenteeism. As a result, student performance increases. Intentionally designed schools are sustainable and built to last.

Designing for Student Safety

Our students' safety and security are at the heart of what we do as educators. As spaces are redesigned, student safety should be essential. The tragic events at Sandy Hook Elementary School in December 2012 (along with far too many other examples) changed the way schools view security. As two former principals—and as dads to our own school-aged children—our hearts ache for the families that lost a part of them that day.

Four years after the Sandy Hook tragedy, a new elementary school opened in Newtown, Connecticut. Safety and security were understandably top priorities throughout the project. Creating the new building was a delicate balancing act for architects, who weighed the need for security and the need to create dynamic learning spaces. Since one of the nation's worst acts of violence occurred on the campus, you may anticipate that they created a campus lined with high walls and metal detectors, but this was not the case. Designers hinged their success on airtight security features that wouldn't communicate an unwelcoming environment.

One of the many security measures, deemed "natural surveillance," focused on offering plenty of sight lines throughout the building and to the outside campus, creating the ability for anyone in the building to report something that seemed out of place. Traffic outside the building was kept to separate areas for visitors and staff, easing and regulating the flow. School bus drop-off and pick-up occurs directly in front of school—providing a spatial buffer and increased visibility. In addition, playgrounds were placed far away from public vehicle access. Inside the school, there are lockable doors in every classroom, unobstructed ground-level views of the outdoors through bulletproof glass, and separate kindergarten and pre-K play areas.

Achieving a new design that was sensitive to the recovering community was foundational throughout the design process. As such, the community played an active and systemic role in the new school's design. For three years, workshop groups—which included teachers, administrators, parents, and first responders—collaborated with the architects. Designers even hosted a series of workshops called KidsBuild!, which invited children into the design process. The children received basic lessons of construction and were able to contribute artwork that was then woven into the campus design (Budds, 2016). The new learning spaces at Sandy Hook Elementary are vibrant, attractive, collaborative, welcoming, and weave in a myriad of seamless security measures to ensure the safety of students and staff.

Key Considerations in Space Design

Among the many methods employed to foster student development, the use of the physical environment is perhaps the least understood and the most neglected.

James H. Banning & Manuel R. Canard (1986)

Between their first day of kindergarten to the day they walk across the stage at high school graduation, American students spend an average of 11,700 hours of their lives in school buildings (Hull & Newport, 2011). College students typically spend an additional 400 classroom hours in post-secondary education buildings (Wellman & Ehrlich, 2003). With such significant portions of our early years spent in such spaces, it's critically important to understand environmental effects on academic performance.

Earthman (2004) conducted a study of the various ways the school environment determined people's comfort levels. The study indicated that environmental comfort embodies four different areas—thermal, luminic, acoustic, and ergonomic—all of which affect a student's ability to focus, engage, and learn. A number of other studies drew the same conclusions and demonstrated a link between school conditions and student achievement (e.g., Bowers & Burkett, 1988; Grangaard, 1995; Hines, 1996). Examples of undesirable conditions are buildings without appropriate HVAC systems, with poor lighting, that are old or noisy, that lack functional furniture, or with some variation or combination of these qualities. As such, the condition of the school building directly affects how well students learn.

Utilizing the latest research in classroom design is a key to developing learning spaces that enhance the teaching and learning process. From the physical layout to what we see, hear, and breathe, a carefully constructed environment promotes maximum attention and engagement. The following are key considerations for educators to keep in mind as they build, design, or update learning spaces.

Design for "Naturalness"

Humans have basic needs for light, air, and safety. These are hardwired into our brains and "create a strong response to natural elements in our environment that we intuitively feel to be nurturing and sustaining" (Barrett & Zhang, 2009). Temperature, light, sound, and air quality are the key aspects of designing a learning environment filled with "naturalness."

Temperature (Thermal)

At one point or another, we've all had the experience of being uncomfortable because of the temperature of the room. Some of us—usually those who teach in traditionally underserved areas—teach in such environments on a daily basis. It's no secret that many of today's schools are over half a century old, and upgrading HVAC systems is particularly expensive in old buildings. As such, air temperature is reported as unsatisfactory or very unsatisfactory in one out of seven, or approximately 14 percent, of U.S. public schools (Alexander & Lewis, 2014).

One of the largest studies to look at the impact of temperature on learning comes from a decades-old report: a 1931 New York State Commission on Ventilation. The commission, which set out to determine optimal temperatures for learning, subjected students to various temperatures and then measured their achievement. The commission reported the following results:

1. Excessively high temperatures produce harmful physiological effects, and an effective temperature range of 67° to 73° F is desirable.
2. Room temperatures of 75° F with 50 percent relative humidity and no air movement cause a definite increase in body temperature and pulse rate and a marked fall in vasomotor tone, affecting the body's ability to perform.
3. Overheating results in less work performed. The study found that 15 percent less work was performed at 75° F versus 68° F with 50 percent relative humidity and no air movement. When the conditions were raised to 86° F with 80 percent humidity, the decrease was 28 percent.

Due to these findings, the commission recommended that schools maintain room temperatures between 68–70° F and a relative humidity of 50 percent with sufficient air movement to eliminate odors and stale air. These standards, now almost a century old, have remained the reference point for school construction. Yet, sadly, many students aren't afforded such optimal learning environments. We have both been administrators in buildings that were more than 50 years old, and we've seen firsthand the negative effects that temperature and poor HVAC systems can have on both students' ability to learn and a teacher's ability to teach.

Practical Tips:

• Work closely with maintenance staff to identify and document temperature-related issues.
• Maximize fresh air and enable air flow throughout the building.

Lighting (Luminic)

Bright, fluorescent lights. Dim, poorly lit spaces. We've all experienced them. Today, many of our students experience these types of spaces on a daily basis as 16 percent of schools with permanent buildings and 28 percent of schools with temporary buildings (i.e., modular classrooms) have natural lighting that is unsatisfactory (Alexander & Lewis, 2014). Quite often, these buildings are found in high-poverty areas, which also raises concerns over equitable learning environments. Such poorly lit spaces also negatively affect student learning outcomes, as it's been shown that students exposed to more natural light performed better than those exposed to less natural light in their classrooms. These findings parallel the results of studies conducted in office and healthcare spaces that show that rooms with a window (and thus have natural daylight) improve employee productivity and patient recovery time (Edwards & Torcelli, 2002).

A study conducted by Heschong Mahone Group (1999) looked at more than 21,000 students in three different states and found that the higher the amount of natural light, the greater a student's attendance, achievement, and overall health. This research shows the importance of keeping the blinds open and shades up and of finding ways to get students the maximum amount of daylight throughout the day.

Traditional classrooms are often designed with fluorescent lighting to offset minimal amounts of natural light, which can be distracting and even cause headaches for some people. Fluorescent lighting should be minimized, and the use of natural lighting should be maximized to provide the highest levels of comfort. When renovating or building new spaces, besides maximizing the available daylight, it's important to add dimmers or the ability to control lighting beyond a simple on-off switch. Likewise, it's also important to minimize glare. Lighting should be flicker free, clean, and of high quality.

Practical Tips:

- Keep windows clear and blinds open to allow for maximum natural light.
- Minimize glare as it can be distracting and has a negative effect.
- Use nonfluorescent lighting to supplement natural light.
- Use lamps to create "warm" lighting, particularly in small-group areas or reading nooks.
- Utilize outdoor learning spaces.
- Ensure spaces used after hours are well lit at all times.

Sound (Acoustic)

A student's ability to hear in the classroom is vital for both student learning and teacher performance (Earthman, 2004). Researchers have long indicated a negative relationship between noise levels and student achievement. How significant is this issue? Unsatisfactory or very unsatisfactory acoustics were reported in approximately one of seven (14%) of U.S. public schools (Alexander & Lewis, 2014). Students with a hearing impairment are also put at an additional disadvantage in a learning environment with poor acoustics. A 1981 study completed by the California

Department of Health Services correlated the effects of noise on student achievement by comparing schools that were near highways with those in quiet neighborhoods. Confirming previous research on the topic, the report concluded a negative relationship between classroom noise levels and reading achievement (Lukas, DuPree, & Swing, 1981). A synthesis of studies pertaining to facilities, student achievement, and student behavior indicated a significant relationship between noise level and student achievement (Lemasters, 1997). The report stated that construction, jet aircraft, sound systems, television, radio, automobiles, and heating and ventilation units have a negative impact on teaching and learning.

Some of these external factors are difficult or impossible for school leaders and teachers to control unless a new building is built. However, it's imperative for school leaders to make conscious decisions in the areas they do control. The location of music rooms and instructional spaces near the cafeteria and gymnasium should be carefully planned, and procedures should be put in place to minimize overcrowded classrooms and noisy hallways that overlap instructional periods.

Practical Tips:

- Work with maintenance staff to identify and document ongoing HVAC needs.
- Carefully consider the placement of classes such as band and chorus where noise is more or less continuous.
- Review building procedures to minimize noise that is irrelevant to learning.

Air Quality

Studies correlate the effect of air quality on a teacher's ability to teach at high levels. Almost one in ten (9%) U.S. public schools have unsatisfactory or very unsatisfactory air quality (Alexander & Lewis, 2014), and low-income schools, which traditionally serve high numbers of students of color, have disproportionately lower air quality (General Accounting Office, 1996). The U.S. Environmental Protection Agency (2000) has estimated that 10 million days of schooling are lost each year by students due to asthma-related illnesses. In a very real sense, poor air quality has a detrimental effect on students' ability to learn while at school. Undoubtedly, many teachers suffer from similar chronic conditions, which negatively affects their attendance rates and both costs districts additional money for substitute teachers and interrupts the continuity of learning. These conditions, and the countless instructional hours lost, have a negative effect on our nation's education system and economy.

Practical Tips:

- Maximize the amount of fresh air in the space.
- Maximize air circulation by keeping windows and doors open or utilizing quiet air movers to circulate fresh air.

Design for Individualization

Most students sit in hard chairs for almost an hour at a time. Quite often, this is the only type of furniture available for student use. As adults, we must ask ourselves if sitting in these chairs, for up to seven hours per day, sounds appealing. Would we do our best work sitting uncomfortably, surrounded by solid surfaces? Of course not, and research backs up what also seems to be common sense. To avoid a sterile, uncomfortable space, student ownership and belonging are critical. When you walk into a space, does it feel like a cookie-cutter, anonymous box similar to the rest of the building, or does it feel like a place where students have ownership? Do displays highlight students and their work? Is there distinctiveness in the learning space design? How can educators design for individualization?

Ensuring Accessibility

Ensuring accessibility for all students goes far beyond ADA requirement adherence. Unfortunately, parents of elementary and secondary school students with disabilities are more likely to report that features of a school's environment (including physical layout) are a barrier to their children's participation (Coster et al., 2013). From physical access to regulating ancillary noise for those with hearing needs to ensuring sanitary food preparation methods for children with food allergies—these are not only legal obligations but also our moral and ethical duty to ensure that *all students*, particularly those with special needs, have the same access and opportunities as their peers.

Practical Tips:

- Seek input from and collaborate with parents of children with special needs on how to better design spaces throughout the building to ensure safety and accessibility.

- Work directly alongside students with special needs and encourage them to offer suggestions and feedback for a more supportive design.
- Seek guidance from community experts and organizations—specifically those that work directly with particular student needs.

The Need for Versatility

Whether you're arranging a single classroom or building a new school, design should incorporate versatile space and furniture so you can shift directions in a short span of time. From moveable walls to easy-to-move furniture, redesigning the learning experience requires teachers to adapt their environments to maximize learning outcomes.

Versatile, modern spaces:

- Contain couches, benches, ergonomic chairs, rocking chairs, ball chairs, beanbags, cafe tables, bistro tables and chairs, adjustable-height tables, and armchairs.
- Promote problem solving, collaboration, and student-student/ student-teacher relationships.
- Allow for continual reorganization of the spaces into various sizes and groups.
- Account for various small-group areas.
- Have comfortable, ergonomic furniture.
- Enable multiple uses.
- Have small, quiet nooks where students can work independently.
- Use durable materials in furniture and finishes.
- Ensure the safety of all students.
- Are easy to monitor by those responsible.

In versatile spaces, you will observe students spending less time in a chair than they do in a traditional school setting. Hellerup School in Finland intentionally designed such a set-up. The number of chairs in the school equals 50 percent of the student population, meaning that students, on average, cannot sit in a chair for more than half the day. Instead, time is spent on stools, on exercise balls, and on the floor or soft seating (e.g., couches, beanbags) (Nair, 2014).

Practical Tips:

- Identify learning zones that support different instructional pedagogies.

- Create spaces for whole-group, small-group, and individual work and reflection.
- Use partitions to create versatile, fast-changing spaces.
- Keep the visual focus away from the classroom door to minimize distractions.
- Ensure furniture purchases are comfortable and ergonomic.
- Consider getting rid of the teacher's desk (as they are typically large and relatively immobile).

The Need for Voice and Choice

Including students in the design of the physical environment can both enhance the space and build classroom community. Gaining students' insight and voice brings a sense of empowerment and ownership, creating a sense of belonging. As adults, we can relate to the desire to work in different types of spaces for different types of tasks. However, we can also understand that our preferences may be very different from our colleagues'. Such preferential differences also exist within the classroom community, exhibiting the need to consider where student voice and choice can play a role in design.

Educators can begin by simply having students communicate "pain points"—those areas of the building or classroom where they don't feel comfortable, that they don't enjoy, or that cause anxiety or stress. School leaders may find themselves surprised at students' responses; areas perceived as a strength for adults may turn out to be a pain point for students.

Practical Tips:

- Form student leadership teams, and challenge them to evaluate all spaces on campus and propose solutions for better space design.
- Seek and leverage student input on building policies and procedures.
- Be a student for a day! Choose a student's schedule to follow for an entire day and evaluate the spaces utilizing a student lens. Alternatively, ask for a parent volunteer to do the same!

The Need for Informal Learning Areas

The "third place" is a term coined by psychologists to describe the setting outside of home and work where socializing, eating, reading, studying, and relaxing with others takes place. It's also where a lot of informal learning takes place and is something traditional schools often overlook—and at times purposefully limit. With the opportunity for informal learning to occur in all areas of the school building, it is important for all learning spaces to promote social and informal interactions (Nair, 2014).

Practical Tips:

- Leverage student voice by asking students what type of learning space they need to learn best.
- Give students a choice in where and how they work.
- Intentionally design a "third place." If outside the school campus, have a conversation with students about how they can design their own spaces for learning.
- Maximize social interactions in informal learning areas.

Be Intentional with Visual Stimuli and Messaging

Various findings link human emotional responses to characteristics in their surroundings. From the colors of students' learning space to the explicit and subtle messages sent to students about what and who is valued through displays, decor, and imagery, visual stimuli and messaging crosses brain science, gender differences, and cultural identities—all of which must be considered when designing spaces.

The Impact of Color

A synthesis of 40 studies that looked at the impact of color on people indicated how colors or "colored environments" have influence over work performances, can cause certain behaviors, can create positive or negative perceptions to tasks, and undoubtedly affect mood and emotions (Jalil, Yunus, & Said, 2012). The synthesis indicated that color can affect our concentration, emotions, and perception of our surroundings. It also showed how a learning environment should be visually stimulating, as learning itself includes various aspects of motivation, mood, and action from the learner. The purposeful use of color can decrease eye fatigue while simultaneously increasing student and teacher productivity. Unfortunately, most schools pay very little attention to the use of color.

For the use of color to be effective, it must be designed intentionally. Classroom colors should be warm yet not distracting. They should always be welcoming to both boys and girls; therefore, it's important to choose monochromatic tones and colors that are gender neutral. The perception of color in a learning space carries visual, emotional, and symbolic effects and should be used to design the learning space's intended purpose (see Figure 4.1).

Practical Tips:

- Avoid the overuse of colors and patterns that can overstimulate learners.
- Avoid the full whitewash look that resembles a sterile hospital space.
- Use bulletin boards as developmentally appropriate teaching tools—not simply decorative spaces.
- Maximize the use of natural, monochromatic earth tones and colors that have a calming effect.
- Reserve bright colors for hallways, stairwells, and common areas.
- Use plants and other natural elements to bring earth tones and nature to life in the classroom.

FIGURE 4.1

Psychological Effects and Properties of Color

Color	Positive Psychological Properties	Negative Psychological Properties	Commonly Used Terms and Phrases
Blue	attentive, calm, cool, comfortable, creative, orderly, peaceful, reflective, reliable, serene, stable, trusting	aloof, cold, lonely, not emotional, sad	*feeling blue, blue Monday, blue ribbon, blue moon, blue collar, blue blood*
Green	attentive, balanced, calm, creative, natural, quiet, refreshed, relaxed	bland, bored, enervated, stagnant	*green thumb, green with envy*
Yellow	cheerful, confident, creative, energetic, friendly, optimistic, visible, warm	afraid, aggressive, angry, anxious, emotionally fragile, fatigued, frustrated	*yellow bellied, yellow streak, yellow journalism*
Red	active, comfortable, courageous, emotional, energetic, excited, eye-catching, passionate, powerful, stimulated, warm	aggressive, angry, dramatic, intense	*red tape, be shown a red card, be out of the red, red hot, caught red handed, saw red, red carpet, paint the town red*

Gender Perceptions

It's vital that both genders are considered in the design process since gender stereotyped colors and themes are typically not the best choice. Research by the University of Washington's Institute for Learning & Brain Sciences has indicated that girls are three times as likely to take a STEM-type course such as computer science if the room looks less "geeky" (Master, Cheryan, & Meltzoff, 2016). Simply put, this study claims that the learning space itself makes a difference in girls' attitudes toward the type of coursework they'd take. The stereotypical perception was that the rooms looked like a place for "nerdy males" and not a place that females would enjoy. In response, the University of Washington changed the color and design of their STEM-area college classrooms to be more gender neutral and reflective of nature. The redesign took about two weeks and had minimal costs. As districts work to redesign the learning experience for all students, they must ensure the learning space remains neutral and comfortable for all.

Practical Tips:

- Ensure visual symbols are representative of both genders and the majority of symbols are gender neutral.
- Seek critical input and feedback from colleagues of the opposite gender.
- Ask male and female students and colleagues for feedback.

Racial and Cultural Perceptions

Symbolic features also have a significant impact on classrooms and student learning. Symbols affect student perceptions as to whether they are valued learners and belong within the classroom. For example, subtle messages to students of color and female students that they may be evaluated based on their race or gender can raise fears that confirm negative stereotypes about a particular group's abilities, thereby lowering learning outcomes (Steele, Spencer, & Aronson, 2002). Fortunately, educators can alter the symbolic aspects of the classroom in a simple, cost-effective manner. It's imperative that classroom symbols are respectful and sensitive to race and gender and promote positive outcomes for *all* students.

Practical Tips:

- Ensure visual symbols are representative of various ethnicities and cultures.

- Seek critical input and feedback from colleagues or community members of different ethnicities, religions, and cultures.
- Solicit feedback from a diverse group of students.
- Ensure that the school entrance is intentionally designed with visual messaging and stimuli in mind. First impressions matter!

Overstimulation and Clutter

According to Fisher, Godwin, and Seltman (2014), off-task behavior lasts 10 percent longer in heavily decorated classes. As such, educators must work to ensure bulletin boards and other wall displays aren't overly distracting and decorations hung from the ceiling don't cause distractions. Distracted students spend more time off task and thus demonstrate smaller learning gains. It's also important that classroom supplies remain organized and don't serve as an additional distraction or lead to a loss in instructional time. As said by Edward Tufte, "Clutter and confusion are failures of design, not attributes of information" (Tufte, 1992). An uncluttered space can help students remain organized and ultimately grant them more control and ownership over the space.

Practical Tips:

- Moderate levels of stimulation are best. Avoid under and overstimulation.
- Eliminate distracting media from classroom walls.
- Decrease visual clutter and overcrowding on walls and bulletin boards.
- Avoid distracting, irrelevant decorations that hang from the ceiling.
- Use wall space intentionally and with a definite purpose.
- Ensure that classroom supplies remain organized for ease of use and minimal distractions.
- If you have material that isn't used all year, share it with a colleague who can put it to use so your space can be better utilized.
- If particular materials aren't being used for long periods of time, find appropriate, out-of-sight places to store them.

The Use of Space Outside Traditional Classroom Walls

The traditional school structure creates an environment in which each classroom space defines a separate, unique learning area that is often unrelated to what's found on the other side of the door. Intentionally designed classrooms extend beyond the traditional 900 square feet of space to reach every corner of the campus. Comprehensive design of learning spaces should also address the commute to and from scheduled classes; informal learning can happen everywhere, including corridors, lobbies, courtyards, and cafeterias. As such, the classroom door should represent a seamless transition from in-class learning to life learning (Wulsin, 2013).

Wireless infrastructure and the power of today's mobile devices enable learning to occur anywhere, any time. Technology also accelerates the notion that learning spaces must reflect a network of connected places beyond the traditional classroom. Where learning is able to seamlessly flow from one space to the next, a sense of community is fostered. As such, it's vital to design and utilize an entire school campus as one large learning space (Kiefer, 2012).

Some school districts, such as Coachella Valley School District in California, have taken this notion to the next level by adding Wi-Fi to school buses in an effort to provide access to students while traveling. Whether students are traveling to a sporting event in a neighboring town or to school early in the morning, school buses have been transformed into powerful learning spaces with an intentional design.

Learning beyond the classroom and bringing the learning outdoors can have many positive effects, as a number of studies have connected nature with the ability to help relieve cognitive fatigue and increase the ability to concentrate. Nair (2014, p. 131) also highlights the following research on the effect of nature:

- Children with symptoms of ADHD are better able to concentrate after contact with nature.
- Play in a diverse natural environment reduces or eliminates bullying.
- Nature helps children develop powers of observation and creativity and instills a sense of peace and being at one with the world.
- Early experiences with the natural world have been positively linked with the development of imagination and the sense of wonder.
- Wonder is an important motivator for lifelong learning.
- Children who play in nature have more positive feelings about one another.
- A decrease in children's time spent outdoors is contributing to an increase in myopia in developed countries.
- Outdoor environments are important to children's development of independence and autonomy.

Whether it's creatively utilizing a courtyard space, turning bus trips into learning opportunities, or knocking down classroom walls to include outdoor learning spaces, thinking outside the traditional 900-square-foot space can provide students with unique, personal learning experiences and opportunities.

Dedicating Spaces to Tinker, Design, and Create

If you build it, they will come, and if you let them build it, they will learn.

Laura Fleming

The intentional design of spaces for students and staff to tinker, design, and create is vital to support the shift to a more personal approach to learning. These spaces can be designed with minimal square footage in a classroom setting, or they can become a focal point of an entire school. This has been seen in the redesign of many library spaces, which now include Makerspaces and areas for STEM-based learning.

The best libraries have always been places where learning was made personal. Even traditional libraries have been learning-focused spaces (not teaching-focused) designed with both collaboration and personalization in mind. What was originally created as a place to store books, access information, and passively consume content can become a hub for innovation when intentionally designed. In these spaces, learning can be transformed.

Laura Fleming, a library media specialist at New Milford High School in New Jersey, has been at the forefront of library redesign. Author of the best-selling book *Worlds of Making: Best Practices for Establishing a Makerspace for Your School* (2015), Fleming has helped districts nationwide think differently about their use of library spaces. Fleming shares the following advice (personal communication, September 8, 2016):

> My philosophy of school libraries centers on fostering a participatory culture. This essentially means that students are provided with as many opportunities to do things and create things as possible. In my libraries, I have provided access not only to information and content but also to the resources, materials, and supplies that

allow my students the opportunity to become creators and not just consumers. It is this philosophy that has been at the core of every library I had a hand in designing.

When designing a library, it is important to ask yourself if you are setting the conditions for your learners to be great. Our spaces need to work best for the children we are creating them for, not just for the adults who are designing them. Asking students to take part in your library design opens the door to genuine, authentic student voice. Empowering students in this way will guarantee that you create a unique learning environment that students need, want, deserve, and value.

The Maker Movement in K–12 has been a revolution in education that has allowed students to move from consumption to creation and to turn their knowledge into action. It promotes learning through doing in an open, social, and student-driven environment. Establishing a physical Makerspace in a school library pulls in some of the excitement from the Maker Movement by creating a unique learning environment that encourages tinkering, play, and open-ended exploration for all.

A dedicated space that creates the conditions to inspire your learners to take risks and innovate will transform your library into a creativity and innovation hub. A personalized approach to planning these learning spaces is key. Proper planning is essential in uncovering a space that works best for your school community. This approach will also ensure that your space is meaningful now and will remain vibrant and sustainable in the future.

Whether you're just getting started with learning space redesign or have already utilized significant resources, leveraging the talents of school librarians is essential. When effective, school libraries can serve as hubs of innovation and the birthplace of your school's redesign.

Blending Physical and Virtual Learning Spaces

With the exponential growth of digital learning experiences, many learning spaces are rapidly moving into the virtual realm. With the development and popularity of full-time online schools and the addition of digital learning opportunities in many traditional schools, school leaders must wrestle with ways to blend physical and virtual learning spaces. Today's students are profoundly immersed in the digital world, which sets them apart from previous generations. Tomorrow's leaders are growing up at a time in which access to technology and information is available in real time. Social media and instant informational gratification are simply a way of life. These students wear more technology than some of their teachers will ever own or use. They treat their multitasking handheld devices as an extension of their bodies. A vast percentage of teenagers have a cell phone, and 80 percent of them report that they sleep with their devices (Pew Research Center, 2010). For a generation whose parents grew up mailing letters to a pen pal around the globe and waiting weeks for a response, the Netflix Generation can seemingly text with their eyes closed and socially network with anyone they meet at any time.

As school leaders intentionally design technology-rich experiences to transform learning, analogous changes should also be evident in the learning space. Simply placing 21st century tools in a 20th century learning environment will have little to no impact. Designing technology-empowered learning spaces means thinking differently about the types of learning opportunities we want and the associated needs of each.

The Need for Power

Adding hundreds, if not thousands, of devices to a school building dramatically increases the need for charging places. Too often, dozens of devices will be added to a classroom without adequate thought given as to where, when, and how those devices will be charged—both overnight and throughout the day. When building or renovating a new space, school leaders must consider adding outlets and modern charging spaces. However, cost can quickly become a barrier since wiring additional electrical outlets can be expensive, so these locations should be carefully and strategically planned.

Rather than assign a locker to every student (as is traditionally done in most secondary schools), school leaders at a 60-year-old high school in Albemarle County, Virginia, asked the school's 2,000 students how many wanted a locker for the coming year. Only 25 students opted for a traditional locker space. Since the move was already in line with their shift toward a more digital approach, school leaders removed the lockers in three hallways and used the newly created space with informal seating, whiteboards, and additional power outlets so students could collaborate and work in what was previously unusable space. The new spaces created a more open feel for the school, and the solution ended up with additional functional space in a building that's well over half a century old (DeNisco, 2015).

With both district-owned and personal devices commonplace in today's schools, the need for power can't be overemphasized. Cafeterias, related arts areas, foyers, and other collaborative spaces should include stations for students to power up throughout the day. These areas are also great locations to promote a school's brand, inclusivity, and relationships. Schools such as New Milford High School and Northfield Middle School, both in New Jersey, have embraced this approach with their intentionally designed spaces.

The Need for Real-time Communication

Modern spaces support dynamic, real-time communication through digital signage and the ability to project content. From interactive touchscreens to large-screen digital displays, the ability to communicate information in real time, whether in a classroom setting or a large-group space, is now an expectation. Upon walking into a school, everyone should be greeted with real-time information with the school brand prominently displayed. In a classroom setting, creating places for students to present and share—both in small groups and to the whole class—will encourage collaboration and high levels of learning. These areas are typically flexible, technology-accessible, multiuse spaces.

The Need for Ubiquitous Connectivity

Discussed in depth in Chapter 6, ubiquitous connectivity is an expectation for intentionally designed schools. We've all experienced the frustration of trying to work in a location with limited connectivity. When connectivity is limited, so is the opportunity to learn. Even though districts have significantly upgraded wireless infrastructure in recent years, there are still locations with "dead zones" or limited broadband speeds. Districts must not only consider classroom spaces but also large-group and informal learning areas. From the cafeteria to the auditorium, particular attention should be paid to ubiquitous connectivity in large spaces where the number of connected devices will far exceed a typical instructional space. Ubiquitous connectivity is a lifeline for progress.

The Need for a Safe, Collaborative Online Space

Learning management systems (LMS) provide online spaces for students and staff to connect and collaborate, both in synchronous and asynchronous ways. With an increase in digital content, the need for some sort of hub or online, shared space grows. A strong LMS empowers teachers to create and share digital content, provide feedback in real time, and ultimately teach students anywhere in the world. These spaces can empower a more collaborative, relevant, real-time, personal experience for students. However, when poorly used, these online spaces can become an expensive digital worksheet graveyard—a digital version of a messy desk full of disorganized paper.

So what might we find in a highly connected learning space of the future? With the acceleration of nanotechnology, biometrics, and artificial intelligence, anything is possible. What was once perceived as science fiction is now seen as outdated technology. Much of the technology that might seem futuristic actually already exists. It's just too cost prohibitive to implement at this time. Advances in technology and a subsequent drop in cost increase what's possible in the classroom. This was the case for computers not too long ago. According to the Bureau of Labor Statistics (2015b), from December 1997 to August 2015, the Consumer Price Index for personal computers and peripheral equipment declined 96 percent, with most of the price decrease occurring between 1998 and 2003—the digital revolution. Simply put, schools are paying less than one-twentieth of what they were less than 20 years prior.

From fully interactive walls to digital, multidimensional work spaces and the use of holograms and augmented and virtual reality, the possibilities are endless and exciting. Such opportunities, although seemingly far-fetched, may be here and affordable before we know it. As breakthroughs in science and technology continue, new opportunities for authentic learning inside learner-centered spaces become possible. As this occurs, the learning is transformed.

Creating Spaces That Work—On a Budget

When school leaders hear some version of the phrase *learning space redesign*, many immediately envision dollar signs and often downplay its potential because of the real issue of limited budgets. However, this doesn't have to be the case, as learning space redesign doesn't have to be costly. A few gallons of paint, time spent decluttering, a few yard sales, and a commitment to thinking creatively can help provide a fresh look, versatility, and tools to complete a learning space redesign. As such, school leaders should start by thinking creatively—not costly.

When considering a redesign, especially in older, more traditional spaces, it's a good idea to start with a small space (such as a reading nook in a classroom) or one larger space (such as a library or foyer). This will lay the groundwork for a new mindset of what's feasible in meeting the needs of modern learners. Many educators have become adept at creating incredible spaces and resources on very limited budgets by thinking differently. So how can we create spaces that work for kids without breaking the bank?

Transform Unused or Underutilized Spaces

Start by reviewing every square foot of unused or underutilized space inside and outside the classroom and school campus. Brainstorm instructional needs that could be taught better in a creative space, and consider unconventional ideas. Ask colleagues to think creatively and envision what could be possible and what it would take to increase instructional opportunities. From small closets to hallways to the backstage of the auditorium, is every square foot being put to maximum use? How can traditionally unused or underutilized spaces become hubs for innovation?

Engage the Community: Ask for Donations

Dealing with a limited budget but driven by a burning desire to create learning opportunities for students to make, create, and design, Samantha Edwards, a digital media specialist at Fogelsville Elementary in Pennsylvania's Parkland School District, knew she needed to find a way to transform her traditional library space. She approached her principal, Tim Chorones, and assistant superintendent Tracy Smith, about her ideas, who in turn pushed her to innovate and take risks to create authentic opportunities for all of her students. Edwards went on to articulate her desire to the parents in her community about wanting to transform the library space to one that focused on higher-order design, problem solving, *and* literacy.

Stemming from conversations she had with her students, Edwards held a "LEGO Drive" and appealed to parents by asking if they were "tired of stepping on LEGO bricks at home" or if they were "ready to clean out a closet to help their child's school." By appealing to the full community of this Title I school, Edwards was able to create a dynamic Makerspace, much of which was donated by students' families. By engaging school families and encouraging students to think creatively, redesign became possible through the donations of time, a few gallons of paint, and used supplies found in the community. One parent with carpentry skills even stepped up to create tables, and many others donated used computers, LEGO bricks, and other design-oriented toys—all of which ultimately found new life in her transformed space. Edwards's low-budget Makerspace caught the attention of the regional PBS station and a local education foundation, which led to a $50,000 grant to replicate the transformed learner-centered experiences in the district's other elementary schools. How can your community support a needed redesign?

Open the Outdoors

With a fixed amount of space inside the school walls, some schools have taken to outdoor spaces to extend learning opportunities. At Walter Bracken STEAM Academy Elementary School in Las Vegas, students have built raised-bed gardens from concrete blocks and pavers, recycled PVC, and tires (Decker, 2016). With the successful redesign of previously unused spaces, the school is looking at ways to build a track on their field for students to use while simultaneously saving water—a critical issue in this desert community. How can you leverage outdoor space?

Find a Hack!

Educators are hacking traditional ideas and creating visually appealing, multifunctional resources for not much money and often sharing them on collaborative online spaces such as Pinterest. One example of a creative hacking solution can be seen in the charging and storage of devices. With the cost of charging carts often exceeding $1,000, some educators have turned to creating their own solutions, using dish racks and power strips to save both money and space. Using hacks such as these also encourages students to creatively problem solve other issues they face. A quick Internet search for classroom hacks will turn up many great ideas. What problems can you solve through a creative hack?

Empower Students to Design and Create

Many times we find ourselves racking our brains to find a solution and never pause to ask our students their opinions. Many students, especially those in vocational education classes, have incredible real-world trade skills. From automotive and cosmetology to carpentry and electronics, today's modern learners have the ability to creatively design and create needed resources. Can traditional coursework for these students be shifted to problem solve issues in their home schools? Doing so builds the community and school culture while also empowering students to solve real-world issues. What problems are your students designing solutions for and solving? How are their learning experiences being transformed?

Still unable to find the needed supplies and materials for a small redesign? Start small, but think big! Some of the ideas in this chapter might immediately be written off by those stuck in traditional settings where anything outside the box is frowned upon. We encourage school leaders to work with their administrative teams, parent and community organizations, and local school board to think differently about how, when, and where design materials come from.

Shop Local and Used

Try connecting with the local Goodwill or Salvation Army to give second-hand materials new life. Form relationships with local managers and explain what, as a school, you're looking for and the student experiences you're trying to design. They might just put you on their speed dial list!

Purchase Seasonally

Develop relationships with local colleges and universities, and offer to purchase used college furniture during graduation week as students leave for the summer—a time when significant money can be saved. During this time of year, graduating students often want to get rid of their belongings and are willing to sell them at a low cost or even donate them to the local school district. It's also a good idea to connect with local big box stores such as Home Depot, Lowes, and Target, and ask them to let you know when seasonal merchandise hits the clearance aisle. Many of these stores take great pride in supporting their local schools and community.

Crowdsource Your Needs

Sites such as DonorsChoose, GoFundMe, and Classwish connect teachers with people willing to donate to school projects. Staff and students can share their online campaign with the world to raise money and support the project.

Whether designing a new building, renovating an old one, or updating even a few square feet of space, every effort should be made to create the conditions where student-centered learning can flourish. It's imperative to understand that each space is inhabited by various teachers with a very specific—*and different*—group of students. As such, there is no one "right way" to design a space. Each space, whether old or new, large or small, traditional or modern, should be designed to maximize a personal approach to student learning. Schools will know that their spaces have been designed successfully when the design positively contributes to the learning process and helps create an authentic, dynamic experience for all.

What type of spaces are in your school? Do the current spaces correlate with the instructional pedagogy you have in mind? What research is currently being used? What do the students think of the current design? Have you asked? Whose learning space is it anyway?

You are part of the solution.

Innovative Practices in Action

Elizabeth Forward School District, Pennsylvania
Bart Rocco, Superintendent
Todd Keruskin, Assistant Superintendent
League of Innovative Schools Model District

In 2009, the Elizabeth Forward School District had over 80 students in outside cyber/charter schools, a 10 percent dropout rate, and was struggling with passing the school budget year to year. The school district needed to make a dramatic change to the traditional teaching and learning happening in the school district. In an effort to begin making significant changes, we partnered with the Grable Foundation and the Entertainment Technology Center at Carnegie Mellon University to take Elizabeth Forward School District from Frontierland to Tomorrowland.

If we wanted to significantly impact achievement, attendance rates, and other factors, we knew we had to shift our mindset and our programming to create an environment where all students wanted to be. The shift also included a shift in our learning spaces. We started the Entertainment Technology Academy at the Elizabeth Forward High School that redesigned an old computer lab into a fun place to learn all about gaming. A series of courses are now offered to high school students in grades 9–12 through an educational partner called Zulama. After students complete a sequence of classes covering the history of gaming, programming, graphic design, and storytelling, the students work with nonprofit organizations in the Pittsburgh region to build apps and video games in the gaming internship class. The Entertainment Technology Academy is changing the culture about what students are learning in school, and they are seeing the direct applications to real-world experiences.

We then moved to redesigning the EF Media Center learning space. This space was modeled after the YOUMedia Center at the Chicago Public Library and was based on the book by Mizuko Ito, *Hanging Out, Messing Around, and Geeking Out: Kids Living and Learning with New Media*. The center is divided into areas where students can relax, use sound or television media equipment, and work on projects. The EF Media Center is still a library in a traditional sense, but it's accentuated with media resources for all students. The EF Media Center also has a cafe where students can drink frozen lattes and enjoy a snack while working on classroom projects or assignments. Students from our life skills programs help as workers in this space as well.

Our next redesigned space occurred at the Elizabeth Forward Middle School where we installed a Situated Multimedia Art Learning Lab, or SMALLab. This was the first installation in a public school. The SMALLab includes an overhead projector, which beams down onto a padded floor, and there are 12 motion-capturing cameras around the room that help create a simulated learning environment for students. When classes attend the lab, they are embedded in learning simulations that are geared toward defined subject areas. Students are learning new skills in a collaborative teaching environment. The activities use gamification as a tool to instruct students on difficult subjects. Today, the district partners with graduate students at the Entertainment Technology Center (ETC) at Carnegie Mellon University to create new simulations for this space!

In continuing the redesign, Elizabeth Forward Middle School created a DREAM Factory, a state-of-the-art Makerspace that is approved through MIT's FAB Foundation. Combining the arts with design, computer science, and technology, the DREAM Factory enables every middle school student to learn about modern technical fields such as robotics, engineering, design, and programming. Students have an opportunity to transform inventive ideas into real objects using a laser cutter, CNC router, 3D printers, microcontrollers, and traditional woodshop equipment.

Our high school then created a new FABLab, which was also approved by MIT's FAB Foundation. In this space, high school students are now being taught prototype skills and learning design using digital fabrication tools.

In 2015, we launched the first Girls Maker Class where female students designed and digitally fabricated projects from an LED wall, furniture pieces, and 3D scanned action figures.

To spread the redesign mindset and opportunities to our elementary spaces, we created a Mobile FABLab in a 28-foot long trailer to engage the four elementary schools in digital fabrication. This Mobile FABLab has laser cutters, 3D printers, vinyl cutters, computers, and traditional woodshop tools to help K–5 students with additive and subtractive manufacturing. This FABLab rotates between the four different elementary schools and is integrated into science, math, art, and even social studies. With this transformation, we now have K–12 Digital Fabrication Curriculum for *all* students.

The Elizabeth Forward School District is using creative and innovative technologies to engage students in high levels of learning. The Entertainment Technology Academy, EF Media Center, FABLabs, and the SMALLab are several ways we have redesigned spaces to help students remain excited about learning and provide technologies for their use that will prepare them for future learning.

After seven years of transformation of the school district, the district now has fewer than 10 students in outside cyber/charter schools and has reduced the dropout rate to fewer than five students per year over the last two years. The school district has been named as an Apple Distinguished Program from Apple, Inc. and in 2013, it was named to Digital Promise's League of Innovative Schools.

(Dr. Bart Rocco has been superintendent of the Elizabeth Forward School District since 2009. As superintendent, Bart's goals are to take a small district with limited resources and "make sure that all children have an opportunity to learn and grow in a safe, caring student-centered environment." While he enjoys developing programs alongside teachers and other administrators, he still revels in children's excitement about learning, especially when he has the time to visit classes and teach writing activities. He says, "The students are the best," a belief that informs his work with the district in "providing amazing educational activities for students that will prepare them for the future.")

(Dr. Todd Keruskin joined the Elizabeth Forward School District in Elizabeth, PA, as an assistant superintendent in 2009 after serving for 13 years first as a physics and math teacher and then as a high school administrator for two other school districts in the Pittsburgh region. THE Journal recognized Dr. Keruskin as one of the top innovative administrators in the country, because of his development of a high school gaming curriculum, FABLabs, converting traditional school libraries into media centers, a 1:1 iPad initiative, personalized learning, and founding the Pittsburgh SMALLab Consortium and Pittsburgh FAB Network.)

5 | Making Professional Learning Personal

🔑 Professional learning must be relevant, engaging, ongoing, and made personal.

If we want to change how students learn, we must change how teachers learn.

Katie Martin

A Look at the Research

The notion of "effective professional learning" is something that has been discussed for decades. A comparison in the philosophies of today's school leaders yields results that fall across a continuum of who controls the learning. Although various studies indicate that the top-down, one-size-fits-all, sit-and-get, hours-based approach to professional learning shows little to no impact on student achievement, many districts continue down this path.

For decades, conventional wisdom has been that if schools could just get teachers the right type and right amount of support, then excellent teaching and learning in the classroom would be in reach. According to a report by The New Teacher Project (2015), school districts are spending considerable amounts of money on teacher development, but little of it is actually making a long-term difference. The two-year study of more than 10,000 teachers and 500 school leaders challenges the widely held perception among school leaders that we already know how to help teachers improve and that the goal of great teaching could be achieved if we just applied what we know on a larger scale. Instead of teasing out and testing specific strategies to see if each produced results, researchers used multiple measures of teacher performance to identify those with the most amount of growth and then looked for common experiences or attributes in their professional learning.

They included a broad definition of professional learning experiences to include efforts carried out by districts, schools, and individual teachers. These experiences and attributes were then compared to teachers who did not improve on the same metrics. Conventional thinking might have predicted concentrations of schools where teachers were improving at every stage of their careers or evidence that particular activities were especially helpful in boosting teachers' growth. At the conclusion of the two-year study, researchers were surprised at their findings:

1. **On the whole, school districts are allocating tremendous time and money to teacher improvement.** Of the districts studied, nearly $18,000 per year per teacher was spent on professional learning, with one district spending more on development than on transportation, food, and security combined. Scaling up these numbers, the researchers estimate that the largest 50 school districts in the United States spend approximately $8 billion annually and approximately 19 full school days per year on professional learning. According to these estimates, this means that for every decade spent in the classroom, a teacher will spend a full year on professional learning. These numbers represent a significant commitment to supporting professional growth.

2. **Despite the sizeable investment in time and money, most teachers did not appear to improve substantially from year to year.** Of the districts studied, and with the significant investment of time and money, one would expect to see a noticeable increase in teacher effectiveness. A review of evaluations from this group indicated that nearly 7 out of 10 teachers remained the same as the previous year, with a portion of that group declining in ratings over the two-year period. What was seen, however, was significant growth during the first few years and minimal growth thereafter. The study found the difference in performance between an average first-year teacher and an average fifth-year teacher was more than nine times the difference between an average fifth-year teacher and an average twentieth-year teacher.

3. **In instances where teachers did improve, there was no statistical connection between their growth and any particular development strategy.** Researchers reviewed dozens of variables

spanning the types of development activities teachers experienced, the amount of time spent on them, the mindsets they
brought to them, and the school where they worked. The study
wasn't able to find a common thread that distinguished the
"improvers" from other teachers.

4. **At scale, school systems are not helping teachers understand
   how to improve—or even that they have room to improve at
   all.** Less than 50 percent of the teachers surveyed agreed that
   they had any weaknesses in their instruction. The vast majority
   of teachers in the study were rated as "Effective" or "Meeting
   Expectations" (or higher), whereas the achievement levels at
   many of the schools showed lower than expected levels of student growth. Furthermore, many of the teachers who earned
   lower ratings seemed to disagree with them, with more than
   60 percent of low-rated teachers giving themselves high performance ratings—showing a disconnect between teacher mindset,
   supervisor insight, and student achievement.

It's easy to point to one study and conclude that a particular district's
approach is different or professional learning plan is superior. Although that
may be the case, at least with respect to this particular study, one could argue
that using teacher evaluation rubrics to measure professional growth is not
an effective research method. However, this isn't the only research study
with these types of findings. At least two other federally funded studies of
sustained, content-focused, and job-embedded professional learning had
very similar findings (Garet et al., 2008, 2010).

One might assume that these researchers recommend saving the allocated time and money for use elsewhere, but this was not the case. Instead,
they encourage a radical step toward upending the current approach to
helping teachers improve—from redefining what "helping teachers" actually
means to a systemic overhaul of the professional learning system. Although
particular growth strategies didn't show universal impact, creating the
conditions that foster growth—not finding quick-fix professional learning
solutions—was seen as key.

The New Teacher Project report (2015) identified the following
recommendations:

- Redefine what it means to help teachers improve.
- Reevaluate existing professional learning supports and programs.
- Reinvent how we support effective teaching at scale.

You may be critical of or not agree with how the aforementioned studies were conducted, the types of variables and outcomes that were measured, or the conclusions themselves. Nevertheless, as school leaders, if we are to model professional growth, it is imperative that we avoid the echo chambers and "group think" so prevalent in some educational circles and regularly challenge our own beliefs and mindset.

A report by Linda Darling-Hammond and others from the School Redesign Network at Stanford University (Darling-Hammond, Wei, Andree, Richardson, & Orphanos, 2009), shared the following:

> In an effective professional learning system, school leaders learn from experts, mentors, and their peers about how to become true instructional leaders. They work with staff members to create the culture, structures, and dispositions for continuous professional learning and create pressure and support to help teachers continuously improve by better understanding students' learning needs, making data-driven decisions regarding content and pedagogy, and assessing students' learning within a framework of high expectations.
>
> Teachers meet on a regular schedule in learning teams organized by grade-level or content-area assignments and share responsibility for their students' success. Learning teams follow a cycle of continuous improvement that begins with examining student data to determine the areas of greatest student need, pinpointing areas where additional educator learning is necessary, identifying and creating learning experiences to address these adult needs, developing powerful lessons and assessments, applying new strategies in the classroom, refining new learning into more powerful lessons and assessments, reflecting on the impact on student learning, and repeating the cycle with new goals. (p. ii)

This comprehensive research analysis out of Stanford makes the case that professional learning can have a powerful effect on improving teacher skills and knowledge—and on student learning if it is focused on important content, embedded in the daily work of professional learning communities, and sustained over time. This particular research analysis indicated that when designed well, high-quality opportunities to help teachers master content, refine their teaching skills, and reflect on their own and their students' performance can help address the needed refinement in teaching and learning in their schools. The report cited one study that claimed, "rigorous research suggests that sustained and intensive professional learning for teachers is related to student-achievement gains" (Darling-Hammond et al., 2009, p. 9). It further went on to claim that professional learning programs that offered an average of 49 hours in a year boosted student achievement by approximately 21 percentile points. Other efforts that involved a limited amount of professional learning (ranging from 5 to 14 hours in total) showed no statistically significant effect on student learning, which indicates that to be effective, *professional learning must be ongoing and systemic*. The research base also made transparent the shortfall of the all-too-common one-time workshops that many school systems tend to provide and that generations of teachers have abhorred.

From the research, Darling-Hammond and her team were able to conclude the following general guidelines for developing an effective professional learning model:

1. Professional learning should be intensive, ongoing, and connected to practice.
2. Professional learning should focus on student learning and address the teaching of specific curriculum content.
3. Professional learning should align with school improvement priorities and goals.
4. Professional learning should build strong working relationships among teachers.

The report also reviewed successful practices outside the United States, citing countries that had been recognized as high achieving on international measures such as the Programme for International Student Assessment (PISA) and the Third International Mathematics and Science Study (TIMSS). The research literature and data on professional learning in high-achieving countries indicate that teachers in highly successful nations tend to have at least four advantages over their U.S. teaching counterparts.

Ample time for professional learning is structured into teachers' work lives. In most high-performing Asian and European countries, classroom instruction takes up less than half of a teacher's working time. The remaining time, up to 15–20 hours per week, is spent on preparing lessons, delivering feedback, grading, meeting with students and parents, and collaborating with colleagues. Most planning is done with colleagues in departmental or grade-level teams. By contrast, U.S. counterparts generally are allocated between 3–5 hours per week for planning, which is often spent working alone rather than collaboratively with colleagues.

Beginning teachers receive extensive mentoring and induction supports. In many high-performing countries, teacher induction programs are mandatory, occur over long periods, and tend to emphasize the building of strong professional relationships between new and veteran teachers.

Teachers are widely encouraged to participate in school decision making. In most high-performing countries, teachers are heavily involved in curriculum and assessment development, and they subsequently guide much of the professional learning they encounter.

Governments provide significant levels of support for additional professional development. Beyond the daily professional collaboration opportunities, many high-performing countries allocate significant national resources to professional learning. Some countries have also gone so far as to establish national professional learning requirements. For instance, the Netherlands, Singapore, and Sweden require at least 100 hours of professional learning per year, in addition to the allocated time during the school day.

In addition to these vast differences with international counterparts, the report indicates additional shortcomings to professional learning in the United States. From a lack of funding to not enough pedagogical depth in activities and tremendous inequities within and between districts—and then combined with nearly half of all teachers indicating a dissatisfaction with the opportunities they're given—it's evident that the traditional sit-and-get model must be radically transformed.

One interesting facet of the findings in the United States is that teachers in elementary schools rated their content-focused professional learning significantly higher than teachers in secondary schools, and they also tended to rate professional learning experiences on other topics higher. This statistic begs the question why there's such a dichotomy in attitudes and mindset between elementary and secondary teachers related to professional learning. Overall, the low survey ratings of the usefulness and relevance of most professional learning activities, combined with teachers' low perceptions of their influence on school policies and minimal time to collaborate with and mentor one another, clearly indicate that the traditional professional learning model is insufficient.

David Cooper (2004) identifies four critical research-based components that help teachers learn new strategies and skills: (1) presentation of theory, (2) demonstration of the strategy or skill, (3) initial practice in the workshop, and (4) prompt feedback about their teaching. He goes on to say that for teachers to retain and apply new strategies, skills, and concepts, they must receive coaching while applying what they've learned. In our opinion, these recommendations and findings simply mirror high-quality instructional practices. If it's good for kids, then it tends also to be good for adult learners.

So what can we glean from these comprehensive research reports and their sometimes contrasting findings?

First, the ownership of the learning matters. When teachers feel disengaged or that the professional learning has little relevance to them, then any time spent will have little to no impact. As seen in other countries' successes, teachers must be a vital part of the professional learning cycle and have both voice and ownership in the process.

Second, to be effective, professional learning must be ongoing and systemic—woven into the very fabric of a school's culture. The sit-and-get, hours-based, drive-by model continues to prove ineffective and a waste of precious resources.

Third, although the basic how-tos may occasionally serve as a launch point, professional learning must focus on student outcomes through improved pedagogy—not on tools. Many of today's in-service days and education conferences are wrought with the complete opposite, as sessions such as "30 Apps in 30 Minutes" reign supreme. Although such sessions can be beneficial for exposure in identifying what's feasible, many remain tool-centric and are devoid of pedagogical purpose.

Fourth, high-quality professional learning must mirror high-quality classroom instruction. Consistent, personal feedback over time is what great teachers do. Great educator growth can occur when professional learning follows a similar model.

Finally, and a microcosm to schooling as a whole, relationships are foundational to sustained professional growth. From mentoring and peer feedback to supervision to connections made with grade-level and departmental colleagues, dynamic, trusting, professional relationships remains key to one's growth.

Professional Development or Professional Learning?

Although some may call it simple semantics, we've chosen to purposefully use the word *learning* rather than *development* throughout the book. We believe that learning is at the core of everything we do as educators. In our opinion, it also insinuates something that is in process—something that's ongoing—whereas development has a different connotation. We're not sure educators wake up each morning looking to be developed, and the term itself seems to indicate a defined beginning and end, contrary to what we know about effective professional growth.

Part of our rationale in using the term *professional learning* relates to the mindset and past experiences of adult learners. Professional development has long been viewed as full-day seminars, lectures, or sit-and-get workshops. Traditionally, these experiences have been passive and less than engaging, and they've been focused on the dissemination of information about concepts such as pedagogical theory, subject matter, or the latest technology tool. Traditional methods rely heavily on timeslots, schedules, agendas, and one presenter speaking to an entire room.

As instructional pedagogy has begun to shift in recent years to a more engaging, collaborative model, so too has the understanding of what's possible when creating authentic professional learning experiences. We believe that the term *professional learning* emphasizes a modern approach that is interactive, engaging, and ongoing rather than one-size-fits-all and completed over a fixed time period. The acceleration of technology has made real-time collaboration around the world feasible and has removed the traditional barriers of space and time. Opportunities (such as Edcamps) where all participants have a voice and choice in their learning shift the model from something being done to teachers to something where they form a vital part—where *learning* is the focus.

A Paradigm Shift: From One-Size-Fits-All to Personal

Less than half of the teachers surveyed in the aforementioned report from The New Teacher Project (2015) indicated that their professional learning was tailored to their personal needs or teaching contexts, and only about 40 percent reported that most of their professional learning activities were a good use of their time. What's interesting is the parallel connection between students' levels of engagement and teachers' levels of satisfaction with their professional learning opportunities (Gallup Student Poll, 2015). Putting the Gallup survey and The New Teacher Project report side by side seems to indicate that elementary teachers report the most satisfaction with their professional learning and have the most engaged students. High school teachers report the least amount of satisfaction with professional learning and, on the whole, have the least engaged students. Are these two findings related or coincidental? You decide.

For years, school leaders have pushed teachers to differentiate or personalize instruction in their classrooms, yet they have hypocritically utilized a one-size-fits-all model for professional learning. At a time when school leaders are expecting teachers to make learning more relevant and personal for kids, they must also model the desired practice. So what practices are districts using to make professional learning more personal for all involved?

Personal Learning Networks (PLNs)

The rise of social media has given educators vast, worldwide platforms to connect and network around the clock. PLNs have helped educators connect on curricular projects across continents, seamlessly collaborate across state lines, and form personal networks of educators with the skills and knowledge needed to support their personal growth.

Professional Learning Communities (PLCs)

Now commonplace in many schools, PLCs operate under the assumption that the key to improving student learning is ongoing, job-embedded learning for educators. Throughout the PLC process, educators collaborate in recurring cycles of inquiry and action research. The most successful PLCs have a shared vision, focus on student learning, and are reflective in their conversations.

Instructional Coaching

Made popular in recent years, instructional coaches who can model lessons and provide feedback and instructional guidance by working "shoulder to shoulder" are able to support a more personal approach for staff. Although they require a significant financial investment, a great instructional coach is one of the most effective ways to help shift a colleague's instructional practice.

Edcamps

The success of Edcamps is built on the philosophy that all voices matter, everyone can lead, and—regardless of title—you are responsible for the ownership of your own learning. Gone are the "death by PowerPoint," presenter-centric sit-and-get sessions. Edcamp discussions are learner driven and personal, with each person making relevant decisions to take owner-ship of their own learning. Virtually every weekend, hundreds of educa-tors voluntarily go to an Edcamp for free and receive no remuneration or hours-based credit. Who isn't intrigued by that? Three keys to the success of this model are educator voice, choice, and the ability to influence the day's outcomes.

Communities of Practice

These types of experiences often grow from existing networks and can take a blended form, connecting face to face or online. Driven by the goal of improving practices by collectively constructing knowledge, such practice is deeply rooted in educator collaboration. For example, educators will often initially connect using some form of social media, form relationships, and utilize various technologies to expand conversations, connect regularly, and grow together both in person and remotely.

Playdates

While collaborating at 36,000 feet on a flight home from a conference, Jennie Magiera, Kristin Ziemke, and some colleagues from Chicago's public school system designed a new type of professional learning event called Playdates: **P**eople **L**earning and **A**sking **Y**: **D**igital **A**ge **T**eacher **E**xplora-tion. These events shift the learning paradigm to one where there are no lecture-style presentations, no presenters, and all sessions are designed to be hands-on and learner-driven. They are designed to create time and space for educators to come together and collaboratively explore the ideas and tools they've always wanted to learn more about. During Playdates, there are no presenters in the room and there is no set agenda; there's simply time to play, tinker, and explore. At the end of the day, educators collaboratively reflect and share their learning from the event during a Play Off. (To learn more about this type of experience, visit bit.ly/playdateconference.)

Vertical Collaboration

To promote collaboration, teacher schedules often enable grade-level or subject-area collaboration. However, the notion of "vertical collaboration," where teachers can connect with colleagues in the grade level or course just below and above their own level yields positive results. Although teaching is traditionally siloed by structure, teachers can gain a valuable perspective beyond their own area of expertise as a result of this experience.

Peer Observation

Rarely, if ever, do teachers have or take advantage of the opportunity to observe their peers. Although it requires a significant amount of trust and shouldn't be supervisory in nature, peer observations and follow-up collaborative conversations give teachers insight into different styles, methods, and instructional practices being used by their colleagues. Naturally, teachers often think that their peers teach just as they do, but those who supervise instruction know this is rarely the case. Enabling peer observation and collaboration with a foundation of trust can foster improved instructional practices.

On-Demand Learning Opportunities

Similar to the notion of high-quality digital content that's readily available for instructional purposes, on-demand content for professional learning can support a more personal approach. Whether it supports basic technology skills or promotes an understanding of differentiated assessments, high-quality content that's available on demand can undoubtedly support teacher growth.

Social media and online communities of practice have made anytime, anywhere professional learning a realistic possibility. Combining the traditional face-to-face format with blended and online opportunities yields more growth opportunities than ever before, both for school districts and individuals. The Office of Educational Technology at the U.S. Department of Education (2014a) proposes five "design principles" for integrating blended and online opportunities into professional learning plans:

- Invest in instruction-related professional learning—online, blended, and face-to-face.
- Tap local educator knowledge and experience and further build capacity for leadership in professional learning.
- Identify research- and standards-based professional learning strategies likely to affect teaching and learning.
- Align professional learning strategies with the continuous improvement process.
- Approach the way professional learning works systemically.

School leaders often find themselves looking for a way to create a positive buzz at the beginning of professional learning time, during lunch, or at the end of the day. How can leaders empower their team to share their voice, ideas, and personal experiences? Try these high energy formats:

Lightning Talks. These short presentations, typically 5–10 minutes in length, empower educators to share their ideas quickly and efficiently. The length of the presentation forces the speaker to articulate their message in a concise manner, remain on point, and remove any unneeded information. Due to the fast pace of such talks, the audience is typically able to maintain focus while also being able to hear from a broad array of people with different presentation styles and messages. Sessions where a series of lightning talks occur are sometimes referred to as a data blitz.

Two styles of lightning talks that add additional parameters include the following:

1. **Ignite Talks:** During an Ignite, the speaker has five minutes to talk about a particular topic. During the presentation, each slide advances automatically every 15 seconds, displaying a total of 20 slides, keeping the brief presentation fast and upbeat!

2. **PechaKucha:** In this fast-paced format, a speaker uses 20 slides, which each display for 20 seconds, making each presentation 6 minutes and 40 seconds long. What began as a presentation format in Japan is now used around the world. In some locations, PechaKucha nights are composed of 8–14 presentations focused on architecture, photography, art, design, and education. This format can also be used in a classroom where students have to pitch an idea, present an invention, or make an argument on a particular topic.

Birds of a Feather. Often formed in an ad hoc manner, and relatively common at education conferences, these informal discussion times find attendees coming together and organizing themselves based on a common interest or topic. Birds of a Feather conversations can promote networking opportunities for participants by giving people who share a common interest space and time to connect, share, and collaborate.

Speed Dating. Modeled after the process of getting people to meet quickly in a social setting, Speed Dating as a professional learning activity can help facilitate a quick exchange of ideas among peers and create a place for collaboration and networking—whether there are 10 people in a room or 500. For example, participants may have four minutes to share their favorite digital engagement tool with a colleague before rotating to the next person in line. Participants leave with new connections, new ideas, and a list of things to explore.

Speed Geeking. A format used to quickly view a number of presentations within a fixed period of time, speed geeking is an offshoot of speed dating and is an excellent way to be able to be part of a number of presentations in a short time period. Presenters are spread out around the perimeter of a large venue, and the audience starts in the center of the space before breaking into groups and spreading out to the different presenters. Presenters then have a short period of time, often five minutes, to share their message. After a few additional minutes for audience interaction and questions, the facilitator restarts the timer, and the group moves to the next presentation.

World Café. World Cafés are designed as a forum for open thinking and the cross pollination of people, experiences, and ideas. They use preset questions aligned to a particular theme, but there are no predetermined answers or solutions, and conversations take place in spaces conducive to small-group conversation (such as round tables). Questions guide the conversations, which take place for a set amount of time—often 20–30 minutes. A "table host" may remain to pass on key insights to the next group so they can build on the previous conversation. Graphic representations or collaborative notes are often used to capture the group think. This structured conversational format facilitates open discussion and links ideas, over time, to the larger group to leverage the collective intelligence of the room.

Moving from Hours-based to Outcome-based Accountability

Hours-based accountability, which is the metric that many—if not most—districts use to weigh professional learning expectations, indicates absolutely nothing about the growth of an educator's instructional practice. Similar to the way a student's attendance only reveals his or her location on Earth on a given school day, measuring professional learning in terms of hours, and not outcomes, yields similar outcomes for staff. How many educators can relate to the following scenarios?

During the spring of her fifth year teaching, Paisley, a 4th grade teacher at the local elementary school, wraps up her day. Soon after the bell rings, she rushes to her car to drive across town for a two-hour workshop that she chose from the district's professional development calendar. Paisley's teacher contract requires 18 hours of professional development time, and she needs two more hours to fulfill her contractual obligations. The following month, during her end-of-the-year evaluation, Paisley shares with her principal the list of workshops she attended, the hours she earned, and how she met her contractual obligation for the year.

Caden, a 20-year veteran, drives to the late September district in-service day. Upon entering the building, he waits in line to sign in for the day to verify his attendance. Caden receives his schedule for the day and attends five sessions, three of which are required, and two of which he is able to choose. Throughout the day, he learns various technology tools and has conversations with colleagues about their science curriculum and that year's state testing. When the clock strikes 3:00 PM, he heads back to the lobby to sign out for the day—verifying his six hours of professional development.

Nick, a first-year teacher, wakes up early on a Saturday morning to drive 30 minutes to a local Edcamp. He's heard a few of his colleagues mention how much they enjoyed their last experience, so he decides to check out one close to home. Over the course of the day, Nick helps lead a session and takes part in five others of his choice—all of which are engaging and discussion-based. After talking to his principal, Bella, about his great experience, she responds, "That's great! I have enjoyed the Edcamp experience as well, but unfortunately those hours *won't be able to count* for your professional development this year."

Having workshops and in-service days are not the issue or the cause of outdated professional learning models. If done well, they can be effective and help shift instructional practice. It's the mindset—*the culture*—that professional learning should be measured in hours and that educators need the same amounts of time and the same activities to grow that is outdated, irrelevant, and ineffective.

So why do districts continue to use this metric? It's simple. Counting hours for a contract and making "accountability" based on seat time is easy to calculate. A one-size-fits-all professional learning day is efficient to organize. However, if we're honest with ourselves, to equate seat time and accountability is teetering on negligence. When we measure seat time, we're measuring the wrong end of the learner (Murray & Zoul, 2015). When it's the hours that are systemically most important, it's the hours they'll value.

A report from the Alliance for Excellent Education reinforces this point by urging that schools move toward more continuous and comprehensive professional learning models as opposed to episodic, hours-based, sit-and-get approaches that fail to change instructional practice in meaningful ways (Thigpen, 2014). So how have districts begun to shift away from the hours-based model?

Model the desired outcomes administratively. School leaders who want to shift the professional learning in a district must begin by leading the way. If the focus is always on what "they" (i.e., teachers) must do and not on what "we" can do to lead and model the way, then growth will be limited.

Shift from a checklist of hours to a critical part of the supervision process. Districts that find themselves deciding which hours "count" and which experiences are meaningful enough to "award credit" to often inadvertently discourage personal growth outside of contracted time. Making professional learning a vital part of the supervision process is key. Focus conversations on instructional pedagogy and learning experiences for growth, not the hours obtained or sessions attended.

Institute microcredentials or digital badging. The concept of microcredentials, or badges, is simple, yet it's a paradigm shift for most educators. Similar to the Boy Scouts or Girl Scouts, educators earn recognition for demonstrating proficiency of key knowledge and skills. Made digital, a portfolio of skills and abilities can be created that is similar to a competency-based instructional model. As opposed to sitting in a workshop to obtain hours, badging requires the demonstration of a target content or skill and focuses on the outcomes instead of the hours spent achieving the skill. Badging is also an incredibly scalable endeavor, as witnessed in large districts such as Houston ISD (Texas) and Baltimore County Public Schools (Maryland).

Recognize nontraditional forms of professional learning as meaningful. From conversations on social media and at Edcamps to networking through various digital tools and apps, informal and ongoing dialogue with other educators can be meaningful, relevant, and occur in real time. It is thus an effective method of professional growth and should be recognized and respected by district leaders.

This is by no means is an all-encompassing list. As school leaders continue to realize that the one-size-fits-all, hours-based approach leads to minimal—if any—instructional shifts, innovation in this area will continue to occur. Intentionally designed schools that want to transform learning value the actual learning and shifts in pedagogy *far more* than the number of hours it took to accomplish the outcomes.

Shifting Practice to Shift Culture

You can't add value to people if you don't value people.

John Maxwell

We believe that a relationship can be seen between the quality and the types of professional learning experiences offered. In traditional professional learning models, teachers are given few, if any, opportunities for input or feedback, experiences are typically passive, and the instructional approach of the development is counterintuitive to high-quality learning. In these settings, teachers are often herded like cattle into large group rooms and talked at for hours at a time for a contracted number of hours per year.

Evidence of a traditional professional learning model:

- Decreased teacher attendance on in-service days.
- The experience is fully planned by administration in a top-down approach, with little to no teacher involvement.
- The experience is designed with a one-size-fits-all approach.
- A mass exodus occurs when the required time is up.
- There is little opportunity for teacher feedback on the experience.
- Professional learning is viewed as a set number of hours or calendar days per year.
- Accountability is measured in hours—not in progress or outcomes over time.
- Supervision conversations focus on experiences attended and hours earned—not on the transformation of instructional pedagogy.
- Professional learning is viewed solely as a district responsibility.

In this type of model, teachers can be left feeling as if they are just a pawn in game where they have no control. Mention the words *professional development time* in these schools and you'll see eyes roll and hear painful groans throughout the faculty room. School leaders often give or are assigned to give the directions for the experience and are rarely seen growing alongside the teachers. During traditional professional learning time, responsibility for the ownership of the learning often rests with the person planning and leading the experience. Culturally, this method can easily create an "us-versus-them" mindset and attitude within the staff, negatively affecting school culture.

A more personal and relevant approach to professional learning, however, can have a positive effect on a school's culture. In these settings, ownership for the learning is assumed by everyone, with school leaders feeling an inherent responsibility to model the way.

Evidence of a personal professional learning model:

- School leaders model the desired growth outcomes.
- Professional learning is viewed as something that is ongoing and systemic.
- Diverse, high-quality opportunities are readily available.
- All learning experiences, both formal and informal, are respected and seen as growth opportunities.
- Internal capacity is built as teachers have various opportunities to lead.
- Ample opportunities exist for both teacher and administrative feedback on experiences.
- Administrators and teachers take advantage of opportunities regardless of the obtainment of hours or need for additional pay.
- Teachers have a voice in planning.
- Accountability is measured in outcomes and growth over time— not in hours earned.
- Supervision conversations focus on transformation in instructional pedagogy—not on the attendance at particular events.
- Professional learning is viewed as a district *and* personal responsibility.

When this type of learning culture exists, staff buy-in takes care of itself, and staff members are a vital part of the planning and carrying out of the experiences. All staff have the opportunity to lead, and a growth mindset becomes apparent. In this type of culture, districts balance the need to focus on districtwide initiatives with the understanding that, just like students, teachers have various levels of need and thus require a more personal approach. When teachers feel as if they are a vital part of the professional learning cycle, then increased ownership for the learning occurs—creating a culture shift in responsibility and passion.

Developing a Learning Culture of Ownership and Empowerment

Be the leader you wish you had.

Simon Sinek

Professional learning in many districts must undergo radical reform, from a model that's outdated and ineffective to one that's personal, empowering, and owned by the learner. How can such a culture of ownership and empowerment be created?

Clearly define and articulate the vision. Do all stakeholders understand the district's direction? How should instruction improve with the time that's invested? How will students benefit? Can the vision be articulated by all staff members? Do staff members help formulate that vision? Is the vision only one year or more long term?

Model: Practice what you preach. How school leaders run faculty meetings and in-service time should be a direct reflection of the type of instruction they seek in the classroom. Anything else is hypocritical. Staff will rise to the level that is modeled for them. Learn alongside your staff members and model expectations for them. Utilize time in an efficient and meaningful manner. Invest time in professional learning—not managerial tasks. Model and share your learning throughout the process.

Learning should be anytime, anywhere. Today's Netflix Generation of students expects content to be available on-demand: anytime, anywhere. Today's schools must work to provide a robust, digital curriculum where high-quality content is available around the clock. As such, and to mirror today's instructional expectations, today's school leaders must work to provide and empower anytime, anywhere learning opportunities for teachers. From professional learning modules to social media, opportunities for learning through high-quality digital content must be available for both kids *and* teachers.

Balance districtwide initiatives with the need for learning that's personal. For decades, school leaders have expected teachers to differentiate for students. Nevertheless, the professional learning philosophy has often been the complete opposite of this expectation. With students, the expectation is to meet them where they are or to teach at the speed of learning, yet current practice for teachers is often a far different approach. Maintain a laserlike focus on the vision while meeting the individual needs of staff members through a more personal approach to learning, which happens only by abdicating some control.

Move from hours-based to outcome-based accountability. What's more important: hours or learning? When it's seat time we measure, it's the hours we value (Murray & Zoul, 2015). But is that what's best for personal growth? Districts that have success in this area are moving professional learning to an integral part of the supervision process where teachers have voice, choice, and ownership in their learning. Teachers should work side by side with supervisors to develop goals that specifically outline a plan for growth, both short- and long-term, and then be held accountable for results. Districts must work to foster a culture of professional learning communities, job-embedded learning, and peer coaching to support teachers in the growth process—not limit what counts in the process. Supervision conversations must move from "I attended . . ." to "I learned and then implemented . . ." Nontraditional forms of professional learning such as Edcamps, social media conversations, and the utilization of digital tools and apps to connect and communicate are valuable experiences for educators. We should no longer hear or say, "That doesn't count."

Shift the culture of professional learning. All staff must recognize that professional learning shouldn't be viewed as set calendar days per school year but as an ongoing, daily culture of learning. Professional learning is a personal responsibility. It's not just a few additional days built into a teacher contract or a handful of after-school workshops. Stop spending the time. Start investing it. Do so every day.

Empower staff to design their own learning. Districts have incredible expertise sitting in their classrooms, yet they often underutilize their staff in the professional growth process. Teachers will see value when they are invested in the design process. Find ways to grow teacher leadership and build capacity in your staff. We trust teachers with children every day, yet we often don't trust them enough to help design their own learning. School leaders who are fearful of abdicating some of this control may very well be standing in the midst of a toxic culture.

Solicit teacher feedback. Teacher voice is prominent in all effective professional learning models. Too often, professional development is something that teachers feel is done to them; it's not something they are a vital part of. Districts need to seek out teacher feedback to see what's working, what's relevant, and what areas still need to grow. Is what you're doing valuable in the eyes of your staff members? What do your best people think? Measure the effectiveness of your model by soliciting feedback from all stakeholders on a regular basis. Adjust and personalize accordingly.

Break down silos: Cross-district collaboration. Traditionally, a highway will divide the types and quality of professional learning opportunities that are available for educators. Our imaginary district borders are known to create educational silos, limiting access and opportunity on both sides. Districts that are leading the way in this area are breaking down the traditional barriers of space and time and working collaboratively with surrounding districts to leverage additional and higher-quality professional learning opportunities for all.

Grow your network. Social media and technology tools offer global networks of educators looking to connect and grow professionally—at all hours of the day—yet it's not about the tool. It's about the network and learning community. Students need school districts to break through the confines of traditional borders to seek opportunity. As has been shared on social media by our good friend George Couros, "Isolation is now a choice educators make."

For learning to be transformed, professional learning must be a core value of all stakeholders and must be an ongoing, outcome-based process that is embedded into the very fabric of a school's culture where accountability and responsibility for growth is high. Our students need and deserve this type of mindset.

You are part of the solution.

Innovative Practices in Action

Dysart Unified School District, Arizona
Gail Pletnick, Superintendent
2016 AASA Arizona Superintendent of the Year

In his book *Drive*, Daniel Pink speaks of the three things that really motivate people: autonomy, mastery, and purpose. In this time of high accountability and ever-changing demands on our educators and staff, employees express concern that they feel less in control professionally and do not feel they have a voice in much of what happens in their professional lives. Equally critical is the need to support teachers and staff as we transform our schools to environments where students acquire the knowledge, skills, and dispositions that prepare them for the innovation age in which they will live—rather than the industrial age our schools presently support so well.

To address these problems of practice, the Dysart Unified School District established a team to explore a 21st century approach to staff development that must be supported by an ever-declining budget. That work resulted in an innovative plan named YourCaLL (Your Community as Leaders and Learners). Through the YourCaLL program, staff members apply the skills of critical thinking, creativity, communication, and collaboration to identify and solve challenges faced in the district. Participants have control over their time, the application of their talent, who they work with, and what they work on. The focus is on self-selection and self-direction in a collaborative work environment. The self-designed staff projects build capacity and increase intrinsic motivation for professional learning while resulting in a product that can be replicated elsewhere in the district. This unique Dysart program raises the integrity and quality of teaching and leadership in the district by empowering staff with meaningful professional learning that is personalized, creates a community of 21st century learners and leaders, and supports the vision and goals of the district.

In its first year of implementation, approximately 30 unique proposals were submitted by YourCaLL teams. For the first round, 13 were selected. Success in this beginning stage of implementation was measured by the quality of the projects and the personalized learning opportunities provided through YourCaLL. A bonus for Dysart were the products created that directly supported the district's strategic plan. As this initiative matures, the structure of the YourCaLL program fosters sustainability, cultivates community, and increases leadership capacity both within the program and across Dysart. To learn more about these projects and the YourCaLL participants, please visit dysart.org/yourcall.

Using the YourCaLL initiative, Dysart staff personalize their own professional learning. Control over the who, the what, the how, and the where of their work engages and empowers participants. Just as personalized learning creates a flexible environment for students, YourCaLL creates options for staff. The YourCaLL participant's learning is not defined by the school day or by hours dedicated to the professional learning calendar but rather can be 24/7. Since people self-select the project, it fits their interests and needs. The teams work collaboratively and creatively, using critical thinking and communication skills. This professional learning experience for the adults in the Dysart system exemplifies the personalized learning environment necessary for our students.

YourCaLL will move into its third year, and we continue to build on our successes and add teams. This initiative has had an impact on our mindset around all staff development. We are viewing the options and opportunities provided by Dysart through this personalized learning lens. Our professional learning equation is to start with the end in mind and add the components in any order and in any combination to personalize the journey. In Dysart, we no longer think about what all staff need but rather about what each staff member needs. This relates not only to content but also to how the professional learning is delivered, when staff members achieve common understandings, and who participates in a learning experience. The professional learning needs and wants of the individual are as valued as the needs and wants of the many. This personalized approach to professional learning ensures equity for all staff.

(Dr. Gail Pletnick has been the superintendent of Dysart Unified School District in Arizona since 2007 and was named as 2016 Arizona Superintendent of the Year. She was elected to serve as the 2017–18 president of AASA, the national superintendents' organization, and she serves as the chair of the EdLeader21 PLC Advisory Committee. Dr. Pletnick and the Dysart Unified School District team have received recognition at the state and national levels for their leadership in personalizing education and their work in preparing students with the knowledge, skills, and dispositions to be future ready. Michelle Benham, director of instructional technology; Teresa Heatherly, director of curriculum and instruction; and Kristie Martorelli, a professional development coordinator, collaborated with Dr. Pletnick on the contribution to this chapter.)

6 | Leveraging Technology

> ⚷ **Technology must be leveraged and used
> as an accelerant for student learning.**

Nothing could be more absurd than an experiment in which computers
are placed in a classroom where nothing else is changed.

Seymour Papert

Learning First. Technology Second.

Educational technology is not a silver bullet. Yet year after year, districts
purchase large quantities of devices, deploy them on a large scale, and are
left hoping the technology will have an impact. Quite often, they're left
wondering why there was no change in student engagement or achievement
after large financial investments in devices. Today's devices *are* powerful
tools. At the cost of only a few hundred dollars, it's almost possible to get
more technological capacity than was required to put people on the moon.
Nevertheless, the devices in tomorrow's schools will be even more robust.
With that in mind, it's important to understand that the technology our
students are currently using in their classrooms is the worst technology
they will ever use moving forward. As the technology continues to evolve,
the conversation must remain focused on learning and pedagogy—*not*
on devices.

Globally, we see a trend in which school leaders are rushing to implement technology in the classroom without a systemic implementation
plan or long-term vision for a shift in instructional pedagogy or mindset.

School leaders must simultaneously formulate a shared vision, empower educators to carry out that vision, and develop a long-term sustainability plan. When implemented well, technology can help close achievement gaps and improve learning outcomes, but when paired with 20th century pedagogy, it can be a substantial waste of money (Darling-Hammond et al., 2014). The proper combination of talented, well-trained teachers and high-octane technology can create authentic and transformed learning experiences for all students.

Designing a Robust Infrastructure

The ability of technology to support personalized learning is dependent on a robust infrastructure. Most teachers have, at some point, tried to teach a lesson where the computers take longer to boot than the activity itself, and the idea of streaming digital content is laughable at best. A flexible, robust infrastructure is imperative to provide the needed opportunities for transformed learning experiences for all students (see Figure 6.1). In order for students to be able to effectively leverage technology in their learning through exploration, design, and creation—and for their teachers to be able to collaborate, network, teach, and assess with real-time feedback—the infrastructure must be reliable and the connectivity ubiquitous.

The National Educational Technology Plan of 2016 outlines four keys for designing a robust infrastructure (U.S. Department of Education, 2015, p. 65):

1. **Ubiquitous connectivity:** Persistent access to high-speed Internet in and out of school.
2. **Powerful learning devices:** Access to mobile devices that connect learners and educators to the vast resources of the Internet and facilitate communication and collaboration.
3. **High-quality digital learning content:** Digital learning content and tools that can be used to design and deliver engaging and relevant learning experiences.
4. **Responsible Use Policies:** Guidelines to safeguard students and ensure that the infrastructure is used to support learning.

Designing a robust infrastructure with ubiquitous connectivity is foundational to creating an effective learning environment where technology can

FIGURE 6.1

Infrastructure to Support Everywhere, All the Time Learning

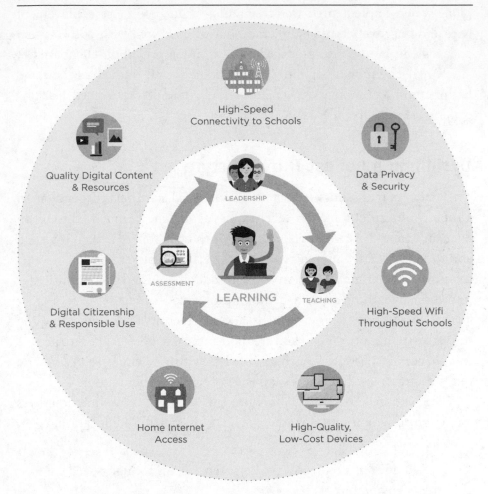

Source: From "Section 5: Enabling Access and Effective Use," by the U.S. Department of Education, Office of Educational Technology, 2015. Available: http://tech.ed.gov/netp/infrastructure

be leveraged and learning transformed. Without such seamless access (or consistent and reliable access to the Internet), students and teachers cannot connect and engage globally or leverage high-quality learning resources.

Although most people consider infrastructure to be synonymous with the boxes and wires found in server closets and networking rooms, it also includes devices used for learning, digital content, and the policies that govern access and use throughout districts. When developing a school district's infrastructure, or when refreshing existing equipment, school leaders should consider the following (Office of Educational Technology, U.S. Department of Education, 2014b, pp. 12–16):

- What is the vision for learning that technology will be supporting?
- What digital tools will be needed?
- What kind of professional learning will teachers and administrators need?
- How much bandwidth will be needed?
- What will the needs of your in-school network be?
- How many and what type of devices are needed?
- What resources are available to fund the transition?

Another large, often overlooked aspect of infrastructure considerations is what's known as interoperability. Quite often, districts will purchase various systems that remain completely separate with an inability to "talk" to each other (i.e., share data between systems). A number of frameworks outline data interoperability standards for different purposes. Districts must consider what programs are in place prior to infrastructure upgrades and should work to streamline the various systems for efficiency in management and security.

The Consortium for School Networking (CoSN) regularly surveys technology leaders through its annual IT Leadership Survey, which provides an overview about how education leaders are leveraging technology and gives insight regarding potential changes in the field. Some of the main insights from the 2016 CoSN survey were as follows:

- Broadband and network capacity was the top priority for IT leaders, replacing assessment readiness as the previous top concern.
- Privacy and security of student data is an increasing concern for IT leaders, with 64 percent saying they are more important than they were last year.
- Nearly 90 percent of respondents expect their instructional materials to be at least 50 percent digital within the next three years.
- Virtually all responders (99 percent) expect to incorporate digital Open Educational Resources (OER) over the next three years, with 45 percent expecting their digital content to be at least 50 percent OER within that timeframe.
- Nearly 80 percent of IT leaders use online productivity tools—the largest use of cloud-based solutions in education.

- District bans on student personal devices are a thing of the past—only 11 percent have banning policies.

CoSN's IT Leadership survey indicates a shift in school technology leader priorities and places a strong emphasis on creating and maintaining a robust infrastructure. To meet the digital demand of redesigned learning experiences, school infrastructure must be working in unison and at maximum capacity. If one or more aspects of the network are underperforming, the digital content and access—and thus the ability to transform learning for all students—will at the very least be inhibited.

Overcoming the Digital Divide: Equity in Access

In a country where we expect free Wi-Fi with our coffee, we should definitely demand it in our schools.

Barack Obama

Bringing technology into a classroom can awaken students to the world outside of it. According to an Alliance for Excellent Education case study of Talladega County Schools (Alabama), when technology is effectively implemented in schools, students become more engaged, are more likely to graduate, attend more classes, and gain marketable tech skills (Hall, Thigpen, Murray, & Loschert, 2015). The case study demonstrates how this predominantly low-income school district dramatically improved student engagement in the classroom and significantly increased high school graduation rates through digitally enhanced, project-based learning. As evidenced in Talladega, such digital learning opportunities hold tremendous promise for students, yet many of today's schools don't have the required connectivity for these opportunities to occur.

The notion of a "digital divide," the term used to describe the gap in access to and use of digital technologies, has been a popular topic of conversation since the turn of the century. Since 2006, metrics indicate that 99 percent of schools have had some sort of Internet connection; however, for many of those districts, the available connectivity has been extremely limited. A report by the State Educational Technology Directors

Association and Common Sense Kids Action indicated that in 2016, 41 percent of schools were still underconnected (Jones & Fox, 2016).

Simply put, students on the "wrong side" of the divide haven't had the same opportunities as their connected peers. For poverty to be disrupted, students must have seamless access to what the world can offer, as connectivity is a lifeline for progress. Fortunately, from the White House to local school districts, the need for robust connectivity for all students has become a priority.

As it relates to the digital divide, schools and students who already have the greatest disadvantage in technology access appear to have another challenge to overcome: the impact hasn't solely been on students but on teachers as well. A report published by the Education Week Research Center (2016) indicates that teachers who are least confident in educational technology tend to work in high-poverty and urban schools. Researchers have found that poor and urban students have consistently been at a disadvantage as it relates to broadband access and the way technology is used, but this report also indicates a gap in teacher perceptions and confidence levels between those working in poor, urban schools and those working outside these environments.

Education Week has reported that only 17 percent of the least confident teachers indicate that their students use devices daily, compared with 50 percent of teachers who feel most confident (Herold, 2016). They also indicate a gap in the use of active technology and personalized learning approaches between these two groups. Examples include

- Parent and student communication tools (37% of least confident versus 49% of most confident).
- Use of digital curricula (17% of least confident versus 47% of most confident).
- Assessment tools (13% of least confident versus 25% of most confident).
- Web-based collaboration tools (13% of least confident versus 23% of most confident).
- Dashboards for student data (16% of least confident versus 27% of most confident).

Furthermore, educators who are least confident indicate they are far less likely than their more confident counterparts to use educational technology for individual and group student projects, educational games, collaborative student work, and research. Essentially, the research indicates that more confident teachers tend to use technology for more effective practices—to explore, design, and create—whereas less confident teachers (higher levels of which are found in poor, urban schools) use the tools less and for less effective instructional practices. Thus, a digital divide exists not just in access but also in teacher confidence levels, which ultimately leads to a wider gap in the effective use of educational technology.

Various supports for school connectivity have been in place for some time. The passing of the 1996 Telecommunications Act signaled the creation of the Universal Service Schools and Libraries Discount Mechanism. As part of this Act, a Universal Services Fund (USF) was established to help schools and libraries connect to the Internet. The USF, made up of four separate programs, is managed by the Federal Communications Commission (FCC) and is funded through telecommunications subsidies and fees passed on to consumers. With each phone and cable bill paid in the United States, USF fees are charged and a portion of proceeds go back to schools and libraries to help fund connectivity. According to the FCC, when established in 1996, only 14 percent of the nation's K–12 classrooms had access to the Internet. This program is commonly referred to as E-Rate.

Over the next few decades, advances in technology significantly shifted the landscape and needs for connectivity in schools. Over time, calls for modernization of the program grew. Updates began in 2010 and continued through 2014 with the adoption of the E-Rate Modernization Order. The FCC took bold steps to update the program to current standards and connectivity needs. The main goal of the 2014 modernization was to close the so-called Wi-Fi gap, and the program began to phase out support for legacy technology services such as web hosting and telephones (Federal Communications Commission, 2014).

As part of the modernization, the FCC also established a variety of connectivity targets for school infrastructure. We believe these updates will prove to have a profound impact on our nation's education system. With significant financial investment and the needed flexibility for district leaders, our schools will be supported in building the robust infrastructure that is needed to properly educate today's learners. High-quality broadband and Wi-Fi are no longer a classroom luxury. Access and connectivity are essential to transform learning and ultimately prepare students for their future. Although great strides have been made to develop the proper infrastructure in our nation's schools, far too many students lose access to connectivity when they leave school campus.

Out-of-School Connectivity and the "Homework Gap"

Trying to navigate today's complex world with telephone service but no Internet access is like using a horse and buggy on the interstate.

Bob Wise

According to the Pew Research Center, of the 29 million households with school-aged children, approximately one out of every six lacks access to high-quality broadband at home (Horrigan, 2015). Almost one-third of households whose incomes fall below $50,000 and with children ages 6–17 do not have a high-speed Internet connection. The data also make it evident that low-income households—especially African American and Hispanic families—make up a disproportionate percentage of the 5 million families without access. Coined the "homework gap" (Rosenworcel, 2015), this means that many of the children sitting in our classrooms lose connectivity the moment they leave school. How does your school handle this issue?

Equity in opportunity isn't something that only affects U.S. school children. The need for connectivity to become a productive member of society has skyrocketed since the beginning of this century. Whether it's continuing your education, applying for a job, or accessing vital information, the ability to connect is critical to take advantage of economic opportunities. As such, government, the FCC, and other organizations have partnered to support those most in need.

In 1985, the Lifeline Program was created to provide a substantial discount on phone service for low-income Americans. At the time, the goal of the program was to "ensure that all Americans had the opportunities and security that phone service brings, including being able to connect to jobs, family, and emergency services" (Federal Communications Commission, 2016a). To participate in the program, consumers must either have an income that is at or below 135 percent of the federal poverty guidelines or participate in one of a number of government assistance programs. In the spring of 2016, the FCC voted to modernize the program and include broadband services for low-income families. This came at a time when 43 percent of the nation's poorest families indicated that they couldn't afford such services. Although it wasn't specifically designed for families with school-aged children, the Lifeline Program and its modernization could bring additional access to millions of our nation's school children. In the years ahead, school leaders should stay up to date with the work of the FCC and changes to the Lifeline Program to see how it may benefit access and connectivity for the students they serve.

Schools are also working locally to close the homework gap, and a number of districts are rising to the top when it comes to innovative connectivity practices. The leadership in the following districts have prioritized this issue and are working to grant connectivity to their students around the clock.

Coachella Valley Unified District in California is a district where 100 percent of the students qualify for free and reduced-price lunch. This southwestern desert community is also known as one of the poorest areas in the United States. Former superintendent Darryl Adams helped put the at-home connectivity issue on the map nationwide. Many of Coachella Valley's students ride the bus for over an hour each way. Simply putting Wi-Fi on buses was not enough for Adams, since when students got home, they would completely lose connectivity. After he noticed that students would park around the district office on weekends to gain connectivity, Adams piloted Wi-Fi on his buses but not just for the transportation to and from school. Adams parked the district's Wi-Fi enabled buses in the poorest neighborhoods overnight so students could remain connected while at home. To address the issue of router batteries losing their charge after a few hours, solar panels were added to extend connectivity. The program began with two buses and will ultimately reach all 90 buses in the district's fleet.

In Washington's Kent School District, equal online access for all students was made a formal priority. As part of the district's Student Technology, Access, and Resources (STAR) Initiative, Wi-Fi enabled kiosks were placed throughout the community in convenient locations—such as apartment complexes, community centers, laundromats, and church lobbies—to support both student and parent access. Students are able to complete classwork, and parents are able to stay up-to-date on student progress at these free kiosk locations. Furthermore, the kiosks broadcast Wi-Fi up to 150 feet, so students can access the school network on district-issued devices.

In an effort to close its connectivity gap, Spartanburg School District Seven in South Carolina (highlighted at the end of this chapter) created a technology-focused website that gives community businesses direct access to becoming a D7 Wi-Fi Hotspot Partner. With such a partnership, students are able to use the district's Wi-Fi hotspot map to seek out locations for free connectivity. The district then shares its Wi-Fi map with the community in an effort to help families get the connectivity they need.

With all of the investments both nationally and locally, many children still remain disconnected while at home. How will your district ensure that those who remain disconnected receive equity in access and opportunity?

Developing a Procurement Process

Traditionally, the notion of procurement has not been an area of strength for school districts. State and local purchasing regulations, combined with a given school district's typical internal protocols, has left school leaders and teachers asking, "Did they really buy that?" A report from the Digital Promise and Education Industry Association (2014, pp. 7–18) identifies the gap between how school and district leaders perceive the procurement process and how providers perceive it. When poor procurement procedures are in place, teachers become frustrated, and the student learning experience suffers.

The report indicates that

- Principals, teachers, and students have limited involvement in purchasing decisions.
- Two out of five providers understand the district's instructional needs and preferred pedagogies.
- Only 29 percent of technology directors trust the credibility of evidence shared by providers.
- Districts rely more on pilots and peer recommendations than on rigorous evidence.
- Only 4 percent of providers agree that ed-tech purchasing procedures meet contemporary needs for product acquisitions.
- Some 37 percent of technology directors indicate that student data privacy and security concerns make purchasing learning technologies difficult.
- Larger districts appear to struggle more with ed-tech procurement and express concerns about timelines and less satisfaction with internal communication throughout the process.

With such an obvious disconnect between providers and school districts, developing high-quality, trusting relationships with providers is critical. Providers should expect to bring verified research and evidence of success to the discussion. District leaders should ensure discussion on learning outcomes, student data privacy, professional learning opportunities, and best practices in implementation. To ensure proper procurement procedures, school leaders should (1) know what they need, (2) discover what's out there, (3) involve the end users, (4) level the playing field, (5) focus on evidence, and (6) design better pilots (Digital Promise and Education Industry Association, 2014, pp. 22–23).

Although larger districts can take advantage of price breaks for larger quantities, smaller districts must often choose from fewer products and services, which in turn drives up prices. With the typical procurement process excluding teachers and administrators, dynamic products and service options often remain unknown. Having teachers and school leaders understand current possibilities is important as policy, technology capabilities, and instructional pedagogy evolve (Katzman, 2016).

For identical devices, however, district purchase pricing is all over the map. The Technology for Education Consortium (TEC) is a nonprofit founded in 2016 to "bring transparency, efficiency, and collaboration to K–12 schools engaged in evaluating and purchasing ed-tech products and services." The TEC (2016) began by collecting and comparing the costs districts were paying for 16 gigabyte iPad Airs with the same standard warranty. In the research done by TEC, prices for the same iPads varied between districts from about $370 to nearly $500 per device. TEC's data also indicated that the prices did not follow a specific pattern consistent with the size of the 40 districts studied and was not connected to the volume of devices purchased (Cavanagh, 2016).

John Carver, the former superintendent of Howard-Winneshiek Community School District in Iowa, uses three fundamental questions that have been essential in building trust with the providers with which his team works. Carver shared the following tips for how his leadership team works through the procurement process (Carver, 2015):

Does the provider understand our core business? Profits, commissions, and shiny features can be placed squarely ahead of learning. Whether it is an LMS, professional development provider, hardware, or software, we listen to whether vendors truly focus on learning. We establish this early on in our conversations with vendors.

How will this solution positively impact my students and the teachers that support them?

Do you have a laser sharp focus on your district's direction? We schools need to define our educational direction and priorities first. Then vendors can be engaged. Exclusively relying on vendors to identify our local needs is not productive. Once defined, trust points are earned with vendors who work laterally to implement change along with us. If you do not know where you are going, valuable resources—money and time—could be wasted relying on a vendor to chart this path for you.

Does the provider put technology before pedagogy? Our mantra in Howard-Winn is: technology should not determine learning; pedagogy should determine learning. After all, pedagogy's Grecian roots mean to "lead a child." Technology is a great delivery vehicle but a terrible leader. Teaching and learning should be driving, while the technology is simply along for the ride. This is our basis for being technology agnostic. No matter what the tool is, learning is defined by the pedagogy. When evaluating vendors, we listen closely to the emphasis placed on pedagogy over features. Does the vendor inquire about our district's learning approach and how we teach? The vendor's solution must complement our approach to learning. We don't need to be told-and-sold how we need to change our pedagogy to use their production/solution. Our focus on pedagogy has made us realize that we can't take a 21st century tool and place it into a 20th century structure and expect our students to be Future Ready.

In an interview for this book, Carver went on to share the following:

The term *buyer beware* is alive and well today as it relates to districts making technology purchases to support learning. Providers are all too happy to sell districts hardware and software and quite often do not have any idea as to what the district really needs. Districts, on the other hand, often get so caught up in the "race" to equip students with digital devices that they make purchases just to keep up with their neighbors.

Districts must take the lead and *not* depend on providers to tell them what they need. Internally, districts need to involve not only educators but also the students in charting the course forward. All stakeholders need to be at the table, engaged in the conversation, with diverse perspectives valued. Pedagogy is not a provider question but the learner's (teachers and students) responsibility. There is no "one-size-fits-all," and a crucial error in personalizing learning is expecting everyone to use the same platform, program, software, and application. Personalized learning needs to be device agnostic, with the learner selecting the appropriate tool, application, or software that meets the learning style and creativity of the individual.

Carver identifies his bottom line as the following:

- Be flexible in selecting devices with no long-term commitments.
- Consider initial purchase cost, service durability, shelf life, memory, and capacity. What is the cost analysis of each device?
- Have a robust infrastructure with proper broadband in place. What good is a device if it cannot connect to Wi-Fi?
- Scope out free applications and open-source textbooks. Only buy as a last resort!
- Have the capacity to remotely control devices for the push out of applications and security is a must.

Designing a Rollout and Selecting Devices

As two leaders in the field who work to support districts with digital conversions, we are often asked, "What type of devices should we buy?" The problem with this question is that it is often their leading question; the initial area that the district is investigating. Districts that are working to purchase devices must not do so to follow the latest fad or because another district across the highway just implemented a particular type of device. All too often, districts lead with this question, when it should be one of the final questions and decisions made in the visioning, researching, planning, and selecting process.

How should a district go about selecting a particular device? We recommend they work through this comprehensive ten-step process to choose which type of device will best suit their desired student learning experience.

1. Create a shared vision for what teaching and learning should look like three to five years down the road. Start by engaging a representative cross section of district stakeholders. Be sure to include teachers from all levels, principals, district office administrators, school board and community members, *and* students. Work collaboratively to answer this question: "What do we want teaching and learning to look like in our classrooms in three to five years?" Use visual organizers and collaborative conversation techniques to clearly outline your district's vision for teaching and learning in the coming years. (Note: The purpose of visioning three to five years down the road is to understand that a pedagogical shift takes time. The goal here should be to identify the teaching and learning you *want to occur* in classrooms throughout the district in the future—not what is currently in place.)

Consider asking these types of questions throughout this step:

- What do we want learning to look like in our classrooms?
- What types of learning experiences do we want our students to have?
- How will we make learning personal for each student?
- What do we want our curriculum to look like?
- What do we want assessment in our district to look like?
- How will we provide anytime, anywhere learning opportunities for *all* students?
- What is our desired student-to-device ratio?

2. Organize and map the core curriculum, resources, and assessments the district is currently utilizing. In a typical school structure, resource decisions are made in silos based on curriculum area, grade, or building level. Too often, few, if any, school leaders have a comprehensive systemwide understanding of what is already in place. During this step, school leaders throughout the district should collaborate to inventory what currently exists, from core curriculum and technology support resources to types of devices already in place. It is to be expected that the average district has dozens, if not hundreds, of resources that could be listed here. The goal is to create an overall map of core curriculum and resources that are regularly used in each area—not to develop an exhaustive list of every website or resource used. Districts must understand what they have in place before they can fully decide where they want to go. Leaders also need to know ahead of time what types of curriculum may not work on particular devices, so having an in-depth understanding of what's currently in place in vital.

Consider asking these types of questions throughout this step:

- What are the core curriculum components for each grade level and department?

- What core technology tools and resources are we currently using in each area?
- What types of devices are we currently using in each area?
- What are the main online content providers that we are currently using?
- Which resources are we paying for and how much do they cost?
- What are our current utilization rates of each paid-for resource?
- Are we using any Open Education Resources (OERs)?

3. Compile and analyze research and evidence. Districts often purchase vast amounts of technology based on little to no research or evidence. It's easy for school leaders to find themselves leaning toward a particular device due to personal use or preference. However, school leaders should press providers on research, evidence, and case studies where the device choice and implementation lead to positive student learning outcomes. Identifying research-based pedagogical methods beyond a provider's marketing material and comparing device capabilities needed to enact the district's defined vision for student learning is paramount in this step.

Consider asking these types of questions throughout this step:

- What research are we analyzing in our decision making?
- What internal and external evidence do we have regarding particular devices?
- What research and evidence can the provider offer?
- How does the research and evidence correlate with our district's vision for teaching and learning?
- Does the information shared by the provider correlate with our independent research and evidence?

4. Assess and understand current infrastructure and broadband capabilities. Year after year, stories become public of districts that purchase a large number of devices without doing a thorough analysis of their current infrastructure or a density study of their current wireless system—rendering devices almost unusable. To understand what's currently feasible, and to avoid a negative implementation experience for both students and teachers (not to mention a public relations nightmare), district leaders must work closely with their technology department to understand current capabilities of the district's infrastructure.

Consider asking these types of questions throughout this step:

- What is our current bandwidth capacity coming into the district and between schools?
- What bandwidth size will we need to implement our vision?
- Will our wireless capabilities and current number of access points be sufficient?
- How many simultaneous devices can our wireless infrastructure currently handle?
- What is our refresh plan for servers, switches, and access points?
- What type of device load can our infrastructure handle at each school?

5. Assess utilization rates and strategize the vision. When district leaders begin assessing utilization rates, they are often surprised by how much they are paying for such little use. Developing a content strategy is imperative, and leaders should begin by prioritizing which tools and resources are currently being used well and which should be removed. It's essential that districts create a flexible budget model in which underutilized resources are reevaluated—and possibly eliminated. Districts should particularly monitor the utilization rates of subscription-based tools and engage in conversations with teachers about what's working and what's worth paying for on a regular basis. The decision making should then move back to the created vision, and stakeholders must wrestle with the types of content and learning tools they will need access to so the district vision can become a reality in the next three to five years.

Consider asking these types of questions throughout this step:

- What resources do our teachers find most valuable, based on the utilization data?
- What resources do we currently pay for that we should abandon?
- Which resources can we negotiate better rates for in the future?
- What types of learning tools and resources might we want to implement in the coming years?
- What feedback have our teachers given in this area?
- What feedback have our students given in this area?

6. Develop set criteria for needed device functionality. What are the nonnegotiables for device capabilities, based on your envisioned student learning experience? In this step, district leaders must carefully dissect functionality needs for the tools and resources they will be using in the years ahead. At a minimum, school district leaders should consider the following:

- **Productivity:** Based on how we want teachers to teach and how we want students to be able to learn, what does the device need to be able to do?
- **Assessment:** What do the devices need to be able to do so we can authentically assess students? What requirements does our state currently mandate for devices used in online assessments?
- **Accessibility:** How will the new devices support our special needs population? Will they provide full accessibility based on the individual needs of our students? Are there particular students with special needs for whom certain types of devices wouldn't work?
- **Ubiquitous Connectivity:** How should devices connect to our network, both on and off campus? What type of device control will we need, and why? Will our new devices be going home with students? If so, what will our filtering policy be? How will we tackle home access issues with a particular device type?
- **Security:** How will we ensure necessary student privacy and security? How can we best protect the device, ensure student privacy, and promote high levels of access and use for learning?
- **Peripherals:** What other technologies (e.g., printers, projectors) do we need these devices to connect to? Do we need to redefine any past practices in this area?
- **Storage:** Will storage be primarily in the cloud or on the device? How will we decide how much storage is needed? Is the need the same for both teachers and students?

7. **Estimate the total cost of ownership, predict refresh cycles, and determine what will be sustainable.** Before spending considerable time on this step, districts must understand what device-to-student ratio is realistic. Since device pricing varies greatly, districts must factor in the cost of the devices they will purchase on top of the "total cost of ownership." They must consider such things as warranty, required software purchases, and so on. Districts must tread carefully when using one-time funding, such as grant money, to purchase devices. It's imperative to ask the question, "When this round of devices needs to be replaced, where will the funding come from?" Districts must get in the habit of taking a hard look at their

technology budget each year and developing sustainable refresh plans for all areas, including infrastructure, devices, and digital content and tools.

Consider asking these types of questions throughout this step:

- Besides the initial purchase, what other costs will the devices have?
- How will we ensure that our refresh plan for infrastructure (servers, switches, wireless, phone system) and devices (student, employee, building level) is sustainable?
- What budget areas will we reduce (or eliminate) if we are going to increase hardware costs?
- How will the devices be deployed and managed? What technical staff do we have (and need) to support this purchase?
- As we purchase more devices, is our cost for copiers, toner, and paper going down? If not, why?
- What is our expected learning return on investment?

8. Pilot, test, and evaluate, soliciting teacher and student feedback throughout the process. Purchasing devices without thorough feedback from students and teachers is an act of negligence. District leaders must gain feedback from those who will be using the tools throughout the learning process. This includes both teachers *and* students. Start by purchasing a variety of types of devices—from tablets to laptops—from different companies. Allow teachers and students to adequately test the various devices in their learning environment, and consider what may or may not be age appropriate. Develop a feedback loop in which teachers and students can share strengths and weaknesses for each type of device. Make sure to pilot the devices with teachers who will provide solid, honest feedback about what works and what creates more of a challenge. Log the feedback in a way that decision makers will have easy access to the information.

Consider asking these types of questions throughout this step:

- What type of feedback are we receiving from our teachers?
- What type of feedback are we receiving from our students?
- Which devices are most age appropriate for each level?
- Which devices will work best with our desired curriculum and assessments?
- How will we plan for personal professional learning for staff?
- What type of training will we need to give students?

- What type of training will we need to give to parents and the community?
- How do the various resources work on the device when it's off campus? How do we plan to support home access and filtering?

9. Analyze, narrow down, ensure compatibility, and plan for scale. Testing a few dozen devices and deploying and managing hundreds (or thousands) of devices are completely different levels of work. As devices are being piloted, the technology team must carefully analyze infrastructure and human capital needs. Teams should log issues that arise and note areas that become more or less manageable with different devices as they project how deployment procedures and device management may work. During this process, teams must ensure adherence to pertinent laws such as FERPA, COPPA, and CIPA (each of which is addressed later in this chapter) as they consider usernames, app management, and resource allocation. Understanding federal and state student data privacy requirements, and having the appropriate privacy policies and guidelines in place, is essential. Once sufficient feedback has been given and the device pilot begins to wind down, planning to scale the deployment becomes paramount.

Consider asking these types of questions throughout this step:

- How will we manage these device types?
- Does our current wireless infrastructure support a mass deployment, or will we need to phase this approach?
- What type of privacy policy do we have in place, or what do we need to develop?
- How will we ensure that we are FERPA, COPPA, and CIPA compliant?
- How will we streamline the purchase and deployment of hardware, software, and/or applications with the various device types?
- Do we need to expand our technology team? If we are sizably increasing the number of devices, how will our team manage the extra time that's needed?

10. Collaborate with other districts, find options, and negotiate the best deal. Technology is one thing that typically gets better and cheaper over time. However, human instinct is often to avoid conflict by pushing for a better price. Leaders making these purchasing decisions should have a "that's not good enough" mentality until they are absolutely certain that the deal they are about to sign is the best offer that they can possibly obtain for students, teachers, and taxpayers. It's imperative that district leaders understand that device quality must absolutely be considered in the decision making. Weighing quality and considering longevity, while ensuring student learning outcomes can be met, is paramount in this step. Districts should leverage or create local, regional, or state consortiums to optimize pricing wherever and whenever possible.

Consider asking these types of questions throughout this step:

- What state and district purchasing guidelines must we follow?
- Where and how can we find better pricing?
- Where do other districts purchase their equipment? Are they getting a better deal?
- Can we join or develop a consortium for better pricing?
- Did we adequately compare pricing, or did we simply purchase what we did last time?
- How are we balancing quality, quantity, and cost?
- When the devices we're about to purchase no longer work, where will the next round of funding coming from?

The process of visioning, analyzing, piloting, planning, and purchasing devices is time consuming and comprehensive. School leaders should utilize this ten-step process on a continuous cycle to ensure they are selecting the best devices for desired student learning outcomes and experiences at a sustainable cost.

The Refresh Cycle

As districts work through the purchasing process, they must strategically develop a refresh cycle for all aspects that make student-centered, personalized learning possible. This includes both core infrastructure, such as servers, switches, and wireless hardware, and office, employee, and student devices. Nothing brings digital learning to a screaming halt like a laptop that takes eight minutes to boot or a continuous rendering while trying to stream a video. In order to ensure ubiquitous connectivity and simultaneous sustainability, district leaders must have a refresh plan that keeps technology devices fresh, enables maximum use, and provides a seamless connection.

Some key benefits to a systemic refresh cycle include:

- Reduced risk of loss of instructional time.
- Increased productivity of students and staff.
- Increased ability to foster the development of needed technology skills.
- Budget predictability in operating expenses.
- Improved visibility and transparency of future upgrade needs.
- Increased network security.

Depending on a district's size, a systemic refresh cycle drives decisions on hundreds of thousands—if not millions—of dollars in annual spending and operating costs. School leaders must balance infrastructure and device spending with operating efficiency, security mitigation, and responsibility for using every budgeted dollar well. When developing refresh cycles, districts should keep the following in mind:

Analyze the hardware landscape. Identify, analyze, and log all aspects of the infrastructure ecosystem. This includes the district core, firewall, servers, switches, data storage appliances, wireless gear, phone system, fiber lines, and district devices. District technology leaders must be in the habit of maintaining an accurate inventory of all aspects of the digital ecosystem.

Predict the life cycle of the various technologies. Balancing the various life cycles of the infrastructure ecosystem can be a daunting—yet necessary—task. With devices needing replacement at a faster rate than servers and wireless gear, developing an 8- to 10-year flexible refresh plan is essential.

Predict replacement and upgrade costs. With the constant evolution of new technologies and cost structure, technology leaders must review approximate replacement and upgrade costs on a yearly basis. Those making purchasing decisions should collaborate with leaders in other districts to ensure their current method of refinement is efficient and cost effective. Staying on top of the latest capabilities is vital. With infrastructure costing millions of dollars, school leaders must continue to press technology departments in ways to do things better and cheaper, while ensuring quality and reliability in the process. From leasing equipment to virtualizing environments to bundling services or working with consortiums, pricing and anticipated need are in continuous flux, yet school leaders must bring stability to the process.

Map the anticipated timeline. Technology leaders must map out the approximate refresh timeline. This ensures long-term planning, which is key to sustainability.

Stay current with federal and state support. Staying up to date with the availability of federal and state funding, in areas such as eRate (Priority 1 and Priority 2), Title 1, and ESSA state block grants such as Title 4, is vital.

Load balance the yearly budget allocation. When it comes to budget, one main goal for technology leaders is to keep costs level. In order to do so, these leaders must load balance their budget according to anticipated costs and timeline. Districts with larger numbers of schools may elect to replace higher-cost items, such as switches and wireless gear, in a phased approach.

Consider the intangibles. As district leaders know, there are certain purchases that occur once a decade at most. Examples include the district phone system and fiber lines. Due to some state laws restricting long-term "saving" for such systems, district leaders are encouraged to work closely with their school boards on plans for the replacement of such systems. This also includes expenses the district may incur due to damage from unforeseen circumstances such as weather-related events. School technology leaders should also work closely with their business office to understand the district insurance coverage for such events.

Beware of one-time funding. School leaders must tread carefully when relying on one-time funding for infrastructure purchases. Understanding that such one-time funding purchases will need to be replaced helps districts avoid disastrous scenarios in the future.

Long-term sustainability of a district's digital ecosystem is essential for student-centered, personalized learning. In order for classroom teachers to leverage technology as an accelerant for student learning, the technology must be reliable and connectivity must be ubiquitous. A systemic refresh cycle that ensures sustainability is essential in developing schools that transform learning.

Ensuring Student Data Privacy

For more than two centuries, student information and data were kept in paper form, often in filing cabinets in a school or district office. During this time, there was little concern over security breaches, improper data sharing, or student privacy issues. Similar to other industries over the past few decades, the vast majority of personal information—for both students and employees—has moved from paper to digital. The move to the digital storage of information has enabled many solutions expected by schools today, including online portals for parents and real-time communication with families. However, the misuse and breach of digital student information has brought data privacy to the forefront.

In 2014, I (Tom) was asked to testify in front of the U.S. Congress, specifically the House Education and Workforce Subcommittee on Early Childhood, Elementary, and Secondary Education and the U.S. Homeland Security Subcommittee on Cybersecurity, Infrastructure Protection, and Security Technologies. A few months prior to the hearing, data breaches at both Home Depot and Target became national news. The congressional hearing focused on levels of access and security and the appropriate use of data by school employees and third-party vendors with which districts partner to provide tools and resources for student learning (Murray, 2014).

Within a few months, the notion of student data privacy went from a topic that was rarely discussed by school leaders to one that was being discussed at length at the federal, state, and local levels. Public concerns regarding student data security and access, as well as new laws enacted at various levels, forced many districts to adopt policies on maintaining and securing student data, appropriate levels of access, and student privacy. For instance, according to the Data Quality Campaign, in 2015 alone, 46 states introduced 182 bills addressing student data privacy, and 15 states passed 28 new student data privacy laws.

Today, several years later, some districts have still done little to no work in this area. These districts remain a few mouse clicks away from finding themselves the subject of national news headlines. Even with proper policies in place, cyber security and human error can still remain an issue. Some examples include the following stories:

- Data breach hits MPISD employees (Borders, 2015)
- Ore. student pleads guilty to hacking district computer (*Campus Security* Staff, 2012)
- Hackers alter students' grades at NC high school, send false transcripts to colleges (Fox 8 Web Staff, 2015)
- Computer system network for Swedesboro-Woolwich school district hacked (Hunter, 2015)
- D.C. accidentally uploads private data of 12,000 students (Stein, 2016)
- Wake schools sent postcards containing social security numbers (WRAL.com, 2009)

Education data are essential to personalize student learning, yet student privacy remains a top priority. With that in mind, the Data Quality

Campaign and the Consortium for School Networking, with the support of numerous other organizations, outlined best practices for school districts and offered the following set of principles to safeguard students' personal information (Student Data Principles, 2014).

1. Student data should be used to further and support student learning and success.
2. Student data are most powerful when used for continuous improvement and personalizing student learning.
3. Student data should be used as a tool for informing, engaging, and empowering students, families, teachers, and school system leaders.
4. Students, families, and educators should have timely access to information collected about the student.
5. Student data should be used to inform and not replace the professional judgment of educators.
6. Students' personal information should only be shared, under terms or agreement, with service providers for legitimate educational purposes; otherwise, the consent to share must be given by a parent, guardian, or student, if that student is over 18. School systems should have policies for overseeing this process, which include support and guidance for teachers.
7. Educational institutions, and their contracted service providers with access to student data (including researchers), should have clear, publicly available rules and guidelines for how they collect, use, safeguard, and destroy those data.
8. Educators and their contracted service providers should only have access to the minimum student data required to support student success.
9. Everyone who has access to students' personal information should be trained and know how to effectively and ethically use, protect, and secure it.
10. Any educational institution with the authority to collect and maintain student personal information should

    - Have a system of governance that designates rules, procedures, and the individual or group responsible for decision making regarding data collection, use, access, sharing, security, and use of online educational programs.
    - Have a policy for notification of any misuse or breach of information and available remedies.

- Maintain a security process that follows widely accepted industry best practices.
- Provide a designated place or contact where students and families can go to learn of their rights and have their questions about student data collection, use, and security answered.

As student data privacy has moved to the forefront in recent years, organizations and companies have worked collaboratively to develop various expectations and guidelines related to student privacy. The Student Privacy Pledge (https://studentprivacypledge.org), developed by the Future of Privacy Forum and the Software & Information Industry Association, was introduced to safeguard student privacy regarding the collection, maintenance, and use of student personal information. The pledge was developed to "concisely detail existing federal law and regulatory guidance regarding the collection and handling of student data and to encourage service providers to more clearly articulate these practices" (Student Privacy Pledge, 2016). School leaders can view which companies have taken the Student Privacy Pledge and make the pledge a point of conversation when working with vendors. Along the same lines, in 2016, CoSN launched the Trusted Learning Environment (TLE) Seal (www.trustedlearning.org). The TLE seal is a mark of distinction for school systems, signaling that they have taken measurable steps to implement practices to help ensure the privacy of student data. CoSN hopes to continue to move the conversation from one that leads with privacy to one that focuses on trust.

Complicating matters for school leaders is the fact that states enact their own laws and school board policies provide additional guidance at the local level. As these federal, state, and local privacy policies evolve over time, it is imperative for school leaders to clearly communicate information about student data and how the district will ensure student privacy. District leaders should consider creating a privacy hub for their community on their school website, where federal law, state law, local policies, and resources for parents can be adequately communicated. Districts must find ways to proactively share such information with parents, and developing a district-specific FAQ for parents is a good start. Consider communicating information such as:

- How does the district use student information?
- What information does the district collect on my child?
- Why does the district collect this information?
- Who has access to information about my child?

- How is my child's information safeguarded?
- What type of security precautions does the district have in place?
- What information is shared with outside providers and why?
- How can I access my child's educational records?

As digital tools evolve, student privacy and safety must remain at the forefront. We recommend that school leaders seek legal advice and work collaboratively with other districts to ensure district practices remain current and mirror federal, state, and local policies.

Federal Laws That Protect Student Data and Privacy

As it relates to student privacy, school district leaders must understand and follow various levels of laws and policies. From regulating online content on the school network to deciphering where districts must obtain parent permission, districts often find themselves lost in a sea of legal acronyms pertaining to the various laws and policies currently in place. Districts must find the balance between encouraging the dynamic use of technology tools, the need for access, and the letter of the law. Although other laws apply, there are four foundational federal laws that affect the use of digital technologies in school districts.

(Legal disclaimer: The information contained in this section does not constitute legal advice and does not contain all of the information, requirements, and exceptions of the various laws. Districts should work with their solicitor for specific questions related to educational law and policy.)

Children's Online Privacy Protection Action (COPPA)

COPPA (15 U.S.C. § 6501–6505) regulates the online collection of personal student information for children under 13 years of age (Federal Trade Commission, 1998). The primary goal of COPPA is to put parents in control of the type of information collected from their children. The FCC, which enforces COPPA, has allowed school officials to act in the capacity of a parent to provide consent to sign students up for online educational programs at school. COPPA allows software companies to track students within their particular program, as licensed by the school district, but prevents software providers from tracking students outside of that environment.

School district leaders must have verifiable parental consent before a vendor (e.g., online provider, app) can collect personal information for any student under the age of 13. This portion of the law is one districts often overlook, especially as well-intended classroom teachers sign students up for data collecting resources independent of the district. When implementing digital learning tools, it's essential that districts have a robust protocol in place to ensure proper parent permission is obtained prior to student information being shared. The protocol must be both efficient and effective as digital tools are imperative in the learning process. Districts with questions regarding this law should refer to "Complying with COPPA: Frequently Asked Questions," the published guidelines from the Federal Trade Commission (2015). For further clarification, contact your district solicitor.

Children's Internet Protection Act (CIPA)

Enacted by Congress in 2000 to address concerns about children's access to obscene or harmful content on the Internet, CIPA (47 U.S.C. § 254) imposes certain requirements on schools and libraries that receive discounts for Internet access or internal connections through the E-Rate program (Federal Communications Commission, 2016b). Schools and libraries must certify that they have an Internet safety policy that includes technology protection measures and that those measures block or filter Internet access to pictures that are (1) obscene, (2) include child pornography, and/or (3) harmful to minors.

Before adopting a new Internet safety policy, schools and libraries must provide reasonable notice and hold at least one public hearing or meeting to address the new policy. As outlined by the FCC, school safety policies must address the following issues (Federal Communications Commission, 2016b):

- Access by minors to inappropriate matter on the Internet.
- The safety and security of minors when using electronic mail, chat rooms, and other forms of direct electronic communications.
- Unauthorized access, including so-called "hacking," and other unlawful activities by minors online.
- Unauthorized disclosure, use, and dissemination of personal information regarding minors.
- Measures restricting minors' access to materials harmful to them.

CIPA has two additional certification requirements (Federal Communications Commission, 2016b): (1) Internet safety policies must include monitoring the online activities of minors; and (2) as required by the Protecting Children in the 21st Century Act, they must provide for educating minors about appropriate online behavior, including interacting with other individuals on social networking websites and in chat rooms, and cyberbullying awareness and response each school year.

It's important for technology departments to have a solid understanding of CIPA requirements. Many districts "lock and block" far more than is required by law, yet districts must ensure adherence to the outlined requirements. We believe that schools should filter only what is absolutely necessary and develop a dynamic digital citizenship program to teach students skills and strategies so they can be both prosperous and safe in a global society.

As important as any law are the skills learned by students to self-monitor their own use. These life skills, which can affect their own safety, are an essential part of the technology use conversation in school. Known most commonly as "digital citizenship," today's modern learners must be able to successfully navigate cyberbullying, privacy, safety, "fake news," and numerous other digital dilemmas. They must also have the proper skillset and mindset to remain safe and make good life decisions. When used properly, learning can be transformed, as technology can help provide incredible opportunities for students to connect and collaborate worldwide.

Family Education Rights and Privacy Act (FERPA)

Regulated by the U.S. Department of Education, FERPA (20 U.S.C. § 1232g; 34 CFR Part 99) protects student privacy by prohibiting the improper disclosure of personally identifiable information derived from education records. FERPA gives parents particular rights related to their child's educational records. Once a student becomes 18 years old, these rights transfer to him or her. Main aspects of this law include: (1) a parent's right to inspect educational records maintained by the school; (2) the right to request that errors in a student's record be amended; and (3) the requirement that schools must obtain written permission from the parent (or eligible student) to release any information from a student's educational record. The law does outline specific cases in which schools may share student information. Examples include school officials with legitimate educational interest, another school to which a student is transferring, accrediting organizations, and purposes of financial aid.

When using digital tools or online educational services, schools and districts must ensure that FERPA requirements are met. To support this process, we recommend school leaders refer to the U.S. Department of Education (2014) issued guidance related to best practices in student privacy and the classroom use of educational technology.

Protection of Pupil Rights Amendment (PPRA)

PPRA (20 U.S.C. § 1232h; 34 CFR Part 98) governs the administration of a survey, analysis, or evaluation of students who are 17 years of age or less. The law's eight protected areas include religious practices, political affiliations, self-incriminating or demeaning behavior, and mental or psychological issues (U.S. Department of Education, n.d.). PPRA also covers marketing surveys and other areas of student privacy, parental access to information, and the administration of certain physical examinations to minors. As it relates to digital learning, school leaders must obtain parent permission before surveying students in these protected areas. For more on PPRA, visit www.familypolicy.ed.gov/ppra.

As districts work diligently to transform learning, adhering to the relevant federal and state laws, as well as local district policies to help safeguard student information, is imperative. Each district policy and practice should promote the dynamic use of digital tools while simultaneously ensuring student data privacy.

Cybersecurity

Every day, businesses, hospitals, government agencies, and universities are targets of wide-scale security breaches, which in turn affect millions of people. From credit card information to Social Security numbers, personal information is scattered around the world. For school districts, outside hackers work to get in, but there are also times when people on the inside cause a breach in the system—from an employee who inadvertently exposes confidential information to a student trying to cause chaos.

District networks are at greater risk than your average business because they are often relatively open, transmit and store a significant amount of personal data, have many access points at multiple locations, and support both district-owned and personal devices. In recent years, the amount of data and devices on these networks have grown significantly, while at the same time, many districts have moved to cloud-based infrastructure solutions. During this time, many districts have had stagnant budgets, yielding limited technology staff and few, if any, dollars allocated toward cybersecurity needs. Passing on safety measures such as network assessments and independent audits may be seen as cost savers in the moment, but doing so could yield dark days ahead.

As it relates to cybersecurity, districts should conduct the following on a regular basis:

- Ensure compliance to federal and state laws as well as to local school board policies.
- Maintain an up-to-date diagram of all electronic district systems (both student and employee), listing types of data contained in each.
- Chart levels of access for each district system, including third-party (vendor) access to student data.
- Categorize and prioritize types of data collected and stored.
- Identify current and needed levels of encryption.
- Conduct a risk assessment to determine possible vulnerabilities.
- Consult with cybersecurity professional, as needed.
- Mitigate identified vulnerabilities.

As cybersecurity issues become more complex, districts must think strategically to ensure the security of the district's network, particularly as it relates to personally identifiable student and employee information. In recent years, a growing number of districts have elected to purchase "cyber insurance"—policies that are geared specifically toward protecting employee and student data, both digital and print, in the event of a security breach.

As district personnel wrestle with cybersecurity needs, they should also work to ensure the following:

1. **Emergency Management Plans:** From security breaches to natural disasters, districts must have up-to-date response plans for possible crises that could occur.
2. **Cross Training:** Leaving all of the knowledge regarding access to a particular system with one person leaves districts one car accident or heart attack away from a districtwide crisis.
3. **Redundant Systems:** Districts often lack redundancy in their networks or, without thought, store primary servers and backups in the same networking room, leaving districts one fire away from losing entire systems.

Intentionally designed schools are as agile as banks when it comes to protecting and strengthening security protocols around student and teacher data. They must also be proactive and up to date in their emergency response procedures and protocols.

Moving from Acceptable to Responsible Use Policies

Concern about student safety while online and use of digital tools is undoubtedly valid. Every educator knows the best and the worst that the human mind has produced can be found somewhere on the Internet. We believe it is our moral obligation as educators to keep students safe, while simultaneously enabling them to create responsible digital footprints. Unfortunately, many school districts' filtering policies were developed before the rise of interactive web tools, social media, and mobile technologies.

We don't want student behavior to simply be acceptable. Neither do we want the digital footprint they create over the course of their lives to only be acceptable. We want students to be responsible for their behavior and footprint. Therefore, we believe that schools should move from "acceptable use" to "responsible use" policies. Acceptable Use Policies (AUPs) are typically written in such a manner that outlines everything a student (or employee) *can't* do. AUPs are often multiple pages long, written in legal terms that few understand, and have little to no relevance to users once they are signed at the beginning of the school year. There is also no possible way to adequately communicate all of the things districts deem inappropriate. Thus, these documents often become vast lists of ways users can get themselves into trouble, followed by an extensive pyramid of possible consequences. Although these policies may satisfy legal requirements, very few people pay attention to the details.

By contrast, Responsible Use Policies (RUPs) typically outline how students (and employees) *should* act. These policies typically promote positive behaviors, expectations, and guidelines. RUPs don't diminish student and employee expectations; they define ownership. We believe such ownership is needed for tomorrow's schools to guide students in developing responsible digital footprints that will follow them for the rest of their lives.

High-quality RUPs

- Lay the foundation for digital citizenship and personal accountability.
- Include input from students, teachers, administrators, school board members, and the community.
- Include school-owned and personal devices.
- Encourage high levels of access.
- Value student and community voice.
- Outline expectations in a positive manner (i.e., "I am responsible for . . .").

- Promote the responsible use of social media.
- Encourage student (and employee) ownership of use.
- Are age appropriate and easy for students to understand.
- Are translated into the languages the school community needs.

High-quality RUPs include information about a variety of areas, such as Internet and software access, e-mail and user account information, filtering and monitoring, privacy expectations, and so on. We believe that regardless of how the plan is developed, districts should work to ensure maximum access, student (and employee) ownership, and relevant stakeholder input.

Boston Public Schools (BPS), which serves over 50,000 students in more than 125 schools, is a district that has worked to customize policies in an effort to make them relevant to students. Students enrolled in BPS are from 135 countries, and approximately 75 percent of all students live near or below the poverty line. As BPS worked to update its policy, staff quickly realized that policy language was not kid friendly, and students were signing off on documents they simply didn't understand. BPS tapped a retired teacher to review policy language and work with high school interns to create student-friendly, grade-level specific policies that kids could understand. In addition, high school students are trained as cyber safety mentors to work with students and the community on Internet safety.

Support Services

In recent years, many school districts have significantly increased the number of district-owned devices in their digital ecosystem. With such an increase in technology, many district technology teams find themselves managing far greater numbers of devices with little to no additional support. Fortunately, as technology has continued to evolve, the role of technology support personnel has also become more efficient. Management consoles, Mobile Device Management Systems, and more robust software solutions have made many tasks more efficient. However, even with such an evolution, districts often find themselves in a position where their technology department is severely understaffed, making it difficult for the required technical support to be in place. A lack in support inhibits innovation and leaves teachers frustrated and without the tools for classroom use.

The best technology departments and support staff have a variety of similar characteristics that promote and enable classroom innovation and personalized student learning.

- **Customer Service Mindset:** Understanding that technology and support staff are in place to enable and support—not lock and block—is key. Having a service-oriented mindset, and understanding that the work of the department is first and foremost to serve students, should be a nonnegotiable. The best support services remove roadblocks and do *whatever it takes* to support high-quality teaching and learning in the classroom.

- **Clear Communication with Stakeholders:** As with any service, there are times when repairs, updates, and orders may take significant time. In these cases, it is vital for support personnel to clearly articulate anticipated timelines and expectations. In districts where support tickets are submitted and no communication occurs for weeks on end, teachers will quickly lose faith in the system and look to circumvent the process. In an ideal scenario, support personnel make some level of follow up within a 24-hour period, sharing any relevant information at that time.

- **Detailed Oriented:** Technology support personnel are often in a position where they oversee and handle millions of dollars in equipment. As repairs occur, orders are received, old equipment is disposed of, and changes are made, it is imperative that proper records are maintained and equipment remains organized.

- **Responsive Problem Solvers:** As teachers work to personalize learning for students in the classroom, they need responsive support to ensure seamless access and connectivity. It's important for technology support staff to clearly outline procedures and protocols and be able to address issues in a reasonable time period. As such, technology support personnel must be responsive to student and staff needs, and they must work diligently to problem solve and navigate issues as they arise.

- **Forward Thinking and Visionary:** Technology support staff must work to stay up to date with the latest technologies, standards, and products. Similar to a teacher working to update his or her pedagogical methods, technology staff must stay current to remain relevant, while always thinking about their decisions in the long term.

- **Cost Conscious:** Being cost conscious and always taking the lowest-priced product are not synonymous. Most districts can probably relate to a time when they purchased something simply because of cost and then later regretted the purchase. The best technology support services constantly look for ways to get more for less. Bundled pricing, consortium purchasing, and constantly evaluating usage rates to ensure a maximum return on investment should be standard practice.

Technology support services can be either great supporters of innovation or tremendous roadblocks. It's imperative that technology leaders maintain a kid-first mindset and work to understand classroom needs *before* making decisions that affect student learning. Getting students involved in the process can also have tremendous benefits.

Leveraging Student Tech Teams

In an effort to support teaching and learning, some school districts have begun empowering students to be part of the support process. Districts are leveraging student capacity in different ways. They're increasing support for teachers and students while simultaneously providing valuable experience for students—particularly those interested in pursuing computer-oriented careers. Some districts leverage student support at the middle and high school levels to troubleshoot basic hardware or software issues. District technology support services must be willing to abdicate some control, yet they still need to set ground rules about what students are able to do independently and where they need to work with district support staff to resolve issues.

School districts such as Burlington, Massachusetts, have witnessed tremendous success with their student involvement, and it's given students additional leadership opportunities while building their technological capacity. Students earn course credit and create digital portfolios as part of a Student Tech Team experience. The student tech team has been a tremendous learning experience for the students of Burlington, and it's also provided additional, no-cost support for teachers and other students, thus benefiting the learning process.

Leveraging technology to support a transformed learning experience is a comprehensive feat that goes far beyond the purchasing of devices. Although robust infrastructure, refresh plans, new devices, and privacy plans may not be glamorous, each aspect discussed in this chapter is vital to the ubiquitous connectivity and access students require and to the sustainability districts need to ensure long-term success.

You are part of the solution.

Innovative Practices in Action

Vancouver Public Schools, Washington

Dr. Steve Webb, Superintendent

2016 AASA Washington State Superintendent of the Year

Vancouver Public Schools (VPS) in Washington State is located just north of Portland, Oregon. Our district enrolls approximately 24,000 students in an increasingly diverse, urban-suburban community. The digital transformation in VPS began with our second-generation strategic planning process, which we call Design II. Launched in January 2007, the process engaged hundreds of staff and community members in shaping the future of our district.

Flexible learning environments for the 21st century emerged as a strategic goal area for Design II, challenging us to think differently about the use of time, space, and technology to maximize learning potential. VPS approached this challenge from a "whole systems" perspective to ensure that our digital transformation was executed in the right way from the very beginning.

To scale this initiative with fidelity and flexibility, we committed to "going slow to go fast." We researched best practices, learned from trail-blazing peers, and developed iterative cycles of inquiry and adjustment. Here is what we learned through our experience:

1. Digital transformation takes time. VPS is in the seventh year of a long-range plan, and we're in the third year of providing mobile learning devices to students in our schools.
2. Starting small is OK. Districts should begin by making strategic investments in infrastructure, well-placed pilots, and capacity building among staff and teachers.
3. Focus on high-leverage, high-yield strategies. To prepare students for their future, we must prioritize giving them access to the learning tools and resources that will promote success in school and beyond.
4. Learning from peers is important, but off-the-shelf solutions are often inadequate. Ultimately, each district's approach is unique to its vision, culture, and resources. Culture trumps strategy every time.

As we work systemically to provide students with personalized access to devices and digital resources, our participation in the Digital Promise

League of Innovative Schools and the Alliance for Excellent Education's Future Ready Schools® initiative has been invaluable. We don't have all the answers, and we can't do this work alone. The League provides a community of practice for diverse educational leaders to advance toward a shared vision of success for every student in America. The Alliance provides a research-based planning and learning tool to build capacity to advance a district's vision for digital transformation. We must develop collective thought leadership around the best practices for improving student achievement.

That's why innovation is not just about the technology. It's about the adaptive skills our graduates need to thrive in a globally connected economy and world. To get this right, educational leaders need to think about digital transformation from a whole-systems perspective and build a culture that encourages ubiquitous leadership and fosters innovation. The goal of creating 21st century flexible learning environments is much more attainable with insight, support, and guidance from peers.

It's also important that what we learn is backed up by what we do. Our collaboration with other League member districts and partners is enhancing our digital transformation: weLearn 1:1. The following are illustrations of how we've leveraged opportunities to learn by networking with colleagues.

- Our friends in Mooresville Graded School District (NC) helped us design, implement, support, assess, and scale up personalized learning environments that will enable all students to achieve college- and career-ready standards. Mooresville's approach to professional learning—instructional technology support, content curation, learning management systems, and resource management—has been integrated into our digital transformation. Above all else, Mooresville showed us the magic that can occur in a culture of learning, love, and leadership.

- York County School Division (VA) connected VPS to the Buck Institute for Education. That relationship helped us launch Vancouver iTech Preparatory, a grades 6–12, STEM-focused school of choice colocated at Washington State University, Vancouver. It also influenced our plans to develop the Center for International Studies at Fort Vancouver High School in partnership with the Asia Society.

- Our district is fortunate to have innovative leaders among our teacher librarians, who are an essential component of our professional learning ecosystem. That's why we've partnered with

Mooresville and Lincoln Public Schools (NE) on Project Connect: a national effort to reimagine the role of the teacher librarian to lead the digital transformation.

- We've learned from pioneering districts such as West Ada Schools (ID) and Utica Community Schools (MI) to inform our blended learning model at the elementary level.
- We've partnered with three visionary districts in the greater Pittsburgh (PA) area—Elizabeth Forward, Avonworth, and South Fayette—to help inform our design thinking as we embark on a capital facility plan that supports the "Maker movement."
- We've used "Wi-Fi on Wheels" to close the homework-broadband connectivity gap. Today, 160 Vancouver bus routes extend learning time for our students. All means all in America's Vancouver.
- Finally, League and Future Ready partners Coachella Valley (CA) inspired Vancouver to scale our vision.

Leveraging learning across similarly focused school systems has enabled Vancouver to scale our digital transformation with fidelity while responding nimbly to new contexts. Vancouver Public Schools is committed to ensuring that every graduate in our community and across America is future ready.

(Steven T. Webb, Ed.D., has served as superintendent of Vancouver Public Schools [WA] since 2008. He was named a 2014 Tech Savvy Superintendent by eSchool News. VPS is a charter member of Digital Promise League of Innovative Schools, and Dr. Webb serves as the chair of the superintendent advisory council. In 2015, the U.S. Department of Education spotlighted Vancouver as one of nine districts nationally in a Future Ready leadership video series.)

Albemarle County Public Schools, Virginia
Vince Scheivert, Chief Information Officer

2015 CoSN CTO of the Year

A young woman with college aspirations that take her beyond her rural life looks at the requirements to complete her application online as a daunting task. For her, getting online means a 30-minute ride to her high school or another public place, since her immediate community has no capability for broadband access. She struggles to complete her application and essay on a hand-me-down smartphone sitting outside the school on the weekend using the school's Wi-Fi connection. This young woman beat the odds and ultimately achieved her dreams, but why did it need to be so difficult? After all, this is the 21st century. As school leaders understand, the virtues of our technological society are not equally available to all communities or every student.

On our superintendent's desk is a wooden carving that says, "All Means All." As educators, if we truly believe that, how can we continue to leave some students with the disadvantage of no Internet connectivity because of the zip code where they live? We knew there had to be a better solution—one that could use some ingenuity and dedication to close this digital divide with wireless technologies.

Albemarle County is geographically diverse and located in central Virginia. Nestling up to our western border is the Blue Ridge Mountain range, and as you travel east, you wind your way through the beautiful countryside of the Piedmonts. In the center of our 726-square-mile county is the urban hub of Charlottesville. This urban/suburban area constitutes roughly 40 square miles. The remaining 680 square miles is lightly suburban but mostly rural. Our urban/suburban areas have broadband Internet access available at a reasonable rate. This works well for the 50 percent of students who live in those coverage areas—but not so well for the other 50 percent who live in more sparsely populated rural areas. Limited access exists, if it exists at all, below the broadband standard. This leaves many students at a distinct learning disadvantage.

Albemarle County, like many school districts, was in the process of formulating curriculum digitalization when we realized we had access to the FCC Educational Broadband Spectrum. This spectrum operates at 2.5 GHz and has the potential to carry large amounts of data when compared to the spectrum used by common carriers. Based on the knowledge that we had a wireless spectrum capable of providing broadband services, our technology department began planning to utilize this resource to bridge or eliminate the digital access gap across our 728 square miles instead of leasing it back to telecom companies as we had traditionally done.

We began by experimenting with different technologies before settling on Long-Term Evolution, commonly known as 4G LTE. Having selected LTE, we shifted our focus to the logistics to achieve a broadband solution.

We tried without success to partner with existing vendors. This led to our search for a more creative solution and partners to bring broadband service to all students. Beginning in the summer of 2015, we began deploying base station equipment at various strategic sites. As of early 2017, this distribution of equipment is providing coverage to 30 percent of the county. Within this new coverage area is a housing community with a large number of migrant residents and economically disadvantaged families. In this densely populated community, which is located in the county's urban ring, we are providing network access via a Wi-Fi connection that utilizes the LTE solution. We now have the ability to prop up hot spots anywhere in the county. In more remote areas where the population is less dense, the LTE solution is providing broadband via a fixed wireless solution.

We will complete our broadband access project by the summer of 2019. By then, *all* middle and high school students will have the same software capabilities for their school-issued laptops, and students will be able to connect to the Internet regardless of their geographical location or the demographics of their family or community. Our ultimate goal will be reached *when all students have the same ability to succeed* in Albemarle County schools.

Recognizing that a lack of service availability in the rural areas affects not only our students but also the public safety capabilities of our county, we turned to our county's public safety departments as natural partners. These departments already owned and operated a number of radio transmission towers strategically located throughout Albemarle. We proposed an agreement: in exchange for access to vertical real-estate on towers, we would provide public safety with connectivity via our LTE platform. This agreement has subsequently saved a considerable amount of money for both of the school division and public safety groups while also increasing services.

For students, families, and those who are served by our public safety departments, *all* will finally mean everyone in every location.

(Vincent Scheivert, the chief information officer for Albemarle County Public School division, has been a leader in the application of state-of-the art technology in K–12 public education classrooms for more than 15 years. Scheivert was the 2015 recipient of the Withrow Award from the Consortium for School Networking.)

7 | Collaborating and Engaging with the Community

> ⚷ Community collaboration and engagement must be woven into the fabric of a school's culture.

Your smile is your logo, your personality is your business card, how you leave others feeling after an experience with you becomes your trademark.

Jay Danzie

A Look at the Research

The correlation between family engagement and student achievement has been studied at length, and the evidence is both consistent and positive. As shared in this chapter, research supports what any educator will confirm: families have a tremendous influence on their children's school achievement. Simply put, when schools, families, and the community collaborate to support student success, students achieve at higher levels, drop out less frequently, and think more positively about their school experience. For learning to be transformed, community collaboration and engagement are essential.

One of the most comprehensive meta-analyses on the topic of school and community connections (80 family engagement studies) found that students with involved parents, no matter what their income or background, were more likely to engage in the following activities (Henderson & Mapp, 2002):

- Earn higher grades and test scores, and enroll in higher-level programs.
- Be promoted, pass their classes, and earn credits.

- Attend school regularly.
- Have better social skills, show improved behavior, and adapt well to school.
- Graduate and go on to postsecondary education.

In addition, the authors identified several studies that found that families of all income and education levels and from all ethnic and cultural groups are engaged in supporting their children's learning at home. However, white, middle-class families tend to be more involved at school, which raises discrepancies related to equity, poverty, and cultural awareness.

The same meta-analysis, looked at the effect of programs and special efforts to engage families and whether they made a significant difference in achievement levels. Several studies indicated that such efforts by the school and teachers do make a significant difference. For instance, teacher engagement and communication to parents were related to consistent, positive gains in student achievement in both reading and math. In researching the correlation between higher-performing schools and success in engaging families from diverse backgrounds, three key practices are evident. Higher performing schools

- Focus on building trusting, collaborative relationships among teachers, families, and community members.
- Recognize, respect, and address families' needs, as well as class and cultural differences.
- Embrace a philosophy of partnership in which power and responsibility are shared.

To summarize their research synthesis, Henderson and Mapp (2002) shared the following:

When parents talk to their children about school, expect them to do well, help them plan for college, and make sure that out-of-school activities are constructive, their children do better in school. When schools engage families in ways that are linked to improving learning, students make greater gains. When schools build partnerships with families that respond to their concerns and honor their contributions, they are successful in sustaining connections that are aimed at improving student achievement. And when families and communities organize to hold poorly performing schools accountable, studies suggest that school districts make positive changes in policy, practice, and resources. (p. 8)

In studying the transition to middle and high school, Nancy E. Hill and Ruth K. Chao (2009) indicate that even though family communication and engagement is often strong in the early years, it tends to decline over time so that by the time students are in high school, family engagement has often fallen off tremendously. Correlating this research with the afore-mentioned Gallup Student Poll (2015) indicates that on the whole, *the longer students are in our education system, the less engaged both they and their families become in our schools*. If we are going to transform learning, then we must disrupt this historical trend.

Also evident in the research is the notion that these engagement trends can be altered. A study of 1,531 low-income, mainly African American children and their mothers living in inner-city Chicago showed that per-sistent encouragement from teachers and other educators at school can act as a lever to reverse the negative engagement trend and promote ongoing, collaborative family engagement (Hayakawa, Englund, Warner-Richter, & Reynolds, 2013). The study indicated a correlation between parent involvement, academic achievement, and children's motivation in one of the nation's neediest communities. Supporting this same notion, Hoover-Dempsey and colleagues (2005) indicated how schools can reaffirm the vital roles that families play and strengthen their feelings of efficacy—both of which increase family and community collaboration and lead to higher rates of student success.

Providing parents with a short, personal message from teachers about their children's schoolwork on a weekly basis has also been shown to increase student performance. A study of teacher-to-parent communication showed that with regular (weekly) communication, parents were empowered to support students' efforts to earn course credit toward graduation (Kraft & Rogers, 2014). The study showed a 41 percent reduction in the number of students who failed to earn course credit. Such teacher-parent communi-cation and engagement shows a definitive effect on students' ability to stay on track as they earn their way toward high school graduation. The desire for this type of parent communication was also verified by the 2015 Speak Up Survey, which received feedback from more than half a million K–12 parents, students, and educators. The survey indicated that 55 percent of parents want to receive text messages from their child's teacher or school, which represented a ten-fold increase from only five years prior when only 5 percent of parents surveyed desired this type of brief communication on a regular basis (Project Tomorrow, 2016). Simply put, collaborating with families in high school is just as important as it is in the early grades, and parents, overall, have a desire for up-to-date, regular communications.

Research also indicated that family engagement was a large factor in where high school graduates choose to attend college and the success they had therein (Smith, Pender, Howell, & Hurwitz, 2012). Evident was the fact that when schools collaborate with families and help them understand the college application process and find a good match, students are more likely to earn a post-secondary degree. We believe this is indicative of the vital role that school counselors play at all levels. In many districts, counselors' caseloads make such community collaboration nearly impossible, as they are often forced to spend more time on managerial tasks and quasi-administrative logistics (e.g., testing coordination) than on the emotional well-being and academic future needs of students. Intentionally designed schools have dynamic guidance departments with counselors who have the ability to lead and better serve students and their families.

In working with thousands of school leaders, we've seen firsthand the continuum of engagement levels and the numerous strategies district leaders use or don't use when engaging with families. As such, it's important for school leaders to reflect on their own experiences and the current methods that schools are using and to identify innovative ways to connect and collaborate with the families they serve.

Parent communication and collaboration should mirror the type of engagement we want to experience with our own children's schools. School leaders must first identify what's possible and then take steps to make it a regular part of their school's culture.

School leaders who intentionally design their schools

- Establish timely, two-way communication and dialogue.
- Create regular opportunities for families to learn together at home.
- Are responsive to cultural differences.
- Work diligently to support families living in poverty.
- Understand that community collaboration is ongoing and systemic—not a few times per month.
- Meet families at their level and communicate accordingly.
- Leverage digital tools to communicate in real time while being sensitive to families with limited or no home access.
- Build trust and relationships to form the foundation of community collaboration.

We have no doubt that supporting family engagement and collaboration is an essential strategy for addressing the achievement gap. All research points to that notion, as do our own experiences as school leaders. Today's school leaders must be intentional in their outreach, communication, engagement, and collaboration with the families and community they serve.

Moving From Engagement to Collaboration

Raising the next generation is a shared responsibility. When families, communities, and schools work together, students are more successful and the entire community benefits.

U.S. Department of Education

In recent decades, what's been referred to as "community engagement" has largely been a one-way dialogue where districts push out information about initiatives and programs to the local community. Once-a-month newsletters, information posted on a website, and robocalls for closures and activities are a far cry from the modes and types of engagement our families need to be a vital part of the school community.

School leaders who are working to transform learning understand that the community is foundational to building successful schools. Therefore, simply "engaging" stakeholders is not enough; similar to instruction, "engagement" can be low level and have minimal impact. Collaboration is not something that only occurs when it's convenient or a pressing need arises. Community collaboration works to challenge the perception of traditional school-community partnerships and is something that is ongoing, systemic, and part of the very fabric of a school's interwoven culture.

The Center for American Progress outlines what it takes to develop "community schools" where school and community leaders collaboratively develop a common vision and strategy for success (Blank, Jacobson, & Melaville, 2012). They outline six key strategies that successful community school initiatives use to build effective partnerships and relationships (p. 2):

1. **Ensure that all partners share a common vision.** The entire community and all involved partners should agree on the same goals and expectations.

2. **Establish formal relationships and collaborative structures to engage stakeholders.** Initiating and sustaining stakeholder participation often requires the creation of structured opportunities, ranging from developing task forces to creating formal agreements.

3. **Encourage open dialogue about challenges and solutions.** To foster shared ownership, stakeholders must engage honestly and constructively with one another to solve problems and make midcourse corrections.

4. **Engage partners in the use of data.** Sharing data enables all stakeholders to understand where things stand and hold one another accountable for making measurable progress.

5. **Create and empower central office capacity at the district level to sustain community school work.** Continued capacity can be created by establishing a high-level management position within a district's central office or by creating an office dedicated to supporting a community school agenda.

6. **Leverage community resources and braid funding streams.** Community schools capitalize on the financial assets of community partners and funding streams to support programs and activities aligned with their common vision.

As schools begin to collaborate with the community in authentic ways—and ultimately create community schools—they should wrestle with the following questions:

- For those in our community who speak poorly about our district, how, where, and why do they do so? What could be done to alter their perception and mindset?
- How can we address the negatives while drowning them out with a continuous flood of positives?
- How do we leverage our community's voice?
- How do we involve those families in our community without children?
- How do we collaborate and partner with local businesses?
- What role does social media and other real-time communication applications play in our collaboration?
- If a community member wants to get involved in the collaboration, how and where could they do so?

- Are there education experts who live in our community and do not work for our school district? How can they join the conversation?
- Do we collaborate with any community organizations that have a similar mission?
- Besides the few minutes at our monthly school board meetings, what regular forums do we provide for community input, feedback, and collaborative problem solving and visioning?
- How do we reach out to our traditionally underserved families to ensure their involvement in decision making?
- How do we ensure innovative ideas are grounded in community values and principles?
- Could the average community member articulate our district's vision? If not, what will we do about it?

In a traditional model of community engagement, districts will "push" their content to the community and there will be little "pull" in return. Community collaboration requires a tactical push-pull balance led by a "do whatever it takes" mindset, so the practice becomes systemic and moves from "share and update" to "create and design."

Investing in Relationships: Building Trust and Transparency

If serving is below you, leadership is beyond you.

Unknown

In many schools, the community,—particularly parents—feels left in the dark. Within their own walls, schools often work diligently to communicate the latest initiatives, results, and grading practices, or they discuss things such as the Common Core State Standards. However, the community is often unaware of such important topics until they hit a friend's Facebook wall, an online gossip forum, or become part of the conversation at the local soccer field. If the community is not aware of or has inaccurate information regarding the latest initiatives and practices, then a sense of distrust and disconnect can easily occur.

The foundation to building dynamic, life-changing relationships with families and the community is *trust*. Gaining the trust of those we serve takes time, yet once established, it can also be shattered in a moment. As school leaders know, it only takes one phone call, one breach of privacy, or a few poorly chosen words to ruin what took years to build—making our communication and collaboration with the community all the more imperative.

Building trust with the community does not happen by chance. School leaders must be intentional, authentic, and genuine while building trust. This also holds true with teacher-student relationships in the classroom. As such, school leaders must prioritize trust building and, in turn, model the desired classroom community to their staff. School leaders who build trust engage in the following activities.

They make child-centered decisions daily. With ongoing negativity about schools highlighted on virtually every news outlet, many families are skeptical of schooling before their first child even walks into a school for the first time. Families must feel that school leaders have their children's best interests at heart and that decisions are made with them in mind, as opposed to what's easiest for adults or a particular interest group.

They are present. Foundational to school leadership is the understanding that we must be present to lead change. This notion doesn't simply refer to our location but mirrors a true reflection of our regular investment in authentic conversations and collaboration.

They display competence. Not much ruins trust faster than a perception that the leader is inept and unqualified to guide the way. This is abundantly evident during each national election cycle when thousands of advertisements and millions of dollars in advertisements are devoted to making candidates seem incompetent and unfit to lead.

They invest in people. School leaders who invest the time and energy and continuously display a commitment to building capacity and leadership in the people around them—from parents to teachers and from coaches to support staff members—will take steps in building long-lasting, trusting relationships with their community.

They create transparency. When the community feels left in the dark or that decisions are being made without their input or understanding, distrust builds quickly. School leaders can create transparency by being honest in all things, communicating clearly, and articulating needs while rejoicing in successes. Schools that create transparency seemingly have glass walls where the community understands what's inside and collaborate on what's to come.

They are reliable and follow through. Actions can build trust or shatter long-standing relationships. Reliable school leaders are accountable for their actions and responsive to the needs of their community. These leaders don't say one thing and do another, nor do they promise something and then not follow through. Reliable leaders are predictable, and there is safety and security in knowing that their words have meaning.

They walk the talk. School leaders who build trust also walk the talk. They are role models for the community they serve, and they lead by example—modeling the desired behaviors and characteristics they want to see from their students. Being human, these leaders will occasionally make mistakes, but they also own their missteps and work diligently to make things right.

They lead with integrity. School leaders who lead with integrity are guided by a moral compass and do the right things for the right reasons, even when no one seems to be watching. These leaders are honest in their relationships with people, and they lead a fair system in which people are treated equitably and with love and respect. They are trustworthy, live the life that they preach, show compassion and empathy for those around them, and lead with servant hearts.

One area where schools have struggled to build trust with their communities has been student data privacy, a topic discussed in depth in the previous chapter. On the whole, we believe that schools traditionally overcollect and underutilize the data for which they become responsible. When we think about the traditional, relatively standard protocol of sending home first-day packets, in which parents are asked to share large amounts of personal family information (much of which the school had in their student information system only a few months prior) and often fill out multiple forms of the same information for each child, we can't help but think how outdated and behind we must appear in the digital age.

Schools that are transforming learning work diligently to build trusting relationships and utilize an empathy lens with respect to the things they ask families to do. Remaining relevant by staying up-to-date and mirroring innovative practices seen outside of school go a long way in building a trust where parents believe their children are in good hands.

Parents and the Community as Partners in the Learning Process

It takes a village to raise a child.

African proverb

One of the most important aspects of intentional design is engaging parents and the community as partners in the learning process. Greater parental and community engagement in a student's life promotes and supports greater student success. The primary responsibility for such engagement falls on the shoulders of school leaders, and their success is rooted in an ability to establish high standards for how they maximize family and community engagement. To be successful, school leaders must develop systemic policies and a dynamic culture that welcomes families, bridges class and cultural differences, listens to parents' ideas and concerns, and promotes fair and open ways to collaborate on improving student achievement (National Association for Family, School, and Community Engagement, n.d.).

Beyond the Bake Sale (Henderson, Mapp, Johnson, & Davies, 2007), which in our opinion is one of the best resources for building parent and community collaboration, identifies four core beliefs that schools must hold in order to form authentic partnerships with families:

1. All parents have dreams for their children and want the best for them.
2. All parents have the capacity to support their children's learning.
3. Parents and school staff should be equal partners.
4. The responsibility for building partnerships between school and home rests primarily with school staff, especially school leaders.

Before school leaders are able to build trusting and authentic relationships with families, schools must believe that parents want their children to succeed and view them as equal partners in the learning process. Thus, we believe that these core beliefs are vital in developing such relationships.

The U.S. Department of Health and Human Services (2011) defines parent and family engagement as building relationships with families that "support family well-being, strong relationships between parents and their children, and ongoing learning and development for both parents and children" (p. 1). In an effort to foster such dynamic engagement, a roadmap known as the Parent, Family, and Community Engagement Framework (PFCE) was developed. Developed in partnership with programs, families, experts, and the National Center on Parent, Family, and Community Engagement, this research-based framework outlines how groups can work together to promote parent and family engagement and children's learning and development.

One of the foundational components of the PFCE Framework is the delineation of parent and family engagement outcomes to support promising child-centered practices such as enhanced school readiness skills, sustained learning, and developmental gains across early childhood education and into elementary school (U.S. Department of Health and Human Services, 2011, pp. 7–16):

- **Family Well-Being:** Parents and families are safe, healthy, and have increased financial security.
- **Positive Parent-Child Relationships:** Beginning with transitions to parenthood, parents and families develop warm relationships that nurture their child's learning and development.
- **Families as Lifelong Educators:** Parents and families observe, guide, promote, and participate in the everyday learning of their children at home, school, and in their communities.
- **Families as Learners:** Parents and families advance their own learning interests through education, training, and other experiences that support their parenting, careers, and life goals.
- **Family Engagement in Transitions:** Parents and families support and advocate for their child's learning and development as they transition to new learning environments, including EHS to HS, EHS/HS to other early learning environments, and HS to kindergarten through elementary school.
- **Family Connections to Peers and Community:** Parents and families form connections with peers and mentors in formal or informal social networks that are supportive and/or educational and that enhance social well-being and community life.
- **Families as Advocates and Leaders:** Families participate in leadership development, decision making, program policy development, or community and state organizing activities to improve children's development and learning experiences.

The PFCE Framework can provide a guide to helping school leaders collaborate with parents and community groups to develop a robust support structure for all students, from birth through graduation, and particularly for those who are traditionally underserved.

Parent engagement and communication do not form a one-way street. A child's education is a community effort and is the responsibility of both the school and the larger community. It's vital that educators understand community values and seek input when making important decisions. The ongoing use of parent steering groups, advisory councils, and feedback mechanisms to provide insight into the thoughts of the community is key. Without being part of the process, it's difficult to be invested in the outcome. Schools that find success in this area understand and respond to the pulse of their communities outside their walls so that learning inside their walls can be transformed.

Family Collaboration and Engagement: A Key to Equity

People don't buy what you do; they buy why you do it.

Simon Sinek

In 2015, 47 percent of white adults held at least a two-year college degree, compared with only 32 percent of African American adults and 23 percent of Latino adults (Ryan & Bauman, 2016). Such disparities often become cyclical in nature. Those with low levels of education most often end up in lower-paying jobs, and some parents have to work two or three jobs just to make ends meet. If we dig deeper and look at families composed of single parents, the statistics are more troublesome. According to the U.S. Census Bureau (2014), almost half (45%) of all single mothers live below the poverty line. More specifically, poverty rates for single mothers are about one in two for African Americans (46.3%) and Hispanics (46.5%), and they're not much better for whites (31.6%) or those of Asian heritage (24.0%). Among all other ethnic groups, American Indian single mothers with children had the highest poverty rate (52.8%). In this context, continuous family collaboration, from birth to career, is an issue of equity.

Also related to equity is the home-school transition. Quite often, children from higher socioeconomic backgrounds enter school with higher average achievement scores than those from lower socioeconomic backgrounds. These gaps can be partially explained by families from low-income households having less access to high-quality preschool opportunities, fewer resources, less social support, and higher family stress. Although these findings are indicative of our nation's major struggle with poverty, schools that foster collaboration and transition activities can help shield children from these risks and minimize gaps. Families with the most economic risks benefit most from home-school transitional activities (Caspe, Lopez, & Chattrabhuti, 2015). Unfortunately, inequities in transition practices remain prevalent, and families that are most in need of transition support are least likely to have access to them.

As we discussed in Chapter 6, it's imperative that we identify, support, and collaborate with those families that have no Internet connectivity at home. As previously mentioned, the Pew Research Center (2015) indicates that 5 million of our nation's children lose Internet connectivity as soon as they leave the school campus. As such, simply placing updated information on a district's website and not communicating the information with those families who don't have access is a practice that leads to a greater educational gap. For learning to be transformed, we must tackle the issue of educational equity head on. If your district isn't sure where to start, consider the following:

- **Identify the need.** Which families are not connected or are underconnected at home? (*Note: Identifying how families connect is key. Some families that live in poverty will claim to have Internet access at home but are referring to a smartphone.*)
- **Seek out available supports.** Collaborate with the community and local nonprofit organizations, and research relevant options for families in need.
- **Design a plan.** Leverage all available resources (including EveryoneOn.org) to design a family support plan. Consider families that speak languages other than English and those that may be undocumented, as additional needs will arise in these areas.
- **Collaborate for understanding.** Families cannot take advantage of an option if they are unaware of it. Use all means necessary to ensure families understand every available option, and clearly articulate the district's support plan, remaining sensitive to each family's privacy. Simply placing resources online for families that don't have access is negligence.

Many families, especially those affected by racial and income inequities and immigrant status, often lack genuine opportunities for school-community engagement. With that in mind, consider the following six family engagement action steps and principles to promote educational equity (Harvard Family Research Project, 2015):

1. Families are fundamental for the well-being of children, communities, and society at large.
2. All community members, especially parents, can direct their strengths to mobilize a social movement for excellence with equity.
3. Families, schools, and communities share the responsibility to work together to raise children with the digital media skills necessary for school and workplace success.
4. Comprehensive educational policies on family engagement are necessary for all children to achieve success.
5. It is necessary to make a shift in evaluation efforts from an emphasis on perspectives from privileged institutions and "experts" to a deeper acknowledgment and active incorporation of different worldviews, including those from cultural/ethnic minorities and economically disadvantaged communities.
6. Parents need support and empowering experiences in order to become advocates and agents of change.

If we are serious about closing the opportunity and educational equity gaps, particularly for our students of color and other traditionally underserved student populations, then we must intentionally design our schools so community collaboration is a foundational thread woven into the very fabric of our educational culture.

Partnering with Businesses and Higher Education

The task of the leader is to get his people from where they are to where they have not been.

Henry Kissinger

When school leaders think about community collaboration, the notion of working with families naturally comes to mind—and rightfully so. However, schools that transform learning go further when investing in relationships to benefit their students. Every business in the United States is located within the boundaries of a local school district. Inside these boundaries is tremendous potential for dynamic relationships that can benefit the local community as a whole. Each school district is unique, with its own culture and context. Intentionally designed schools collaborate with local businesses and higher education programs to create authentic learning opportunities for the students they serve.

Leveraging such aspects of the community shouldn't be viewed as an exclusive benefit for the school district; community businesses need highly skilled workers who are trainable and can thrive in the local work environment. When such workers are readily available (from the school system), businesses spend much less time and money retraining new workers, which in turn leads to higher productivity rates and greater profits. In a similar way, students who are better prepared for local higher education programs are in need of less remediation and enable greater opportunities for the institution itself.

MC^2 STEM High School is located in the Cleveland Metropolitan School District, one of the most economically challenged school districts in the country. In 2011, the average high school graduation rate was just 60 percent. With true intentional design, MC^2 STEM was created through public-private partnerships with a number of local organizations. The intent was to provide students with an integrated, STEM-focused curriculum that was amplified through real-world experiences. Feowyn Mackinnon, the visionary principal of this urban high school, recalls a time, shortly after helping to open the school as a teacher, when every structure they had known was turned upside down (personal communication).

> As part of Cleveland Metropolitan School District's (CMSD) push to develop more STEM-focused schools, MC^2 was launched in 2008. The pillars of this school are STEM, project-based learning, mastery, flexible schedules, year-round schooling, and innovation. All of these things were not taught in my preservice classes in my college education program, and all of these things were the reasons students throughout Cleveland decided to come to MC^2 High School. In planning for the school's opening, we were concerned that "magnet type schools" often end up becoming isolated from their surrounding neighborhoods, because of their themed structure and selective admission practices. We knew we had to do better and our kids needed more.

We decided to open our doors to any student who wanted to attend. There was no entrance criteria, no GPA requirement, and no essay—all we requested upon entrance was an interest and a desire. We existed in a district that had only previously offered large, comprehensive high schools to the 40,000 kids in Cleveland. One hundred percent of these kids were living in one of the poorest cities in the United States, 100 percent qualified for free and reduced-price lunch, and 100 percent were previously told that "you get what you get and you don't get upset" on a regular basis. These kids deserved more options and needed additional opportunities. Thankfully, our district took notice.

We began by brainstorming all of the places in the city that related to STEM subject areas—headquarters of the lighting division of General Electric, the science museum, the colleges—and simply said, "How can we work with them?" Through a myriad of partnerships, which would create relevant, real-world opportunities for students, MC^2 STEM High School became one of a number of new opportunities in CMSD. Our doors were open, our mission was clear, our curriculum was messy by design, and our team was getting its hands dirty every day to figure out a way to make this new approach work for kids.

After the first year of implementation, a large reduction in force throughout CMSD led to all but one team member from MC^2 STEM High School losing their positions for the first half of the following year. It was the will of the staff, the determination of the kids, and our incredible partnerships that sustained our newly created environment and saved it during its most difficult days. The staff and our various community partners accepted the challenge of keeping MC^2 an innovative space for our kids. Our students asked for the education they deserved. They wanted the projects, the hands-on learning, and the challenge. They would accept nothing less. We had to find a way to provide that for them. So we did whatever it took to make it happen.

Today, CMSD has a number of STEM-focused high schools, yet MC^2 is the only school that doesn't require prerequisite courses or minimum test scores for admission. The school serves about 400 students, all of whom qualify for free and reduced-price lunch. Teachers teach all of the subjects required by Ohio's state standards through integrated, transdisciplinary project-based learning. Grading is mastery based, and every student is graded on understanding rather than seat time. Students must achieve 90 percent or above on each learning outcome in order to receive credit and continue to work toward the required competencies, whether it takes six months or two years.

Due to the vast community partnerships and incredible collaboration, students attend classes at campuses embedded in business and college sites around the city—from Cleveland State University to the Great Lakes Science Center to GE Lighting's Nela Park campus. At any given time, you can see students from MC^2 immersed in workshops with tutors from NASA, in mentorship programs with engineers from GE Lighting, or in internships at a variety of local businesses. Relevance and real-world opportunities are prevalent. The student learning experience has been completely transformed.

It's not by chance that in one of the neediest areas of the country, MC^2 can proudly claim a graduation rate of 97 percent and more than half of its alumni completing at least one year of higher education after graduation. Having persevered through far more turmoil than most districts can even fathom, the success of MC^2 comes from much more than mere community "engagement." It has taken true community collaboration to yield their level of success. Using a combination of colocated college campuses, experts from local industries, and collaboration with more than 85 local business and community groups, this school in the heart of Cleveland is thriving.

What businesses are part of the fabric of your community? What higher education institutions are nearby or serve a number of your students after graduation? How can you partner with them to transform learning in life-changing ways?

Digital Communication: Leveraging Real-Time Opportunities

In the absence of knowledge, people make up their own.

Joe Sanfelippo and Tony Sinanis

The days of the monthly classroom newsletter, quarterly report cards, and occasional conferences comprising a "sufficient" form of communication are long gone. In a time when technology makes real-time communication efficient and feasible, schools have the ability to use a mobile app to provide information at parents' fingertips, use communication tools to provide instant notifications, promote access to student progress through online portals, and so on. Intentionally designed schools utilize the latest technology to provide real-time dialogue and communication with parents by meeting them where they are, including digital spaces (Sheninger, 2015a).

Ask parents to find the most recent school newsletter, and chances are you'll get a puzzled look. Ask them to pull up their Facebook feed, and they'll do so at a moment's notice. Looking for a picture? Check Instagram. Schools that maximize real-time opportunities are leveraging various social media outlets—by creating Facebook pages to share news, using Instagram to share pictures, or taking advantage of a hashtag on Twitter to build school pride.

Learning to use social media can enhance your school's public image, your community collaboration, and your ability to transform students' learning (Sheninger, 2015a).

Five Tools to Support Digital Leadership

Digital leadership is about meeting your stakeholders where they are and engaging them in two-way communication. It is also about becoming the storyteller-in-chief to take control of public relations while creating a positive brand presence (Sheninger, 2014). School leaders can leverage social media tools to improve school communication and support community collaboration. Some of the most effective tools include the following examples:

- **Blogs:** Simply put, a blog is a 21st century newsletter. Blogs can provide two-way engagement and enable leaders to integrate multimedia content to make stories pop. There's no better medium for sharing strategies, ideas, and success stories. Platforms such as Blogger, Medium, and Wordpress make blogging seamless.
- **Digital Photo Sharing:** Images can quickly capture and highlight student work, facility enhancements, and student and staff accomplishments. During classroom observations, leaders can snap photos of student projects and then post them to platforms such as Instagram or Snapchat. From an Instagram account, school leaders can easily share photos across other platforms such as Twitter and Facebook.

- **Video Platforms:** Creating a YouTube channel enables school leaders to capture and share learning and social activities in real time. Through tools such as Ustream, Periscope, Facebook Live, and YouTube Live, school leaders can share live school events such as concerts and presentations.
- **Twitter:** Tweets can be a dynamic combination of text, pictures, videos, and links to websites. By creating a hashtag for their school or district, school leaders can share a searchable conversation on any issue with stakeholders. Established hashtags can help gain exposure for positive stories.
- **Facebook:** Facebook can easily become a school leader's digital storytelling hub. Parents, students, alumni, and community members will begin to congregate in this virtual space, enabling real-time collaboration. Leaders can set up pages to support two-way communication, while highlighting the many great things that happen in their schools every day.

As with any digital tool (and as we discussed in the previous chapter), student data privacy is imperative and should be considered before use. However, when used effectively, these tools—which will evolve in the coming years—can help create sustainable relationships as district leaders share their schools' stories.

Developing Your Brand: Sharing Your Story

Your brand is what people say about you when you are not in the room.

Jeff Bezos

Each day, in every school, great things happen. Each day, in every one of *your* schools, great things happen. How does your community know about it?

Branding has been a commonly used marketing term in business environments for decades. Companies such as McDonald's, Coca-Cola, and Disney have brands that are recognized by billions of people worldwide, from toddlers to senior citizens. The most successfully branded companies have slogans that can be recited years later; have logos that are instantly recognizable; and bring about thoughts, feelings, or emotions upon recognition. Intentionally designed schools strive for the same.

In recent decades, companies have worked diligently to develop a digitally recognizable brand to remain relevant. In 2016, marketers were set to spend more than two-thirds (70%) of their total budget on digital marketing channels. The majority of marketers were also looking to increase their social media advertising budgets in the next 12 months, with companies seeing an increased return on investment for their social media efforts. Some 82 percent of marketers also agreed that social media marketing had become core to their business (Hutchinson, 2016). But what about schools? If businesses have spent millions of dollars on research for developing a brand and continue to invest more in online and social media marketing, shouldn't schools do the same?

Developing a districtwide brand is far more than coming up with a catchy slogan, getting people to wear school colors, or handing out t-shirts with a district hashtag. Developing a brand, and remaining true to that message, is critical to building a collaborative community. By developing and enhancing their brand, school leaders can move past misperceptions of their work by providing a necessary reality for all stakeholders to embrace and celebrate. Unlike businesses, an educational brand has nothing to do with selling; it has everything to do with showcasing the work of students, staff, and leaders in an effort to become more transparent and collaborative. School leaders who intentionally design collaboration strategies understand the importance of branding in improving and creating learning opportunities for their students.

If you don't tell your school's story, someone else will. When community communication is poor, school leaders roll the dice, which typically results in a negative story. When community members have little to no information, they will often fill in the gaps with the few rumors or half-truths they hear. Traditionally, schools have not done a good enough job of highlighting the amazing work of staff and students, and as a result, they've paid the price. However, by becoming the storyteller-in-chief, school leaders can turn the tide and take control of public relations. Our stories have incredible power, and we must do a better job as leaders to share them.

The most important and crucial outcome of a brand presence in education is building powerful community relationships in ways that were not possible before social media. Let the amazing work in your school turn perceptions into reality by developing a well-known brand that your school community can believe in, stand behind, and live daily.

Someone is telling your school's story every day. Is it you?

You are part of the solution.

Innovative Practices in Action

Spartanburg School District 7, South Carolina
Dr. Russell W. Booker, Superintendent
2015 AASA South Carolina Superintendent of the Year

Spartanburg School District 7 is located in the heart of upstate South Carolina and is one of seven neighboring school districts in the county. From a birds-eye view, Spartanburg is a growing city with progressive initiatives taking place in every pocket of the community and a populace that's long been committed to advancing educational and professional opportunities for its citizens.

Yet drill down a little deeper and the demographics in our district reflect a deep-seated and lingering poverty that is still widespread in the South. Of the 14 schools in our district, the majority are well over the 90 percent poverty rate—a challenge that took on a whole-new meaning with the advent of technology and the burgeoning gap of accessibility. In District 7's earliest discussions about the importance of closing the digital divide, we came to the conclusion that leveling the playing field for our students was more than a good idea; it was essential to fulfilling our mission to inspire and equip our students for meaningful lives of leadership and service. And so, with a visionary school board at the helm and with support from administrators, teachers, parents, and local community partners, we took the road less traveled and set out to transform teaching and learning (in and out of the classroom) by putting the power of technology in the hands of every single student in grades 3–12.

In April 2013, District 7 launched an ambitious and comprehensive 1:1 program called 7Ignites. As one of the few districts in the state to take such a leap at the time, we knew our leadership on this front would be as broadly assessed as our objectives for student achievement. Today, we can proudly report that our digital immersion has far exceeded our expectations. Our belief that every child should be afforded an equal opportunity to succeed, in school and beyond, has been affirmed by heightened levels of student and faculty engagement, by innovative advances in curriculum design, by notable gains for children with disabilities, and by numerous national organizations that have commended our progress.

In our work to embrace the landscape of 21st century learning, District 7 has been fortunate to work alongside community partners and nonprofit entities equally committed to the success of our students. When we dealt with the challenge of limited Internet access for children in low-income housing, two local congregations stepped forward with innovative solutions (and grant money in hand) to solve the problem. By creating hot spots in their churches, and by offering up kid-friendly spaces for extended learning opportunities, many more students now have access to Wi-Fi during after-school hours. Since then, similar initiatives have followed suit, including a partnership between our local housing authority and national education vendor, Kajeet. Working together on behalf of our children, the two organizations paved the way to place Wi-Fi hotspots in the common areas of four nearby housing complexes. Expanding that effort with a new Wi-Fi HotSpot Partner program, we're inviting local business and retail owners to brand their spaces as welcome places for District 7 students to connect to the Internet.

Although the support of the wider Spartanburg community has been essential in our commitment to blended learning, the most pivotal endorsement of 7Ignites has come from our own employees. Teachers who were fairly new to using technology in the classroom have made it a priority to embrace new curriculum opportunities. Technology integration specialists embedded in every school in the district are coaching, mentoring, and coteaching with their peers, ensuring that day-to-day professional learning advances our ongoing implementation. From IT experts at the district level right on through to teachers in the classroom, our digital conversion is seen by everyone involved as a mission-centric imperative to prepare our students for the world of work. Our objectives along the way have been well received by parents, students, and faculty alike, but perhaps most surprising is the national recognition we've garnered from organizations such as AdvanceED, the League of Innovative Schools, Apple, and Common Sense Media. Pointing to our district as a best practice model, both Apple and AdvanceED have singled us out as more effective than most in leveraging technology to advance student outcomes. Most recently, The Seventy Four, a national nonprofit news group, spent time in the district to capture a poignant story about two of our special-needs students who are making tremendous strides through the added benefits of our digital immersion.

Accolades aside, I'm convinced the district's journey to transform teaching and learning through technology was strengthened by our early and careful attention to the planning process for 7Ignites. Acutely aware that a misstep could result in a costly debacle, we took painstaking efforts to evaluate the pros and cons of moving in one direction versus another. We scrutinized learning objectives and aligned our plans in such a way that every aspect of our work was mission guided.

Were we wary? Yes! But more than that, we were worried—worried that the growing digital divide in our district would be a fundamental detriment to our students. And so, with inspired determination, we challenged the audacity of inaction with a bold decision to champion our children. The payoff has been a powerful thing to witness and an exciting reminder that embracing risk in education is often where the greatest lessons are learned.

(Dr. Russell W. Booker has served as the superintendent of Spartanburg County School District 7 since July 2010. His dynamic brand of leadership has catapulted the district into the national spotlight in recent years and garnered the respect of colleagues far and wide. Named South Carolina Superintendent of the Year by the South Carolina Association of School Administrators in 2015, Dr. Booker has been instrumental in a wide variety of progressive initiatives during the course of his tenure with District 7.)

8 Leading the Charge

 Schools that transform learning are built to last as financial, political, and pedagogical sustainability ensure long-term success.

There are no secrets to success. It is the result of preparation, hard work, and learning from failure.

Colin Powell

The Process of Change

This entire book lays the groundwork for leading transformative change. The eight keys we've laid out in this book, grounded in research and scalable in practice—combined with the words of wisdom and experience from over a dozen nationwide leaders—give you the tools necessary to courageously lead change in your school and across your district. Yet, talk is cheap. If there's one thing we traditionally do well in many education circles, it's that we admire the problems—for which there are plenty. Those who continue to admire these problems year after year will continue to suck the energy right out of the next great idea in your school. It is now time to act.

There is always a great deal of discussion about change in education in order to better prepare students for success, and we have most certainly added to that discussion. The stakes have only become higher as the rapid changes in a globally connected, automated world are far outpacing the changes seen in our schools. The proliferation of technology is making it much more difficult to engage our students in meaningful higher-order tasks. This is not to say that authentic, impactful changes are not evident in schools around the world. Through our work with school leaders, and through various social media outlets, we have seen many amazing examples of student learning experiences that have been completely transformed. The first-person Innovative Practice in Action sections throughout this book have provided compelling examples of how school leaders, regardless of the challenges they faced, have intentionally designed their schools. However, we'll be the first to note that these success stories tend to be isolated pockets of excellence rather than evidence of systemic transformation across an entire system, district, or school. For a full systemic shift to occur, school leadership must model the way. The responsibility is yours.

As seen throughout the book, technology and its use in our schools is only one area that must be addressed. Other elements embedded in school culture cloud our vision about what is necessary and possible. Issues such as the status quo, traditions, mindset, fear, apathy, funding, infrastructure, and time seem to consistently rear their ugly heads. These real challenges morph into excuses that, if allowed, will ultimately inhibit the change process. We often "Yeah, but . . ." ourselves right out of innovative and transformative ideas. Every single school faces these types of challenges on a daily basis. The good news, however, is that these real challenges are not insurmountable. If you feel it is important enough, you will find a way to make it happen. If not, then human nature will help you will make an excuse. The process of change is driven by a desire to focus on solutions rather than excuses. We must be willing to see through another lens and remove our typical way of thinking, to alter our own mindset, and to redefine what's possible.

Change isn't easy, and it certainly won't happen quickly. Many of the best examples of sustainable change have resulted from an organic, grassroots approach. The ability to initiate, manage, and create sustainable change relies on a leader's ability—your ability—to understand it as a process as opposed to an event. This type of mindset takes vision, planning, patience, and perseverance. If sustainable change is the goal, then it is important to clarify the what, why, and how—followed by a clear metric of success.

What

This seems like a simple step, yet quite often, the change process stalls because we identify far too many issues that need to be addressed. Change paralysis then ensues. To simplify the process, we must look at objective data, which should come in various forms. A review of relevant and up-to-date objective data will help give you a clear focus that can later be used to articulate the why. Some forms of data that can help you identify the needed changes are

- Achievement (e.g., standardized scores, local measures)
- Attendance rates
- Graduation/promotion rates
- Discipline referrals
- Facilities inventory
- Technology audit
- Perception (i.e., find out what kids and staff think needs to change)

We must dive deeper and ask better questions to determine what it is that needs to change. We can't simply ask educators in our school or community how well we are meeting the needs of today's learners. Instead, we must ask our learners how well our school is meeting their needs and then adjust accordingly.

Why

Once you have some evidence to identify what needs to change, the next step is to build a broad coalition of support. Aligning supporting research is a sound approach to building a compelling rationale for why the change is needed. This, combined with what the evidence indicates, will build a foundation to move the process in a positive direction. When tackling the why, it is also important to consider the following questions and mitigate potential issues while providing a greater focus:

- Why have previous transformation attempts not been sustainable in our school?
- What are other schools in our region doing to move the needle?
- Are we meeting the needs of today's modern learners and preparing them for their future? How can we improve in doing so?

How

This is where you need to roll up your sleeves and be prepared to get dirty. Change rarely succeeds through top-down mandates, directives, buy-ins, or unilateral decisions. Creating a process that involves an honest feedback loop and building consensus are imperative. Forming a comprehensive, inclusive leadership group that includes key naysayers, antagonists, and resistors, as well as those who are already working to lead the change, is key. Naysayers cannot continue to be a part of the problem; they must be active contributors to a solution. Continuously leaving them on the sidelines will only promote their desire to undermine the change process. Present the evidence and supporting research, and work together to build a shared vision and strategic plan for the identified change. These groups must be part of the solution; if they aren't, long-term, sustainable change will be difficult, if not impossible. As the leader, you must be prepared to make some tough decisions along the way. Your students need you to be strong and have the courage to do what it takes.

Success

Over time, a strategic plan for change should bear positive results. If the expected results are not obtained, take time to reflect and reevaluate to improve your outcomes rather than simply scrapping the idea and giving up.

This change process recipe can be applied to virtually any initiative, from a district's homework policy to a mobile learning rollout or changes with the school schedule. Courageous leadership and the perseverance to continually improve are critical to creating a better learning culture for all students and ultimately, to transform learning.

Actions over Opinions

Action expresses priorities.

Mahatma Gandhi

Seemingly everyone has an opinion as to what needs to change in education. *Change* and *reform* have undoubtedly become two of the most overused educational buzzwords in recent years. In fact, as we shared in the Introduction, there has been a call for change in education in the United States since the founding of the nation. Today, you can hear conversations about change in schools, during face-to-face conversations with educators, at the dinner table, and—most emphatically—in social media spaces. Virtually all of these conversations have some merit to them. It goes without saying that education, schools, and professional practice need to change in order to provide learners with the necessary skill sets to succeed in the future. As the world evolves, so too must the system that prepares people for it. This type of change is no easy feat.

Since the overall structure and function of schools have remained relatively unchanged for nearly a century, there is a great deal of work that must be done to redesign the learning experience at scale. This, combined with the onslaught of reforms and mandates enacted by individuals who have no business trying to "reform" education, make the process of actually enacting the needed change much more difficult. We must persevere for the students we serve. There is no other option.

Today's conversations regarding change are a dime a dozen. Within these conversations, there are an endless array of opinions about what needs to happen for change to occur. In some of these same conversations, suggestions about how to implement the change are given. Opinions, suggestions, ideas, and even strategies are great to discuss—in theory. These discussions can make for great conversational catalysts. However, simply offering your opinion and stating what should be done falls short of the intended outcome. Real, meaningful, and sustainable change that is capable of transforming schools and school culture comes from taking action in ways identified throughout this book—not just by talking about it. The time to act is now!

Your leadership must not be defined by the title on your business card but by the actions you take to create meaningful, authentic, transformed learning experiences for every student you serve. Every school leader has the capacity to lead, but initiating sustainable change hinges on one's ability to move from talk and rhetoric to action. The process seems simple to those who get caught up in the constant conversation, but change leaders understand the many challenges associated with what may be the most difficult thing to do in education. We believe that change leadership focuses on these specific elements:

- Identifying the problem and articulating why the change is needed.
- Developing a plan of action to provide stakeholders with a sense of how to effectively implement needed changes.
- Ensuring all support structures are in place to increase the success of the initiative so it becomes sustainable.

- Implementing the plan through action and monitoring the process throughout.
- Evaluating and providing indicators of success. If the change process fails, then reflection is paramount in order to improve the plan.

We encourage you to reflect on these elements the next time you engage in a conversation about change or school transformation. How will you empower others to become change leaders to help create schools that better work for kids? The world is full of opinions but is lacking in the definitive actions that are needed to transform teaching, learning, and leadership. Be the change you wish to see in education—through your actions, not just your words. The time is now.

Against the Flow Leadership

If you think you can or you think you can't, you're right.

Zig Ziglar

We have discussed the need for change, along with proven strategies that lead to success, throughout this book. It's important to remember that change is uncomfortable, which is why this book is grounded in an array of applicable strategies aligned to research- and evidence-based results. We absolutely agree that the process is not absent of difficult challenges. Sustainable change becomes even more difficult when the main adversary is the one we see every morning in the mirror. It is our own mindset, which can at times work against our own best intentions. Instead of taking risks, we often naturally revert back to playing it safe. As fear takes hold and we become uncomfortable, it's natural to retreat to safety—as humans, our brains are hardwired with this failsafe mechanism. Therefore, what was built to protect us in nature can easily hold us back from implementing innovative ideas that can transform learning for kids.

In many cases, human nature compels us to take the easiest possible path to success. As we know, structures are often put in place that make it difficult to deviate from a prescribed path, especially in a centuries-old K–12 education structure. It is easy to go with the flow and follow the crowd if success has already been defined for us. In recent decades, the mindset of many educators and stakeholders has been that a successful school or district is one that achieves through quantitative measures. Over time, institutional practices that have historically been implemented and sustained for the sole purpose of preserving the status quo have become a detriment. As such, past practice might be the single most negative factor perpetuated by fixed mindsets, as seen in the notion "We've always done it this way." We can do better. We must do better.

In order to improve on our current practice, we must reflect on past practice. Courageous leadership involves going against the flow and using fear as a catalyst to face and rise above challenges. Instead of enabling the status quo to dictate the learning culture of a school, critical reflection is employed to disrupt professional practice, grow, and improve. This requires us to ask some difficult questions. Leaders who choose to lead against the flow ask these types of critical questions about their school's learning culture:

- How well are we meeting the needs of today's modern learners?
- How does a particular policy positively affect student learning? If it doesn't, then why is precious time spent developing and enforcing it?
- Do our policies reflect our desired learning outcomes?
- Are we more concerned about traditional grading practices or about learning?
- Does the homework assigned at our school improve learner outcomes? How do we know?
- How does the current supervision process of observation and evaluation ensure accountability while improving instruction and leadership?
- How do we know that our investments in educational technology are actually improving student learning and achievement? What supporting evidence do we have?
- How are our teachers empowered, supported, and encouraged to lead?
- Do we hold ourselves accountable for implementing ideas and strategies learned through professional learning?
- How do I as a leader model what I'm asking from my staff?
- How do I personally affect the culture of my school?

These are the types of questions that not only enable us to reflect but also force us to objectively evaluate what is and isn't working in our schools. Systemwide, there are a number of aspects of a traditional school culture that are broken and can no longer be ignored. Examples include traditional grading metrics, the use of homework, hours-based professional learning, digital drill and kill, prohibitive policies, and the traditional supervision process. Ingrained over time, these traditional compliance-driven systems create a learning culture that will not adequately prepare students for their future. It is our responsibility to lead the change!

What is encouraging, however, is the great number of high-octane leaders who are swimming against the flow, fighting the current, navigating the waters, and doing so daily to intentionally design the schools kids need. These leaders are transforming learning in their schools.

Are you one of them?

Designing a Plan for Transformation

You don't have to have it all figured out to move forward.

Unknown

Transformation begins with you. To be part of the solution, your transformation must begin from within. Transformative change begins with a spark, a passion, or the deep desire to do whatever it takes to achieve a more meaningful outcome.

Change at the individual level is also where it is sustained so it can become embedded in a school's or district's culture. All educators and students must believe they have the capacity to lead change—*and be empowered to do so*. School leaders can support such empowerment by removing barriers to the change process, eradicating the fear of failure, providing autonomy, and enabling teachers to drive change at the classroom level. As a school leader, your hardest but most gratifying work may be the ability to empower your colleagues to take risks and change.

Several conditions for leading and managing complex change are put forward in what has widely become known as Knoster's Model (Knoster, Villa, & Thousand, 2000). This model explores and dissects existing organizational change models to create a simple tool that can be used by school leaders to drive sustained, programmatic change. In short, if a school or district has a well-articulated vision, the needed skills, appropriate incentives, adequate resources, and an aligned plan, then complex change can occur.

Vision + skills + incentives + resources + an action plan = sustainable change. If any one of the components for managing complex change is not present, then the change process may be inhibited or lead to issues of confusion, anxiety, resistance, frustration, or a feeling that the organization is simply running on a treadmill. Do any of these symptoms sound familiar?

We believe that school leaders can identify symptoms present in their school culture and subsequently use this model to objectively understand what is stifling the transformation. Although the model may seem simplistic, it is a powerful lens through which we can link symptoms present in a school with components of managing complex change. To do this, let's flip the model and begin with the outcomes.

Confusion can be the result of a lack of vision. When many staff members are confused, the vision may be missing or have been communicated poorly. The question of "Why are we doing this?" is a direct indication of a muddied vision. We should note that it is possible for a leader to have a dynamic vision, but when it's communicated poorly, confusion still ensues.

Anxiety can be the byproduct of a missing skillset. We believe that by nature, many teachers are perfectionists. They want to do well. They want their students to be successful. Nevertheless, when leaders ask them to change, a feeling of anxiety can occur if they don't think they have the skills needed to obtain the new outcome. An overabundance of anxiety will undoubtedly stifle growth and innovation.

Resistance can derive from a lack of incentives. Every school leader has worked with resistant staff members at some point in their careers. Personal desires and mindsets set the tone, and incentives help provide a compelling reason to change. Seeing student success with the use of a new method can provide the needed incentive to change one's own practice. This area can also be indicative of the "What's in it for me?" question and mindset.

Frustration will occur when there is a lack of needed resources. We have all wanted to initiate something but have been unable to do so because of missing resources. This may come from financial struggles, but it can also come from something such as a lack of time. In these cases, we may know what we want to do, but we don't have the capacity to get it accomplished without additional resources.

Running the treadmill can be a result of not having a systemic action plan. Passionate leaders with a great vision and necessary resources are not enough to obtain the desired outcomes. A plan of action, shared with all and easily understandable, is vital to achieve the desired results. Herein lies one of the top issues in schools today. Teachers are often told where to go and provided with some training and resources, yet they are not sure of the steps to take to achieve the desired outcomes. Running on a treadmill, or feeling like a mouse in a spinning wheel, can be a clear indication of the need for a cogent action plan.

In some schools, the problems can be so significant that there are multiple missing links, which can easily create toxic school cultures where transformation efforts are bound to fail. When designing a plan for transformation, school culture, empowered by trusting relationships, provides the needed foundation for change. School leaders set the tone for school culture. They must know the strengths of the current system yet also reflect honestly about the system's current needs.

We have both been part of more school district strategic planning processes than we care to remember, and we can recall hundreds of hours spent discussing, developing mission statements, and being forced to experience the loudest person in the room getting his or her way. Quite often, the goals that developed were based on one person's opinion and not grounded in any sort of evidence. Transformative change does not occur based on the opinion of a few. To be sustainable, it must be grounded in evidence and be a core belief of many.

Designing such a plan for sustainable transformation includes using an objective lens to analyze numerous metrics. Such change must be based on feedback from many sources, including students, the community, teachers, and other school leaders. Gaining feedback from a large group of stakeholders, and analyzing such metrics through the lens of inclusive, collaborative leadership teams, sets the stage for consensus building.

As district leadership teams work through a visioning and planning process, it's easy for natural blinders and positive opinions of our own work to lead us to a myopic view of what's needed. Transformative change will push even the most innovative school leaders out of their comfort zone. Such change cannot occur without constructive feedback and an honest reflection of the current reality. We encourage district teams to utilize a systemic planning process (such as the one shared in Appendix A) to guide their visioning and action planning moving forward.

Avoiding Initiative Overload

In business, some estimates indicate that 70 percent of change initiatives fail. That's right. Research has shown that up to 7 in 10 corporate initiatives have not led to sustainable change (Blanchard, 2010). We believe that these numbers could easily correlate to education, and the percentages may even be worse.

A general understanding that the student learning experience must be transformed has created incredible opportunities for the future yet has simultaneously caused significant turmoil. As school leaders work to redesign their schools, they must be careful not to immerse themselves, their teams, and their students in an alphabet soup of initiatives. In our experience, initiative overload is one of the primary reasons that transformational change fails.

Throughout this book, we've presented a plethora of research, evidence, stories, and practical steps to transform learning, but school leaders cannot lead change in all areas, at all times. It's easy for leaders to get excited about what could and should be, especially for those who are most passionate about creating new innovative opportunities for students and staff. Although well intended, too many ongoing initiatives can easily dilute the effectiveness of sustainable change. Avoiding initiative overload by maintaining a laserlike focus on what evidence indicates is required is essential for sustainable growth and transformation.

Leading transformational change isn't easy. But our kids are worth the effort.

Built to Last: Ensuring Sustainability

Leadership is about making others better as a result of your presence and making sure that impact lasts in your absence.

Sheryl Sandberg

It seems like every year, school-related stories hit the news and leave us asking, *"They did what?"* From purchasing short-term devices on long-term bonds to unethical decisions by school leaders to large swings in political power at the local, state, and federal levels, some change initiatives fail due to poor decision making by school leaders. These events often lead to mandated change over which stakeholders have no control. In every district, school leaders must make smart, student-centered decisions to ensure the long-term sustainability of progress. As we see it, this type of sustainability encompasses three key areas: financial, pedagogical, and political.

Financial Sustainability

Budgets have remained stagnant for a number of years, so the need for financial sustainability comes as no surprise. Districts have been working to balance budgets from one year to the next, and in many areas, this has led to difficult times. State funding issues. The layoff of teachers. Higher class sizes. Cuts to professional learning. We've all heard these stories. In some places, these stories seem to be a yearly occurrence.

The purchase of technology is often one of the heated debate topics around budget time. One of the most comprehensive research studies on the topic studied almost 1,000 schools that had implemented high levels of technology. The study found nine key implementation factors that were strongly linked to educational success, one of which states that "properly implemented technology saves money." The report indicates, "Substantial evidence shows that technology has a positive financial impact, but for best results, schools need to invest in the reengineering of schools, not just technology itself. Properly implemented educational technology can be revenue-positive at all levels—federal, state, and local. Project RED respondents report that technology contributes to cost reductions and productivity improvements—the richer the technology implementation, the more positive the impact" (One-to-One Institute, n.d.). To ensure sustainability, districts must work diligently to review vendor contracts, analyze resource utilization rates, and fight for lower or consortium pricing *every year*. For the most part, technology should get better and cheaper over time.

Although grants and other supplemental funding sources can serve as catalysts for initial implementation, these types of one-time funding mechanisms are not a reliable part of a long-term plan. For example, when districts purchase a large number of devices, especially when using a grant or bond, they must be able to answer the question of where the funding stream will come from for replacements down the line. Use caution, particularly around large purchases, until those types of questions can be answered. Being vigilant about financial sustainability isn't only the responsibility of school business managers and school board members. Financial sustainability is the responsibility of *every* school leader.

Pedagogical Sustainability

As school leaders understand, teachers at the classroom level have the greatest impact on achievement. To redesign the learning experience and sustain those practices in the long term, we must invest in the capacity of those who have the greatest effect. Building pedagogical sustainability comes from ongoing, systemic, personal professional learning opportunities and empowering teachers to be leaders. Although the average teacher tenure far surpasses that of a school administrator's, retirements, maternity and paternity leaves, school budgets, and other factors do lead to teacher turnover. As new teachers join a school's learning culture, the need for sustained pedagogical practices comes into light. Schools that are intentionally designed have induction, mentoring, and support programs in place to build capacity in new teachers—and dynamic professional learning opportunities to build additional capacity in veteran teachers—so the redesigned learning experience can be sustained over time.

Political Sustainability

The school structure in the United States is composed of more than 15,000 individual school districts. Each district has its own unique culture, community, and local politics that factor into decision making. Layered on top of that is the political structure at the state level, where legislatures, governors, and state secretaries of education make decisions that affect each local district. Changes at the federal level also affect state and local decision making and obligations. With the average district superintendent remaining in the same position for just over three years, and the average principal with a similar tenure in any given building, leadership changes are inevitable. Compounded by regular changes on the school board, it's no wonder that many districts struggle to maintain a consistent vision and plan for the long term.

Political sustainability is grounded in trusting relationships. From the school board and district superintendent to individual parents and an elementary principal, political sustainability is built *one relationship at a time*. School leaders must work diligently to build trusting relationships so sustained transformation can occur. When parents, community, or school board members feel left in the dark or a severe lack of trust, things can get ugly fast. However, when trusting relationships are built, political sustainability has a chance to flourish and positively affect student achievement.

To develop political sustainability, school leaders must build capacity and empower people other than themselves. A leader's legacy can be seen in the capacity that remains when he or she leaves. When a school leader retires, moves to another district, or changes positions, who is left to lead the charge? The best school leaders build capacity and empower others to take the torch and continue running, long after their departure.

Is your district's transformation built to last?

Making it Happen

Leadership is the capacity to translate vision into reality.

Warren Bennis

There is no silver bullet when it comes to intentionally designing schools to transform learning, nor is there only one right way to do so. The key to transformational change and intentional design is to build a dynamic school culture by comprehensively planning, investing in and empowering your students and staff, leading by example, and modeling the desired outcomes. As a leadership team, speak with one voice about the needed change, guide the way, and ensure that your people are an integral part of the process. Their voice, experience, and insight matter. Transformational change will only occur with them—not when it's done to them. Collaborative leadership for intentional design involves building a great team, empowering your people to run, arming them with the needed tools, and building positive, trusting, long-lasting relationships with all stakeholders.

Authentic, trusting relationships are the mortar that cements the foundation to transformational change. It is the experience of authentic, trusting relationships that ultimately propels our progress and makes meaningful, long-lasting sustainable change possible. These relationships are the foundation to all of our work as school leaders and, ultimately, the glue that binds together the eight keys for unlocking tomorrow's schools. If we lose sight of this, we have lost our way. Relationships are the heart of transformation. If the key to real estate is "location, location, location," then the key to leading people and disrupting the education system is "relationships, relationships, relationships" (Whitaker & Zoul, 2008).

We can no longer wait. Time is of the essence. We cannot design and lead schools for the world we grew up in. We must intentionally design schools that are relevant for the world our students will live in long after we're gone. Creating the schools that our kids need will not happen by chance. It is *our* responsibility to make it happen. The schools our kids need are, and always will be, intentionally designed. It is in these schools that learning is transformed. Together, we can do this.

You are part of the solution.

Appendix A: Future Ready Schools®

Future Ready Schools® (FRS) is a bold effort to maximize digital learning opportunities and help school leaders move quickly toward preparing students for success in college, career, and citizenship and is offered free for school districts. Beginning with a systemic planning process, FRS helps districts develop the human and technological capacity needed to personalize student learning. The Alliance for Excellent Education, a bipartisan, nonprofit organization located in Washington, DC, leads this effort alongside a vast coalition of more than 60 national and regional partner organizations.

Future Ready Schools® helps district leaders plan and implement personalized, research-based digital learning strategies so all students can achieve their full potential. It is the belief of FRS that every student deserves a rigorous, personalized learning environment filled with caring adults and student agency. Thus, districts must leverage digital technologies to accelerate high-quality teaching and learning. Nationwide, thousands of district superintendents have signed the Future Ready District Pledge (www.futureready.org/pledge), indicating their commitment to develop the human and technological capacity needed to personalize student learning.

The backbone of FRS is the Future Ready Framework, a robust structure for digital learning's vision, plan, and implementation. The research-based framework emphasizes collaborative leadership and creates an innovative school culture where teaching and learning can flourish. Planning and implementation focuses on the seven key areas (called gears) of the framework. This framework keeps personalized student learning at the heart of all decision making. The seven gears include

- Curriculum, Instruction, and Assessment
- Personalized Professional Learning
- Robust Infrastructure
- Budget and Resources
- Community Partnerships
- Data and Privacy
- Use of Space and Time

Copyright 2015 Alliance for Excellent Education

For more on Future Ready Schools®, including the free Interactive Planning Dashboard©, Leadership Hub, and events for school leaders, visit www.futureready.org.

Appendix B: Communicating a Concept with Instagram

(This assignment and rubric were developed by Joanna Westbrook.)

The aim of the Instagram Project is to challenge you to communicate a concept from *A Raisin in the Sun* through the use of visual images. You will choose a theme/concept statement from the statements we generate or address in our Socratic Seminar in class. Once you have chosen that statement, you will produce a series of photos that you will post to Instagram in the form of a photo essay.

Requirements:

1. **Identify the concept in the play.** The first two photos will portray the concept as it is expressed in at least two specific lines from the play. In your comment for both photos, you will quote the lines accurately and include the parenthetical documentation for the act, scene, and page number. Group members will represent the characters in the photos, and the tableau you create must be true to both the stage directions and visual spectacle of Lorraine Hansberry's play.

2. **Connect the concept from the play to your world/life.** The next three photos will portray the concept as it is demonstrated in the world around you. In your comments for these photos, you must articulate how the concept is connected to the play and to contemporary society. Note that you can either agree or disagree with the statement.

3. **Portray Hansberry's spectacle.** On the day we take the photos, you must have assembled and planned the props you will use to convey both the details of the play and the ideas you want to communicate. *You must be prepared for the photos.*

4. **Divide responsibilities.** You will work in a group of three students. Each group must have at least one student with a smartphone. Each group member must be responsible for the planning/staging/arrangement/comment of at least one photo in the collection you submit. Divide tasks and be fair. *Do your bit!*

Theme/Concept Statements:

1. If you work hard enough, you can achieve your dreams.
2. Discrimination is a reality in our world.
3. Men and women have equal opportunities.
4. Success equals having a lot of money.
5. It is honorable to sacrifice for the sake of someone else.
6. Sometimes we have to make a morally questionable choice to do what is right.
7. A family without extra money is more difficult on a man than on a woman.
8. Poverty level has little impact on quality of life.
9. Meeting family obligations is more important than individual desires.
10. People should be willing to do a job they hate to provide for their family.

*Note that each theme statement can also be negated. For example: "Hard work is not enough to achieve your dreams."

Category	4: Excellent	3: Good	2: Acceptable	1: Incomplete
Literal Representation	Information is relevant and specific. Students visually portray two specific moments in the play where the concept is demonstrated. The staging of the moment is visually accurate, insightful, and based on the language of the play.	Information is relevant and specific. Students visually portray two specific moments in the play where the concept is demonstrated. The staging of the moment is visually accurate and based on the language of the play.	Information is relevant but not as specific as a 3 or 4. Students attempt to visually portray only one specific moment in the play where the concept is demonstrated OR one is lacking in some key aspect. The staging of the moment may be inaccurate in some way.	Information is incomplete or irrelevant. Student does not seem to understand how the words of the play link to the chosen concept.
Originality	Product shows a large amount of original thought. Ideas are creative and inventive. All five photos are visually interesting and compelling.	Product shows some original thought. Work shows new ideas and insights. Most of the photos are visually interesting.	There is little evidence of original thinking. The photos are inconsistent in their visual interest.	Product is incomplete or unfinished. Unclear if any thought has gone into the design.

Category	4: Excellent	3: Good	2: Acceptable	1: Incomplete
Attention to Detail	Students have used correct punctuation and complete sentences, grammar, and spelling in the accompanying comments.	Students have mostly (no more than two errors) used correct punctuation and complete sentences, grammar and spelling in the accompanying comments. Errors do not distract from the content.	Students have sometimes (three or four errors) used correct punctuation and complete sentences, grammar, and spelling in the accompanying comments. Errors do not distract from the content.	Errors distract from the product. Five or more errors in grammar, punctuation, or spelling.
Requirements	All requirements are met and exceeded.	All requirements are met.	One requirement was not completely met.	More than one requirement was not completely met.
Workload	The workload is divided and shared equally by all team members.	The workload is divided and shared fairly by all team members, though workloads may vary from person to person.	The workload was divided, but one person in the group is viewed as not doing his/her fair share of the work.	The workload was not divided OR several people in the group are viewed as not doing their fair share of the work.
Gallery Walk	Interesting and well-rehearsed with smooth delivery that holds audience attention.	Relatively interesting and rehearsed with a fairly smooth delivery that usually holds audience attention.	Delivery not smooth, but able to hold audience attention most of the time.	Delivery not smooth and audience attention lost.

Related Common Core State Standards

RL.9-10.2: Determine a theme or central idea of a text and analyze in detail its development over the course of the text, including how it emerges and is shaped and refined by specific details.

W.9-10.1: Write arguments to support claims in an analysis of substantive topics or texts, using valid reasoning and relevant and sufficient evidence.

SL.9-10.5: Make strategic use of digital media in presentations to enhance understanding of findings, reasoning, and evidence and to add interest.

Appendix C:
District and School Highlights

Throughout this book, you've heard from some of the finest educational leaders in the world. Many of these school leaders have rightfully been recognized as Superintendents and Principals of the Year. They have broken through barriers, overcome obstacles, and helped families break the chains of poverty. From coast to coast, these leaders and the teams inside their schools have intentionally redesigned the student learning experience. In these schools and across these districts, *learning has been transformed.*

1. Albemarle County Public Schools, Virginia
2. Coachella Valley Unified School District, California
3. Dysart Unified School District, Arizona
4. Elizabeth Forward School District, Pennsylvania
5. Fogelsville Elementary School, Parkland School District, Pennsylvania
6. Greenwood Elementary School, Wayzata Public Schools, Minnesota
7. Lockport City School District, New York
8. MC² STEM High School, Cleveland Metropolitan School District, Ohio
9. Spartanburg 7 School District, South Carolina
10. Talladega County Schools, Alabama
11. Vancouver Public Schools, Washington
12. Vista Unified School District, California
13. West Port High School, Marion County Public Schools, Florida

References

Abramson, P. (2012). 17th annual school construction report. Retrieved from http://school planning.epubxp.com/i/74777-feb-2012

Alexander, D., & Lewis, L. (2014). *Condition of America's public school facilities: 2012–13* (NCES 2014-022). Washington, DC: U.S. Department of Education, National Center for Education Statistics.

Banning, J. H., & Canard, M. R. (1986). The physical environment supports student development. *Campus Ecologist.* Retrieved from www.campusecologist.com/?s= The+physical+environment+supports+student+development

Barrett, P., & Zhang, Y. (2009). *Optimal learning spaces: Design implications for primary schools.* Salford, UK: Design and Print Group.

Barrett, P., Zhang, Y., Davies, F., & Barrett, L. (2015). *Clever classrooms: Summary findings of the HEAD Project (Holistic Evidence and Design).* Salford, UK: University of Salford, Manchester.

Barrett, P., Zhang, Y., Moffat, J., & Kobbacy, K. (2013). A holistic, multi-level analysis identifying the impact of classroom design on pupils' learning. *Building and Environment, 59,* 678–689.

Baur, C., & Wee, D. (2015). Manufacturing's next act. *McKinsey & Company.* Retrieved from www.mckinsey.com/business-functions/operations/our-insights/manufacturings-next-act

Bendici, R. (n.d.). Schools build for the future. *District Administration.* Retrieved from www.districtadministration.com/article/schools-build-future

Blanchard, K. (2010). Mastering the art of change. *Training Journal.* Retrieved from www.kenblanchard.com/img/pub/blanchard_mastering_the_art_of_change.pdf

Blank, M., Jacobson, R., & Melaville, A. (2012). *Achieving results through community school partnerships: How district and community leaders are building effective, sustainable relationships.* Center for American Progress. Retrieved from https://cdn.americanprogress. org/wp-content/uploads/issues/2012/01/pdf/community_schools.pdf

Borders, G. (2015, January 21). Data breach hits MPISD employees. *The Daily Tribune.* Retrieved from www.dailytribune.net/news/data-breach-hits-mpisd-employees/ article_051ec5d0-a1d2-11e4-b1c7-afde4a6d4ed1.html

Borman, G. D., Benson, J. G., & Overman, L. (2009). A randomized field trial of the Fast ForWord language computer-based training program. *Educational Evaluation and Policy Analysis, 31*(1), 82–106.

Bowers, J. H., & Burkett, C. W. (1988). Physical environment influences related to student achievement, health, attendance and behavior. *Council of Educational Facility Planners Journal, 26,* 33–34.

Branson, R. (2014). Look after your staff. Retrieved from www.virgin.com/richard-branson/ look-after-your-staff

Bringuier, J. C. (1980). *Conversations with Jean Piaget.* Chicago: University of Chicago Press.

Bromberg, M., & Theokas, C. (2016). *Meandering towards graduation: Transcript outcomes of high school graduates.* The Education Trust. Retrieved from http://edtrust.org/resource/ meandering-toward-graduation

Budds, D. (2016). The school an entire town designed: Rebuilding Sandy Hook Elementary. *Fast Company.* Retrieved from www.fastcodesign.com/3062562/the-school-an-entire-town-designed-rebuilding-sandy-hook-elementary

Bureau of Labor Statistics. (2015a). Employment Projections Program. Retrieved from www.bls.gov/emp/ep_table_104.htm

Bureau of Labor Statistics. (2015b). Long-term price trends for computers, TVs, and related items. *The Economics Daily*. Retrieved from www.bls.gov/opub/ted/2015/long-term-price-trends-for-computers-tvs-and-related-items.htm

Campus Safety Staff. (2012, November 19). Ore. student pleads guilty to hacking district computer. *Campus Safety Magazine*. Retrieved from www.campussafetymagazine.com/article/ore-school-hacker-pleads-guilty-to-computer-crime

Carver, J. (2015, December 8). The 3 trust questions to ask any ed-tech vendor. *eSchoolNews*. Retrieved from www.eschoolnews.com/2015/12/18/editors-picks-2015-no-ten-the-3-trust-questions-to-ask-every-ed-tech-vendor

Caspe, M., Lopez, M. E., & Chattrabhuti, C. (2015). Four important things research tell us about the transition to school. *Harvard Family Research Project*. Retrieved from www.hfrp.org/family-involvement/publications-resources/four-important-things-research-tells-us-about-the-transition-to-school

Cavanagh, S. (2016, March 15). New tech consortium research probes iPad pricing for school districts. *EdWeek Market Brief*. Retrieved from https://marketbrief.edweek.org/marketplace-k-12/new-tech-consortium-to-probe-ed-tech-prices-policies-across-k-12-districts

Cheryan, S., Ziegler, S., Plaut V., & Meltzoff, A. (2014). Designing classrooms to maximize student achievement. *Behavioral and Brain Sciences, 1*(1), 4–12.

Chui, M., Manyika, J., & Miremadi, M. (2016). Where machines could replace humans—and where they can't (yet). *McKinsey Quarterly*. Retrieved from www.mckinsey.com/business-functions/business-technology/our-insights/where-machines-could-replace-humans-and-where-they-cant-yet

CollegeBoard. (2016). SAT program participation and performance statistics. Retrieved from http://research.collegeboard.org/programs/sat/data

Consortium of School Networking. (2016). 2016 IT leadership survey report. Retrieved from www.cosn.org/itsurvey

Cooper, D. (2004). *Professional development: An effective research-based model*. Retrieved from www.washingtonstem.org/STEM/media/Media/Resources/Professional-DeveloPment-An-Effective-Research-Based-Model-COOPER.pdf

Coster, W., Law, M., Bedell, G., Liljenquist, K., Kao, Y.-C., Khetani, M., & Teplicky, R. (2013). School participation, supports and barriers of students with and without disabilities. *Child: Care, Health and Development, 39*, 535–543.

Covey, S. (2009). Leadership is a choice, not position: Stephen Covey. *Business Standard*. Retrieved from www.business-standard.com/article/management/leadership-is-a-choice-not-a-position-stepen-r-covey-109020300076_1.html

Darling-Hammond, L., Wei, R. C., Andree, A., Richardson, N., & Orphanos, S. (2009). *Professional learning in the learning profession: A status report on teacher development in the United States and abroad*. Dallas, TX. National Staff Development Council.

Darling-Hammond, L., Zielezinski, M., & Goldman, S. (2014). *Using technology to support at-risk students' learning*. Stanford, CA: The Alliance for Excellent Education and Stanford Center for Opportunity Policy in Education.

Davis, E. (2015, April 22). *Want kids to pay attention in class? Give them standing desks*. Vital Record. Retrieved from https://vitalrecord.tamhsc.edu/want-kids-to-pay-attention-in-class-give-them-standing-desks

Decker, K. (2016, March 18). *Transforming used school spaces into something amazing*. *Edutopia*. Retrieved from www.edutopia.org/blog/transforming-unused-school-spaces-amazing-kathleen-decker

DeNisco, A. (2015). Lockers give way to charging stations. *District Administration*. Retrieved from www.districtadministration.com/article/lockers-give-way-charging-stations

Digital Promise and Education Industry Association. (2014). Improving ed-tech purchasing. Retrieved from digitalpromise.org/wp-content/uploads/2014/11/Improving_Ed-Tech_Purchasing.pdf

Dornhecker, M., Blake, J., Benden, M., Zhao, H., & Wendel, M. (2015). The effect of stand-biased desks on academic engagement: An exploratory study. *International Journal of Health Promotion and Education, 53*(5), 271–280.

Dougherty, S. (2016). Career and technical education in high school: Does it improve student outcomes? *Thomas Fordham Institute*. Retrieved from https://edexcellence.net/publications/career-and-technical-education-in-high-school-does-it-improve-student-outcomes

Dynarski, M., et al. (2007). *Effectiveness of reading and mathematics software products: Findings from the first student cohort.* Washington, DC: U.S. Department of Education, Institute of Education Sciences.

Earthman, G. I. (2004). Prioritization of 31 criteria for school building adequacy. Baltimore, MD: American Civil Liberties Union Foundation of Maryland. Retrieved from www.schoolfunding.info/

The Economic Times staff. (2015, July 27). China sets up first unmanned factory; all processes are operated by robots. Retrieved from http://economictimes.indiatimes.com/news/international/business/china-sets-up-first-unmanned-factory-all-processes-are-operated-by-robots/articleshow/48238331.cms

Education Next. (2016). Results from the 2016 Education Next poll. Retrieved from http://educationnext.org/2016-ednext-poll-interactive

Education Week Research Center. (2016). Teachers and technology use in the classroom: Exclusive survey results. Retrieved from www.edweek.org/media/teachers-and-technology-use-in-the-classroom.pdf

Edwards, L., & Torcelli, P. (2002). *A literature review of the effects of natural light on building occupants.* Golden, CO: National Renewable Energy Laboratory.

FairTest. (2015). 2015 SAT score report reaction. Retrieved from www.fairtest.org/2015-sat-score-report-reaction.

Federal Communications Commission. (2014). Modernizing the E-rate Program for schools and libraries. Retrieved from www.fcc.gov/document/fcc-releases-e-rate-modernization-order

Federal Communications Commission. (2016a). FCC modernizes Lifeline program for the digital age. Retrieved from www.fcc.gov/document/fcc-modernizes-lifeline-program-digital-age

Federal Communications Commission. (2016b). Children's Internet Protection Act. Retrieved from www.fcc.gov/consumers/guides/childrens-internet-protection-act

Federal Trade Commission. (1998). Children's Online Privacy Protection Rule ("COPPA"). (1998). Retrieved from www.ftc.gov/enforcement/rules/rulemaking-regulatory-reform-proceedings/childrens-online-privacy-protection-rule

Federal Trade Commission. (2015). Complying with COPPA: Frequently asked questions. Retrieved from www.ftc.gov/tips-advice/business-center/guidance/complying-coppa-frequently-asked-questions

Ferlazzo, L. (2016). Response: EdTech has over-promised & under-delivered. *Education Week Teacher*. Retrieved from http://blogs.edweek.org/teachers/classroom_qa_with_larry_ferlazzo/2016/03/response_ed_tech_has_over-promised_under-delivered.html

Fisher, A., Godwin, K., & Seltman, H. (2014). Visual environment, attention allocation, and learning in young children: When too much of a good thing may be bad. *Psychological Science, 25*(7), 1362–1370.

Fleming, L. (2015). *Worlds of making: Best practices for establishing a makerspace for your school.* Thousand Oaks, CA: Corwin.

Fox 8 Web Staff. (2015, November 5). Hackers alter students' grades at NC high school, send false transcripts to colleges. Retrieved from http://myfox8.com/2015/11/05/hackers-alter-students-grades-at-north-carolina-high-school

Fullan, M. (2001). *Leading in a culture of change.* San Francisco, CA: Jossey-Bass.

Gallup Student Poll. (2015). Engaged today: Ready for tomorrow. Retrieved from www.gallupstudentpoll.com/188036/2015-gallup-student-poll-overall-report.aspx

Garet, M. S., et al. (2008). *The impact of two professional development interventions on early reading instruction and achievement.* Washington, DC: National Center for Education Evaluation and Regional Assistance, Institute of Education Sciences, U.S. Department of Education.

Garet, M. S., et al. (2010). *Middle school mathematics professional development impact study: Findings after the first year of implementation.* Washington, DC: National Center for Education Evaluation and Regional Assistance, Institute of Education Sciences, U.S. Department of Education.

Gelbrich, J. (1999). Education in the revolutionary era. *Oregon State University, School of Education.* Retrieved from http://oregonstate.edu/instruct/ed416/ae2.html

General Accounting Office. (1996). *School facilities: America's schools report differing conditions.* Washington, DC: Author. Retrieved from www.gao.gov/products/HEHS-96-103

Gershenson, S., Holt, S., & Papageorge, N. (2015). *Who believes in me? The effect of student-teacher demographic match on teacher expectations.* Upjohn Institute Working Paper 15-231. Kalamazoo, MI: W.E. Upjohn Institute for Employment Research. Retrieved from http://dx.doi.org/10.17848/wp15-231

Girls Who Code. (2017). Mission and vision. Retrieved from http://girlswhocode.com/about-us

Gonen, Y. & Campanile, C. (2015. December 15). City to close failing schools for the first time. *New York Post.* Retrieved from www.nypost.com

Goodwin, T. (2015). The battle is for the customer interface. *TechCrunch.* Retrieved from https://techcrunch.com/2015/03/03/in-the-age-of-disintermediation-the-battle-is-all-for-the-customer-interface

Grangaard, E. M. (1995). *Color and light effects on learning.* Washington, DC: Association for Childhood Education International Study Conference and Exhibition. ERIC Document Reproduction Service No. ED 382 381.

Gustafson, B. (2015). *A phenomenological study of professional development in the digital age: Elementary principals' lived experiences.* Doctoral dissertation. Retrieved from ProQuest (3648959).

Hall, S., Thigpen, K., Murray, T., & Loschert, K. (2015). Building a foundation: How technology-rich, project-based learning transformed Talladega County Schools. *Alliance for Excellent Education.* Retrieved from http://all4ed.org/wp-content/uploads/2015/04/Talladega.pdf

Hargreaves, A., & Fink, D. (2004). The seven principles of sustainable leadership. *Educational Leadership, 61*(7), 8.

Harvard Family Research Project. (2015). *Promoting educational equity through family engagement: The King legacy.* Retrieved from www.hfrp.org/hfrp-news/news-announcements/promoting-educational-equity-through-family-engagement-the-king-legacy

Hayakawa, M., Englund, M. M., Warner-Richter, M., & Reynolds, A. J. (2013). Early parent involvement and school achievement: A longitudinal path analysis. *NHSA Dialog: The Research-to-Practice Journal for the Early Childhood Field, 16*(1), 200–204.

Henderson, A., & Mapp, K. (2002). A new wave of evidence: The impact of school, family, and community connections on student achievement. *National Center for Family & Community Connections with Schools, Southwest Educational Development Laboratory.* Retrieved from www.sedl.org/connections/resources/evidence.pdf

Henderson, A., Mapp, K., Johnson, V., & Davies, D. (2007). *Beyond the bake sale: The essential guide to family-school partnerships*. New York: New Press.

Herold, B. (2016, June 27). Teachers in high-poverty schools less confident about ed tech, survey finds. *Education Week*. Retrieved from http://blogs.edweek.org/edweek/DigitalEducation/2016/06/teacher_tech_confidence_high_poverty_schools.html?r=813673874&cmp=eml-enl-dd-news1&preview=1

Heschong Mahone Group. (1999). Daylighting in schools: An investigation into the relationship between daylighting and human performance. Retrieved from http://h-m-g.com/downloads/Daylighting/schoolc.pdf

Heuer, R., & Stullich, S. (2011). Comparability of state and local expenditures among schools within districts: A report from the study of school-level expenditures. Retrieved from www2.ed.gov/rschstat/eval/title-i/school-level-expenditures/school-level-expenditures.pdf

Hill, N. E., & Chao, R. K. (2009). *Families, schools and the adolescent: Connecting research, policy, and practice*. New York: Teachers College Press.

Hines, E. W. (1996). Building condition and student achievement and behavior. Unpublished doctoral dissertation, Virginia Polytechnic Institute and State University.

Hoover-Dempsey, K. V., et al. (2005). Why do parents become involved? Research findings and implications. *Elementary School Journal,106* (2), 105–130.

Horrigan, J. (2015). The numbers behind the broadband "homework gap." *Pew Research Center*. Retrieved from www.pewresearch.org/fact-tank/2015/04/20/the-numbers-behind-the-broadband-homework-gap

Hull, J., & Newport, M. (2011). Time in school: How does the U.S. compare? *Center for Public Education*. Retrieved from http://centerforpubliceducation.org/Main-Menu/Organizing-a-school/Time-in-school-How-does-the-US-compare

Hunter, W. (2015, March 24). Computer system network for Swedesboro-Woolwich school district hacked. *CBS Philly*. Retrieved from http://philadelphia.cbslocal.com/2015/03/24/computer-system-network-for-swedesboro-woolwich-school-district-hacked

Hutchinson, A. (2016). New data shows 82% of marketers believe social media marketing is now core to their business. *Social Media Today*. Retrieved from www.socialmediatoday.com/marketing/new-data-shows-82-marketers-believe-social-media-marketing-now-core-their-business

Institute for Computing Education at Georgia Tech. (2013). Detailed data on pass rates, race, and gender. Retrieved from http://home.cc.gatech.edu/ice-gt/556

Ismail, S. (2014). Exponential organizations: Why new organizations are ten times better, faster, and cheaper than yours (and what to do about it). New York: Diversion Books.

Ito, M. (2013). *Hanging out, messing around, and geeking out: Kids living and learning with new media*. Cambridge, MA: MIT Press.

Jalil, N., Yunus, R., & Said, N. (2012). Environmental colour impact upon human behavior: A review. *Procedia, Social and Behavioral Sciences, 35*, 54–62.

Jones, R., & Fox, C. (2016). State K–12 broadband leadership: Driving connectivity and access. Washington, DC: State Educational Technology Directors Association. Retrieved from www.setda.org/wp-content/uploads/2016/04/Broadband_2016.4.11.16_updated.pdf

Katzman, J. (2016, April 8). K–12 procurement is hell: Let's fix it. *Huffington Post*. Retrieved from www.huffingtonpost.com/john-katzman/k12-procurement-is-hell-l_b_9711606.html

Keynes, J. M. (1930). *Essays in persuasion*, New York: W.W. Norton.

Kiefer, A. (2012). Learning per square foot. *American School & University*. Retrieved from http://duetresourcegroup.com/userdata/userfiles/file/KI-99178_Learn-Square-Foot_white-paper.pdf

Knoster, T., Villa, R., & Thousand, J. (2000). A framework for thinking about systems change. In R. Villa and R. Thousand (Eds.), *Restructuring for caring and effective education: Piecing the puzzle together* (93–128). Baltimore: Paul H. Brookes.

Kohn, A. (1999). *The schools our children deserve: Moving beyond traditional classrooms and "tougher standards."* Boston: Houghton Mifflin.

Kolb, D. (1984). *Experiential learning: Experience as the source of learning and development.* Englewood Cliffs, NJ: Prentice-Hall.

Kouzes, J., & Posner, B. (2009). To lead, create a shared vision. *Harvard Business Review.* Retrieved from https://hbr.org/2009/01/to-lead-create-a-shared-vision

Kraft, M. A., & Rogers, T. (2014). The underutilized potential of teacher to parent communication: Evidence from a field experiment. *Harvard Kennedy School.* Retrieved from http://scholar.harvard.edu/files/mkraft/files/kraft_rogers_teacher-parent_communication_hks_working_paper.pdf

Kuhn, T. S. (1970). *The structure of scientific revolutions.* Chicago: University of Chicago Press.

Kurzweil, R. (2014). Don't fear artificial intelligence. *Time.* Retrieved from http://time.com/3641921/dont-fear-artificial-intelligence

Leithwood, K., Louis, K. S., Anderson, G., & Wahlstrom, K. (2004). *How leadership influences student learning: A review of research for the Learning from Leadership project.* New York: The Wallace Foundation.

Lemasters, L. K. (1997). A synthesis of studies pertaining to facilities, student achievement, and student behavior. Unpublished doctoral dissertation. Blacksburg, VA: Virginia Polytechnic Institute and State University.

Lieberman, M. (2012). Education and the social brain. *Trends in Neuroscience and Education.* Retrieved from www.academia.edu/2790088/Trends_in_Neuroscience_and_Education

Lowther, D. L., Ross, S. M., & Morrison, G. R. (2003). When each one has one: The influences on teaching strategies and student achievement of using laptops in the classroom. *Educational Technology Research and Development, 51*(3), 23–44.

Lukas, J. S., DuPree, R. B., & Swing, J. W. (1981). *Effects of noise on academic achievement and classroom behavior.* Office of Noise Control, California Department of Health Services.

Marzano, R. J. (2003). *What works in schools: Translating research into action.* Alexandria, VA: ASCD.

Marzano, R. J., Waters, T., & McNulty, B. A. (2005). *School leadership that works: From research to results.* Alexandria, VA: ASCD.

Master, A., Cheryan, S., & Meltzoff, A. (2016). Computing whether she belongs: Stereotypes undermine girls' interest and sense of belonging in computer science. *Journal of Educational Psychology, 108*(3), 424–437.

Maslow, A. H. (1943). A theory of human motivation. *Psychological Review, 50*(4), 370–396.

McLeod, S. (2014). Lev Vygotsky. *Simple Psychology.* Retrieved from www.simplypsychology.org/vygotsky.html

Mediratta, B., & Bick, J. (2007). The Google way: Give engineers room. *The New York Times.* Retrieved from www.nytimes.com/2007/10/21/jobs/21pre.html

Mezirow, J. (1998). On critical reflection. *Adult Education Quarterly, 48*(3), 185–199.

Morrisey, M. (2000). Professional learning communities: An ongoing exploration. Austin, TX: Southwest Educational Development Laboratory.

Moser, L. (2016, April 5). We're graduating more students than ever, but are they prepared for life after high school? *SchoolED.* Retrieved from www.slate.com/blogs/schooled/2016/04/05/high_school_students_aren_t_prepared_for_college_and_careers_says_education.html

Mouza, C. (2008). Learning with laptops: Implementation and outcomes in an urban, under-privileged school. *Journal of Research on Technology in Education, 40*(4), 447–473.

Murray, T. (2014). Using data safely and effectively to strengthen student performance: A report prepared for the House Subcommittee on Cybersecurity, Infrastructure Protection, and Security Technologies and House Subcommittee on Early Childhood, Elementary, and Secondary Education. *Alliance for Excellent Education*. Retrieved from http://all4ed. org/wp-content/uploads/2014/06/062515TomMurrayTestimony_Written.pdf

Murray, T., & Zoul, J. (2015). *Leading professional learning: Tools to connect and empower teachers*. Thousand Oaks, CA: Corwin.

Nair, P. (2014). *Blueprint for tomorrow: Redesigning schools for student-centered learning*. Cambridge, MA: Harvard Educational Publishing Group.

Nation's Report Card. (2014). Technology & engineering literacy (TEL). Retrieved from www.nationsreportcard.gov/tel_2014/#

National Association for Family, School, and Community Engagement. (n.d.). *District policy*. Retrieved from http://nafsce.org/resources/?_sft_resource_types=research-paper-or-report&_sft_resource_topics=community-engagement#policy

National Center for Educational Statistics. (2013). High school longitudinal study of 2009. Retrieved from http://nces.ed.gov/surveys/hsls09

National Center for Educational Statistics. (2015). *National assessment of educational progress (NAEP)*. Retrieved from http://nces.ed.gov/nationsreportcard/about/natadministered.aspx

National Center for Educational Statistics. (2016). Public high school graduation rates. Retrieved from https://nces.ed.gov/programs/coe/indicator_coi.asp

National Commission on Excellence in Education. (1983). *A nation at risk: The imperative for educational reform*. Retrieved from www2.ed.gov/pubs/NatAtRisk/index.html

New Teacher Project. (2015). *The mirage: Confronting the hard truth about our quest for teacher development*. Washington, DC: Author.

New York Commission on Ventilation. (1931). School ventilation and practices. New York: Teachers College, Columbia University.

Office of Civil Rights, Civil Rights Data Collection. (2014). Data snapshot: School discipline. Retrieved from http://ocrdata.ed.gov/Downloads/CRDC-School-Discipline-Snapshot.pdf

Office of Educational Technology, U.S. Department of Education. (2014a). The future ready district: Professional learning through online communities. Retrieved from http://tech. ed.gov/futureready/professional-learning/future-ready-district

Office of Educational Technology, U.S. Department of Education. (2014b). Future ready schools: Building technology infrastructure for learning. Retrieved from http://tech. ed.gov/futureready/infrastructure

Office of Educational Technology, U.S. Department of Education. (2016). National education technology plan. Future ready learning: Reimagining the role of technology in education. Retrieved from http://tech.ed.gov/netp

One-to-One Institute. (n.d.). Project Red: The findings. Retrieved from http://one-to-oneinstitute.org/findings

Organisation for Economic Co-operation and Development. (2012). *Programme for International Student Assessment (PISA) results from PISA 2012*. Retrieved from www. oecd.org/unitedstates/PISA-2012-results-US.pdf

Organisation for Economic Co-operation and Development. (2015). New approach needed to deliver on technology's potential in schools. Retrieved from www.oecd.org/education/new-approach-needed-to-deliver-on-technologys-potential-in-schools.htm

Organisation for Economic Co-Operation and Development. (2017). About. Retrieved from www.oecd.org/pisa/aboutpisa

Pew Research Center. (2010). Millennials: A portrait of generation next. Retrieved from www.pewsocialtrends.org/2007/01/09/a-portrait-of-generation-next

Pew Research Center. (2014). AI, robotics, and the future of jobs. Retrieved from www. pewinternet.org/2014/08/06/future-of-jobs

Pew Research Center. (2015). The numbers behind the broadband "homework gap." Retrieved from www.pewresearch.org/fact-tank/2015/04/20/the-numbers-behind-the-broadband-homework-gap

Plympton, P., Brown J., & Stevens, K. (2004). High-performance schools: Affordable green design for K–12 schools. *National Renewable Energy Laboratory*. Retrieved from www.nrel.gov/docs/fy04osti/34967.pdf

Porter, E. (2015, November 3). School vs. society in America's failing students. *The New York Times*. Retrieved from www.nytimes.com/2015/11/04/business/economy/school-vs-society-in-americas-failing-students.html

Prime, J., & Salib, E. R. (2014). Inclusive leadership: The view from six continents. *Catalyst*. Retrieved from www.catalyst.org/knowledge/inclusive-leadership-view-six-countries

Project Tomorrow. (2016). *Speak Up 2015 research project findings*. Retrieved from http://www.tomorrow.org/speakup/pdfs/speakup-2015-social-media-use-in-school-and-out-august-2016.html

Purcell, K., Heaps, A., Buchanan, J., & Friedrich, L. (2013). How teachers are using technology at home and in their classrooms. *Pew Research Center*. Retrieved from www.pewinternet.org/2013/02/28/how-teachers-are-using-technology-at-home-and-in-their-classrooms-2

Reilly, S. (2016, February 14). How troubled teachers cheat the system. *USA Today*. Retrieved from www.usatoday.com/media/cinematic/video/80373852/how-troubled-teachers-cheat-the-system/

Riazi, D. (2016, March 4). NYC public schools are still segregated. *NYU Local*. Retrieved from www.nyulocal.com/nyc-public-schools-are-still-segregated-f75e7720bff3

Roberts, C. (2008). Developing future leaders: The role of reflection in the classroom. *Journal of Leadership Education, 7*, 116–129.

Rosenworcel, J. (2015, June 15). Bridging the homework gap. *Huffington Post*. Retrieved from www.huffingtonpost.com/jessica-rosenworcel/bridging-the-homework-gap_b_7590042.html

Ryan, C., & Bauman, K. (2016). Educational attainment in the United States: 2015. *United States Census Bureau*. Retrieved from http://www.census.gov/content/dam/Census/library/publications/2016/demo/p20-578.pdf

Ryan, J. (2009). Leadership success always starts with vision. *Forbes*. Retrieved from www.forbes.com/2009/07/29/personal-success-vision-leadership-managing-ccl.html

Saad, L. (2016). U.S. education ratings show record political polarization. *Gallup*. Retrieved from http://www.gallup.com/poll/194675/education-ratings-show-record-political-polarization.aspx

Sax, L. J., et al. (2015). Anatomy of an enduring gender gap: The evolution of women's participation in computer science. *Braid Research*. Retrieved from https://braidresearch.gseis.ucla.edu/wp-content/uploads/2016/06/AERA-CS-Presentation.compressed.pdf

Schleicher, A. (2016), *Teaching excellence through professional learning and policy reform: Lessons from around the world*. Paris: OECD Publishing.

Schon, D. (1983). *The reflective practitioner*. New York: Basic Books.

Schwab, K. (2016). The fourth industrial revolution: What it means, how to respond. *World Economic Forum*. Retrieved from www.weforum.org/agenda/2016/01/the-fourth-industrial-revolution-what-it-means-and-how-to-respond

Scott-Webber, L., Strickland, A., & Kapitula, L. (2014). How classroom design affects student engagement. *Steelcase Education*. Retrieved from https://www.steelcase.com/content/uploads/2015/03/Post-Occupancy-Whitepaper_FINAL.pdf

Seith, E. (2016). 'Ignore Pisa entirely,' argues topic academic. *TES*. Retrieved from www.tes.com/news/school-news/breaking-news/ignore-pisa-entirely-argues-top-academic

Seijts, G. (2013). Good leaders never stop learning. *Ivey Business Journal*. Retrieved from http://iveybusinessjournal.com/publication/good-leaders-never-stop-learning

Sheninger, E. (2014). *Digital leadership: Changing paradigms for changing times*. Thousand Oaks, CA: Corwin.

Sheninger, E. (2015a). Transforming your school with digital communication. *Educational Leadership, 72*(7). Retrieved from http://www.ascd.org/publications/educational-leadership/apr15/vol72/num07/Transforming-Your-School-with-Digital-Communication.aspx

Sheninger, E. (2015b). *Uncommon learning: Creating schools that work for kids*. Thousand Oaks, CA: Corwin.

Sipe, J., & Frick, D. (2009). *Seven pillars of servant leadership: Practicing the wisdom of leading by serving*. Mahwah, NJ: Paulist Press.

Smith, M. (2016, January 30). Computer science for all. *The White House Blog*. Retrieved from www.whitehouse.gov/blog/2016/01/30/computer-science-all

Smith, J., Pender, M., Howell, J., & Hurwitz, M. (2012). A review of the causes and consequences of students' postsecondary choices. *College Board*. Retrieved from http://research.collegeboard.org/sites/default/files/publications/2014/9/literature-causes-consequences-students-postsecondary-choices.pdf

Steele, C. M., Spencer, S. J., & Aronson, J. (2002). Contending with group image: The psychology of stereotype and social identity threat. In M. P. Zanna (Ed.), *Advances in experimental social psychology* (Vol. 34, pp. 379–440). San Diego, CA: Academic Press.

Stein, P. (2016, February 11). D.C. accidentally uploads private data of 12,000 students. *The Washington Post*. Retrieved from www.washingtonpost.com/local/education/dc-accidentally-uploads-private-information-of-12000-students/2016/02/11/7618c698-d0ff-11e5-abc9-ea152f0b9561_story.html

Strauss, V. (2016, January 20). How bad are conditions in Detroit public schools? This appalling. *The Washington Post*. Retrieved from www.washingtonpost.com/news/answer-sheet/wp/2016/01/20/how-appalling-are-conditions-in-detroit-public-schools-this-appalling/?utm_term=.8f5a98737c80

Student Data Principles. (2014). 10 foundational principles for using and safeguarding students' personal information. *Data Quality Campaign and Consortium for School Networking*. Retrieved from www.studentdataprinciples.org/the-principles

Student Privacy Pledge. (2016). About the pledge. Retrieved from http://studentprivacypledge.org

Taylor, D. (2014). How do leaders get their organizations from vision to action? *Thinking Business*. Retrieved from www.thinkingbusinessblog.com/2014/11/20/how-do-leaders-get-their-organizations-from-vision-to-action

Technology for Education Consortium. (2016). TEC district snapshot report. Retrieved from www.techedconsortium.org/wp-content/uploads/2016/06/TECDistrictSnapshotReportJune2016wChromebooks.pdf

Thigpen, K. (2014). Creating anytime, anywhere learning for all students: Key elements of comprehensive digital infrastructure. *Alliance for Excellent Education*. Retrieved from http://all4ed.org/wp-content/uploads/2014/06/DigitalInfrastructure.pdf

Tufte, E. (1992). *Envisioning information*. Cheshire, CT: Graphics Press.

U.S. Census Bureau. (2014). Poverty status, food stamp receipt, and public assistance for children under 18 years by selected characteristics: 2014. Retrieved from www.census.gov/hhes/families/data/cps2014C.html

U.S. Department of Education. (2014). Protecting student privacy while using online educational services: Requirements and best practices. Retrieved from http://ptac.ed.gov/document/protecting-student-privacy-while-using-online-educational-services

U.S. Department of Education. (2015). *National Education Technology Plan*. Retrieved from www.tech.ed.gov/netp

U.S. Department of Education. (2016). Chronic absenteeism in the nation's schools. Retrieved from www2.ed.gov/datastory/chronicabsenteeism.html#intro

U.S. Department of Education. (n.d.) Protection of Pupil Rights Amendment (PPRA). Retrieved from http://familypolicy.ed.gov/ppra

U.S. Department of Health and Human Services. (2011). *The Head Start parent, family, and community engagement framework*. Retrieved from http://eclkc.ohs.acf.hhs.gov/policy/im/acf-im-hs-11-06

U.S. Environmental Protection Agency. (2000). *Indoor air quality and student performance*. Washington, DC: Author.

Van Note Chism, N. (2002). A tale of two classrooms. *New Directions for Teaching and Learning, 92*, 5–12.

WRAL.com. (2009). Wake schools sent postcards containing social security numbers. Retrieved from www.wral.com/news/education/story/6547340

Warschauer, M. (2007). A teacher's place in the digital divide. Retrieved from http://gseweb.oit.uci.edu/person/warschauer_m/docs/tpdd.pdf

Watson, J., & Gemin, B. (2008). *Using online learning for at-risk students and credit recovery: Promising practices in online learning*. Vienna, VA: North American Council for Online Learning.

Wellman, J. V., & Ehrlich, T. (2003). Re-examining the sacrosanct credit hour. *Chronicle of Higher Education, 50*, B16.

Whitaker, T., & Zoul, J. (2008). *The 4 core factors for school success*. New York: Routledge.

White House. (2015a). Fact sheet: Obama administration announces more than $375 million in public and private support for next-generation high schools. Retrieved from https://obamawhitehouse.archives.gov/the-press-office/2015/11/10/fact-sheet-obama-administration-announces-more-375-million-support-next

White House. (2015b). Remarks by the president at Every Student Succeeds Act signing ceremony. Retrieved from https://obamawhitehouse.archives.gov/the-press-office/2015/12/10/remarks-president-every-student-succeeds-act-signing-ceremony

White House. (2016a). Fact sheet: President Obama announces high school graduation rate has reached new high. Retrieved from https://obamawhitehouse.archives.gov/the-press-office/2016/10/17/fact-sheet-president-obama-announces-high-school-graduation-rate-has

White House. (2016b). Economic report of the president: Together with the annual report of the Council of Economic Advisors. Retrieved from https://obamawhitehouse.archives.gov/sites/default/files/docs/2017_economic_report_of_president.pdf

Wilson, M. (2016). Standing desks for kids? It's not as crazy as it sounds. *Fast Company*. Retrieved from www.fastcodesign.com/3063353/evidence/standing-desks-for-kids-its-not-as-crazy-as-it-sounds

World Economic Forum. (2016). The future of jobs: Employment, skills and workforce strategy for the fourth industrial revolution. Retrieved from www3.weforum.org/docs/WEF_Future_of_Jobs.pdf

Wulsin, L. R. (2013). Classroom design: Literature review. Prepared for the Special Committee on Classroom Design, Princeton University. Retrieved from www.princeton.edu/provost/space-programming-plannin/SCCD_Final_Report_Appendix_B.pdf

Yuki, G., & Mahsud, R. (2010). Why flexible and adaptive leadership is essential. *Consulting Psychology Journal Practice and Research 62*(2), 81–93.

Zheng, B., Warschauer, M., Lin, C. H., & Chang, C. (2016). Learning in one-to-one laptop environments: A meta-analysis and research synthesis. *Review of Educational Research, 86*(4), 1–33.

Index

The letter *f* following a page number denotes a figure.

About the Authors

 **Eric C. Sheninger** is a senior fellow and thought leader on digital leadership and learning with the International Center for Leadership in Education. Prior to this, he was an award-winning principal at New Milford High School. Under his leadership, his school became a globally recognized model for innovative practices. Eric oversaw the successful implementation of several sustainable change initiatives that radically transformed the learning culture at his school while increasing achievement.

His work focuses on leading and learning in the digital age as a model for moving schools and districts forward. Eric has emerged as an innovative leader, best-selling author, and sought-after speaker. His main focus is purposeful integration of technology to facilitate student learning, improve communications with stakeholders, enhance public relations, create a positive brand presence, discover opportunity, transform learning spaces, and help educators grow professionally.

Eric has received numerous awards and acknowledgements for his work. He is a CDE Top 30 award recipient, Bammy Award winner, NASSP Digital Principal Award winner, PDK Emerging Leader Award recipient, winner of Learning Forward's Excellence in Professional Practice Award, Google Certified Innovator, Adobe Education Leader, and ASCD 2011 Conference Scholar. He has authored and coauthored five other books on leadership and technology.

He has also contributed to the Huffington Post and was named to the NSBA 20 to Watch list in 2010 for technology leadership. *Time Magazine* also identified Eric as having one of the 140 best Twitter feeds in 2014. He now presents and speaks internationally to assist other school leaders to embrace innovative practices and effectively utilize technology. His blog, A Principal's Reflections, was selected as Best School Administrator Blog in 2011 and 2013 by Edublogs. It was also recognized with an Editor's Choice Content Award in 2014 by Smartbrief Education.

Eric began his career in education as a science teacher at Watchung Hills Regional High School. He then transitioned into the field of educational administration as an athletic director, supervisor of physical education, vice principal, and principal in the New Milford School District. Eric received his M.Ed. in Educational Administration from East Stroudsburg University, a B.S. in Biology from Salisbury University, and a B.S. in Marine/Environmental Science from the University of Maryland Eastern Shore. Connect with him on Twitter at @E_Sheninger and at ericsheninger.com.

Thomas C. Murray serves as the director of innovation for Future Ready Schools®, a project of the Alliance for Excellent Education, located in Washington, DC. He has testified before the U.S. Congress and works alongside that body and the White House, the U.S. Department of Education, state departments of education, corporations, school districts, and leaders throughout the country to implement student-centered, personalized learning while helping to lead Future Ready Schools and Digital Learning Day. Murray serves as a regular conference keynote speaker and was named the 2015 Education Policy Person of the Year by the Academy of Arts and Sciences, one of 20 to Watch in 2016 by the National School Board Association, and the 2017 Education Thought Leader of the Year by PR with Panache. He has also trained thousands of school leaders nationwide throughout his career.

Murray's experiences in K–12 digital leadership, which include implementing a 1:1 program, BYOD, blended learning, and a public K–12 cyber school (where he served as the director of technology and cyber education for the Quakertown Community School District in Bucks County, Pennsylvania), have been recognized nationally by Forbes.com, *THE Journal*, *District Administration* magazine, Project Red, *Tech & Learning* magazine, the Innosight Institute, Edsurge, eSchool News, and iNACOL, among others. He has also been featured on Digital Learning Day in both 2013 and 2014. Previously, he was the recipient of the Blended Schools Network Leadership Award, named one of the top 16 "forward thinking edtech leaders in the country," named one of the "top 100 influential voices in education," and has been featured in various magazines and television shows.

In 2015, Murray coauthored and released *Leading Professional Learning: Tools to Connect and Empower Teachers*. A former school principal and teacher, Murray is regularly recognized as one of the top influencers, thought leaders, and bloggers in school leadership and educational technology. He is also the cofounder of #edtechchat, an educational technology Twitter forum where hundreds of educators from around the world collaborate each week. Murray lives in eastern Pennsylvania with his wife and two children. Connect with him on twitter at @thomascmurray and at thomascmurray.com.

WHOLE CHILD
TENETS

1 **HEALTHY**
Each student enters school healthy and learns about and practices a healthy lifestyle.

2 **SAFE**
Each student learns in an environment that is physically and emotionally safe for students and adults.

3 **ENGAGED**
Each student is actively engaged in learning and is connected to the school and broader community.

4 **SUPPORTED**
Each student has access to personalized learning and is supported by qualified, caring adults.

5 **CHALLENGED**
Each student is challenged academically and prepared for success in college or further study and for employment and participation in a global environment.

THE WHOLE CHILD

ASCD's Whole Child approach is an effort to transition from a focus on narrowly defined academic achievement to one that promotes the long-term development and success of all children. Through this approach, ASCD supports educators, families, community members, and policymakers as they move from a vision about educating the whole child to sustainable, collaborative actions.

Learning Transformed relates to the **supported** and **challenged** tenets. *For more about the ASCD Whole Child approach, visit* **www.ascd.org/wholechild.**